The Emergence of the Modern Coptic Papacy

The Popes of Egypt

A History of the Coptic Church and Its Patriarchs from Saint Mark to Pope Shenouda III

Edited by Stephen J. Davis and Gawdat Gabra

Volume One

The Early Coptic Papacy

The Egyptian Church and Its Leadership in Late Antiquity

Stephen J. Davis

Volume Two

The Coptic Papacy in Islamic Egypt

641–1517

Mark N. Swanson

Volume Three

The Emergence of the Modern Coptic Papacy

Magdi Guirguis and Nelly van Doorn-Harder

The Emergence of the Modern Coptic Papacy

MAGDI GUIRGUIS
NELLY VAN DOORN-HARDER

A National Egyptian Heritage Revival Book

The American University in Cairo Press
Cairo New York

This paperback edition first published in 2022 by
The American University in Cairo Press
113 Sharia Kasr el Aini, Cairo, Egypt
One Rockefeller Plaza, 10th Floor, New York, NY 10020
www.aucpress.com

First published in hardback in 2011

ISBN 978 1 649 03245 4

[Library of Congress Cataloging-in-Publication Data applied for]

1 2 3 4 5 26 25 24 23 22

Designed by Sebastian Schönenstein

Contents

Acknowledgments		vii
Editors' Preface		ix
Technical Notes		xi
Part One	**The Coptic Papacy under Ottoman Rule (1517–1798)** *Magdi Guirguis*	
	Introduction	3
1	Exercising Authority: Patriarchs and Public Policy (Pope John XIII to Pope Matthew III, 1484–1646)	11
2	Contesting Authority: Patriarchs and Coptic Notables (Pope Mark VI to Pope Mark VIII, 1646–1798)	31
Part Two	**The Modern Coptic Papacy (1798–2011)** *Nelly van Doorn-Harder*	
	Introduction	55
3	Preparing for Reformation (Pope Mark VIII, 1797–1809; Pope Peter VII, 1809–52)	61
4	Educating Egypt (Pope Cyril (Kyrillos) IV, 1854–61; Pope Demetrius II, 1862–70)	73

5	Redefining Authority (Pope Cyril (Kyrillos) V, 1874–1927)	87
6	Leading in the Midst of Political Change (Pope John XIX, 1928–42; Pope Macarius III, 1944–45; Pope Yusab II, 1946–56)	111
7	Reviving Tradition, Reviving the Church (Pope Cyril (Kyrillos) VI, 1959–71)	127
8	Negotiating Political Landscapes (Pope Shenouda III, 1971–)	155
9	Reforming the Church for the Twenty-first Century (Pope Shenouda III, 1971–)	173

Works Cited: Primary Sources 189
Works Cited: Secondary Sources 193

Notes 207
Index 251

Acknowledgments

I had the idea of writing a book about the Copts in the Ottoman period many years ago, at which time I began to pay more attention to the archival sources kept at the National Archives in Cairo. While I was doing this, Dr. Gawdat Gabra nominated me to participate in the series of the history of Coptic popes, which would be published by the American University in Cairo Press, to write about the Ottoman period (1517–1798). Although I prefer not to deal with Copts through the narrow aspect of religion or the religious institution, I welcomed the idea and began to prepare my contribution. I would like to take this opportunity to thank Gawdat Gabra and Stephen Davis, the general editors of this series. In late 2003 I received a grant from Aziz and Lola Atiya for Coptic studies, which was crucial for researching my contribution to this book. I owe many thanks to Nayra Atiya for her encouragement and support. My thanks are also due to the friends and colleagues at the Ottoman seminar that takes place at the Egyptian Society for Historical Studies. Their discussions and comments during many sessions of this seminar were very helpful. I would particularly like to mention Raouf Abbas, Nelly Hanna, Mohamed Hakim, Nasser Ibrahim, Husam Abdul Mu'ti, Sabri al-Adl, Sabri al-Dali, and Nasser Uthman. I am also grateful to the staff at the Egyptian National Archives, especially Mrs. Najwa Mahmoud.

Magdi Guirguis

Writing this part of the three volumes on the popes of the Coptic Church allowed for many occasions of vigorous discussion and challenged many of my assumptions about modern Coptic history. This exercise took much longer than anticipated and I am deeply grateful to the American University in Cairo Press for their patience and gentle reminders. I equally owe thanks to Stephen Davis for his impeccable editorial eye, and to Gawdat Gabra and Michael Shelley for helping to sort out the tedious details. I especially thank Mark Swanson for generously sharing his wealth of historical information. Thanks to the generous invitation of Salima Ikram, Faiza Heikal, and Dean Ann Lesch, I was able to spend the Fall 2005 semester as the Coptic Chair at AUC, a stay that provided opportunities to collect local materials and resulted in new and renewed friendships with Egyptian colleagues. I fondly remember brainstorming over ample cups of tea with Mary Assad, Vivian Fahmy, Samir Morcos, Nabil Abd el-Fattah, Magdi Guirguis, Mariz Tadros, Father Bishoy el-Antony, and Sisters Aghape and Rauth from the Convent of St. Mary in Beni Soueif. Keen Jesuit observers of the Copts, the late Father Maurice Martin and Fathers Christiaan van Nispen tot Sevenaer and Jacques Masson never tired of sharing their insights. His Holiness Pope Shenouda III and Bishop Musa granted several interviews. Bishop Serapion of Los Angeles and Hawaii, Bishop Suriel of Melbourne, Father Arsanios from the Coptic Church in Amsterdam, and Father Arsanios from Charlotte, North Carolina, patiently helped clarify details of church procedures. I thank them all. Dr. Elhamy Khalil graciously shared with me his book on the Coptic diocese in California, which provided invaluable insights into the community's growth outside Egypt. Laurice Iskander, Vivian Ibrahim, and Febe Armanios took time to comment on the manuscript. Finally, this writing would not have been possible without the friendship and encouragement, given during long car trips through the desert, of Kari Vogt and Magda Kamel.

Nelly van Doorn-Harder

Editors' Preface

As editors of the *Popes of Egypt* series, we take great pleasure in seeing this third and final volume come to fruition. This book is the result of a fine collaboration of efforts: we would like to thank its co-authors, Magdi Guirguis and Nelly van Doorn-Harder, for their expertise and the many years of research that they put into this project, and our associate editor, Michael Shelley, for his good humor and meticulous attention to detail as he helped fine-tune the manuscript at different stages in preparation for publication.

This final volume is groundbreaking on several levels, but especially with regard to the light it sheds on the sometimes cooperative, sometimes conflictual relationship that developed between the Coptic pope and the Coptic laity from the Ottoman period to the present. The period covered between these pages was marked by an ever-changing leadership landscape: at times the laity stepped up to serve as the public face of the Coptic Orthodox Church; at other times, the pope has reasserted and redefined his authority. The emergence of the modern Coptic papacy is largely the product of this shifting terrain.

In tracing the complex social lines of the relationship between the Coptic pope and the Coptic laity during the Ottoman period, Magdi Guirguis (Faculty of Arts, Kafr al-Sheikh University, Egypt) has done scholarship a tremendous service by examining a number of unpublished documentary archives found in Egyptian museums, libraries, and collections. In the past, the study of these sources has been complicated and hindered by difficulties in legibility and problems related to manuscript order and preservation. As a result, scholars have often shied away from the challenge of deciphering their content, and our knowledge of the period from 1517 to 1798 has suffered as a result. By delving into these archival materials, Guirguis was able to document many new historical details about the economic, social, and religious life of the Copts and their papal leadership during this period.

Nelly van Doorn-Harder's task in writing a history of the modern Coptic papacy was equally difficult. If study of the Ottoman period is characterized by the inaccessibility of sources, scholars who study the history of the Coptic Orthodox Church from the nineteenth to the twenty-first century find themselves virtually awash in data. Inundated with such a vast reservoir of evidence, van Doorn-Harder faced a very distinct set of challenges in writing her chapters. A large part of her success in tackling those challenges was the way she marks this burgeoning of sources—the multiplication of media itself—as a factor that has indelibly stamped the social formation of the modern Coptic Church and its leadership. Whether tracing the rise of Coptic reform movements and their relation to developments in Egyptian governmental policies, highlighting revivals in monasticism and pilgrimage among the Copts, or analyzing the complexities of Christian–Muslim relations in Egypt, van Doorn-Harder demonstrates how the Coptic papacy has evolved in accordance with these new dynamics, even as the authority of the pope's office has continued to be marked by traditional ritual and institutional forms.

Over the past forty years, Pope Shenouda III (1971–) has overseen the transformation of his church into a globalized communion that spreads from Egypt to the far ends of the earth, including Europe, North America, and Australia. His eventual successor will therefore be charged with the responsibility of providing leadership to a Coptic Orthodox Church that is at the same time both national and multinational in character. This volume tells the story of the church that Pope Shenouda III's successor will inherit—a story about the making of the modern Coptic papacy.

Stephen J. Davis and Gawdat Gabra, editors

Technical Notes

Arabic words and names are transcribed without macrons or sublinear dots, but the reader who knows Arabic should have no difficulty in deciphering them. For some words that have an established English spelling, such as sheikh and caliph, that spelling has been used. For names of patriarchs/popes that have a common English equivalent, such as Cyril, John, Mark, Matthew, and Peter, the latter has been used. Finally, in the case of certain Arabic names, we have allowed for occasional variation in our transliteration scheme, in order to accommodate common Egyptian usage. For example, we use Ibrahim al-Gawhari instead of Ibrahim al-Jawhari, Girgis al-Gawhari rather than Jirjis al-Jawhari, and Butrus al-Gawli instead of Butrus al-Jawli. We trust this will not cause serious difficulties for the reader.

With respect to dating, whenever both a Hijri year (AH) and a western year (AD) are given for a particular event, the Hijri year is stated first. When only one year is given, it may be assumed to be a western year unless otherwise indicated.

Michael Shelley, associate editor

Part One

The Coptic Papacy under Ottoman Rule

(1517–1798)

Magdi Guirguis

Introduction

Filling a Historical Gap

The Ottoman period of Egypt's history has been neglected for a long time. Negative ideas about this era have long been entrenched in the curricula of Egyptian schools and universities, and most scholars of Egyptian history continue to pass over this period lightly. For a century and a half, the school of Egyptian historical study sponsored by the ruling family of Muhammad 'Ali (1805–1952) conformed with western Orientalists to stigmatize the Ottoman era as a period of stagnation, backwardness, and ignorance. Each had its own reasons: the ruling family was insistent on showing that Muhammad 'Ali had created a modern state out of a cultural void. Orientalists, for their part, wanted to prove that modern Egypt was established when it was given the opportunity to interact with the west, first through the French Expedition (1798–1801), then through the western cadres on which Muhammad 'Ali depended.

To complicate matters, researchers did not have access to the Ottoman archives in Istanbul until after the Second World War. After that, Ottoman studies in general began to be regarded with more esteem. Research on non-Muslim communities in the Ottoman Empire increased, but did not always give consideration to Egypt. No one is to be unduly blamed for this oversight, however, as the available Coptic sources are scattered, disorganized, difficult to find, and hard to access. Moreover, the abundant sources in the Egyptian archives are characterized by illegibility and disorderliness, causing many researchers to shy away from delving into them, besides other difficulties pertaining to the formulation of legal documents, which constitute the bulk of these collections. For these many reasons, there are very few large-scale studies about the Copts during the Ottoman period, and those that exist are too often characterized by inaccuracy.

When it comes to the history of the Egyptian patriarchs, in particular, by the late fifteenth century the tradition of writing the biographies of the Coptic popes had come to a virtual standstill. Indeed, the biographies of the fifteen patriarchs spanning the period from 1484 to 1809 cover only about thirty pages in the published edition of *History of the Patriarchs of the Coptic Church of Alexandria*.[1] Subsequent Egyptian scholarship on the sources has done little to supplement this picture, with the exception of Kamil Salih Nakhla's work, which he recorded on the basis of information collected about the patriarchs from manuscripts found scattered in different monastic libraries.[2] Even his important work, however, suffers from a lack of documentation, as well as a number of factual errors.

Nakhla's failure to document sources adequately is endemic to Egyptian historiography on this period: historians have all too often been forced to rely on earlier, minimally documented sources, and the cycle continues. In Nakhla's case, he depends to a great degree on the work of Ya'qub Nakhla Rufayla, who mentions important information reported by no one else about periods before his time but does not always identify the sources for this information.[3] By way of example, Nakhla relates an account from Rufayla concerning the Monastery of St. Anthony in the Red Sea area: "In 1484 Arabs of Upper Egypt attacked the monasteries of St. Anthony and St. Paul and killed all the monks that were in them, and they remained deserted for about eighty years."[4] However, documentary evidence clearly indicates that the monastery of St. Anthony did not stop functioning for this period of time: a chain of *waqfs* (endowments) for the monastery make clear that its administration continued apace. According to *fiqh* (Islamic jurisprudence), there can be no *waqf* for a Christian place or building in and of itself, but a *waqf* is permissible for the people residing in it. These documents, therefore, can be considered as evidence that there were monks living in the monastery during the dates mentioned.[5] Moreover, what travelers have recorded about the monastery also confirms the inaccuracy of what Rufayla has said and which other historians have quoted.[6] Other examples of errors found in the writings could be produced here. All of this is to say that caution is required when using such sources.[7]

The considerations outlined above make writing about the Copts during the Ottoman period a somewhat risky undertaking—one that requires careful scrutiny of the sparse records of this period. In the writing of these chapters, therefore, I had to search out new sources of information belonging to this period, in the hope of getting a wider perspective on the role of the patriarchs than that offered by traditional ecclesiastical sources. My search took me to materials preserved in the Egyptian archives, many of which were not studied systematically heretofore. In the end, there were three main documentary collections that proved especially valuable for my investigative research:

1. Records of the shari'a courts preserved in Dar al-Watha'iq al-Qawmiya in Cairo. This is a collection of over ten thousand records from seventeen courts in Cairo and six courts in the remaining provinces of Egypt, covering the period from 1520 until the end of the nineteenth century. This collection is a living daily record of the reality of Egyptian society, embracing all classes and confessions. Some of the courts specialized in certain matters, which makes them a unique source of historical material.

2. Diwan al-Ruznama records at Dar al-Watha'iq al-Qawmiya in Cairo, the records of Rizq (Rizaq) Ihbasa (Ihbasiya) and al-Jayshiya in particular. This collection is particularly important as regards the history of the monasteries, their financial allocations, the dates of their destruction, and their restoration. They cover the period from 1382 until the end of the eighteenth century.

3. Archives of the Coptic Orthodox Patriarchate in Cairo, which preserves over seven thousand documents concerning *waqf*s as well as the affairs of churches and monasteries.

Finally, I also accessed numerous assorted manuscripts from Egyptian monasteries and churches, more than 70 percent of which date back to the Ottoman period (whether originals or copies).

The Theoretical Framework

In the nineteenth century, in one court case in al-Minya in Upper Egypt, one Muslim and two Coptic witnesses stood before a judge. It was necessary for a witness to know the basic tenets of his own religion in order for his testimony to be accepted at court. When the judge asked the Muslim witness about his religious knowledge, he answered that he did not know how to pray. The two Copts also said that they did not know anything about religion. They were only peasants who were told that they belonged to *al-nasara* (the Christians). Because of their lack of knowledge, the judge turned the three of them down and refused to accept their testimony.

Moving ahead to the late twentieth century, I can relate the following story from my own experience. My family was living in Fayoum province (a hundred kilometers south of Cairo) in a big village surrounded by many small villages. I was young, religious, and had the opportunity of preaching on numerous occasions in the years leading up to 1984. In that setting, I saw that Coptic villagers knew nothing about the basics of their religion. In most villages, if you asked a Copt to recite the Lord's Prayer, he would start reciting the first chapter of the Qur'an, just as Muslims do, believing it to be part of his own faith tradition. The majority of these people were not baptized and had never seen a priest in their life.

There is an explanation for why the Coptic Church as an institution had so little influence over the Copts in rural society. Around the year 1200 the number of churches in Egypt was 2,048, while the monasteries numbered 834. In 1430, the churches numbered 193, the monasteries seventy-four. In the late sixteenth century, there were 112 churches and five monasteries. Almost all of the surviving churches were located in major or provincial cities. Only a very few large villages had churches. This means that most Christians in rural society did not have any link with the church. They were totally isolated. When we talk about the Coptic community, it is difficult to locate these people within this framework.

What is also amazing is that many Coptic peasants were not paying the *jizya* (poll tax) required of minority religious communities since the early centuries of Islamic rule. As a result, they did not fall into the category of *ahl al-dhimma* (a protected people).[8] In many documents from Islamic village courts, there is no mention of *dhimmi* (protected people) or *nasrani* (Christians) to describe Coptic individuals. This, in fact, is another problem related to the interpretation of the documentary sources used in this study. In general, most historians of the Ottoman period rely primarily on the city records, which in my view represent the state discourse. However, these records do not give a picture of how everyday life in the villages was organized.

From the perspective of the Ottoman state, the Copts were dealt with as though they were one group—a community defined by their religion, with one main responsibility toward the state, the payment of *jizya*. Officially, the Copts had a religious leader who was responsible for their affairs. And yet the archives indicate that there were Copts who had no relationship whatsoever to the church or to religion. These archival sources show that some Copts during the period we are studying actually stood in opposition to the church, without necessarily denying or forgoing their religious identity. Naturally, there were other social allegiances competing for their time and energy. For example, Copts, like other Egyptians, belonged to *tawa'if* (professional and crafts guilds). These guilds had their own special characteristics and their own rules of conduct that members were expected to follow.

I believe that these historiographical problems—the urban biases of official sources and historians, and the sometimes tenuous relationship between identification and practice that those official sources obscure—also apply to the study of 'Islamic society' in general. What do we mean when we refer to Islamic society? Many studies on the 'history of Islamic society' have in fact focused almost exclusively on Islamic cities. But results and conclusions from these studies have been generalized and applied to Islamic society as a whole, without taking into account that about 70 percent of the population was living in rural society.

What does all this mean for Part One of this book? It means, very simply, that it is about the history of an institution (the church) and its leaders, and not about the identity or experience of all Copts during the Ottoman period. Many social, cultural, and political aspects related to the Coptic community and its leaders will be addressed, but the primary focus is on the history of the institution, with particular attention to the Ottoman state's relationship with a "religious community."

The Copts and the Ottoman State

In general, the relationship between the successive "Islamic governments" and *ahl al-dhimma* was shaped within the context of what came to be known as *'aqd al-dhimma* (the covenant of protection). Regardless of its source (it is attributed to the Caliph 'Umar ibn al-Khattab, ca. 586/90–644) or the degree of adherence to its letter and spirit within each generation, it remained the fundamental legal reference point whenever necessary. Although this covenant did not touch on the internal organization of the Coptic community and the manner of its representation before the government, the situation of the Coptic community with respect to the broader society was governed by this status designation.

Accordingly, the role of the popes in managing the affairs of the Copts was also governed by those same circumstances. Notwithstanding, the authority granted to the popes was neither stable nor clear-cut. Subject to the political, social, and cultural fluctuations of Egyptian society, papal authority would expand or contract. Sometimes the state itself would try to usurp the prerogatives of the popes, while at other times the state would make efforts to affirm and support the power and authority of the Coptic papacy.[9]

Until the end of the Mamluk period (1517), the Coptic pope was responsible for the affairs of the Coptic community before the government. He was issued a *tawqi'* (decree of appointment),[10] which stipulated his functions and mandates. These decrees give us a theoretical understanding of the papal public role as authorized by the state. In a *tawqi'* for Pope Benjamin II (1327–39), for example, we find the following stipulations:

> He shall be consecrated as their patriarch in the manner of those who preceded him and whose residence was in Egypt . . . governing by the laws of his religion, dispensing justice within his community according to the rules of his faith, exerting his utmost to permit and prohibit what is necessary according to the gospel, in such a manner that his honorable view would prevail in all circumstances, and the lowly and the mighty would not do anything except by his abundant instruction, and he shall appoint for them the bishops and priests who are diligent in their religion and their trustworthiness, and who do not perform any of their business except with his approval, and he should enjoin the members of the monasteries and churches to offer up suitable prayers for him for the duration of his days, and not to exceed any limit or design or do anything that has not been deemed appropriate by him.[11]

In another *tawqi'* for one of the popes at the close of the Mamluk period we find the stipulation: "He shall proceed according to what they profess with regard to selling, breach of contract, inheritance, and marriage."[12] From these decrees we see clearly the extent of the authority granted the popes to deal with all matters related to their community. However, we should view these decrees with caution, for although they may express the avowed policy of the rulers, they do not necessarily correspond to reality on the ground.

When Sultan Muhammad al-Fatih (the Conqueror) captured Constantinople in 1453, he appointed the Greek Orthodox patriarch and gave him general authority over his followers in all spiritual and civil affairs.[13] The patriarch became one of the eminent people of the state who had his own banner (like the governors of the provinces). He was given the title of Millat Pasha and Wali over the Orthodox people, and enjoyed important tax-related, administrative, and judicial mandates.[14] Sultan Muhammad al-Fatih did not take long to apply this system to the Armenian subjects of the Ottoman state as well. He appointed for them three patriarchs, giving them the same rights he had granted the Greek Orthodox patriarch. This procedure might have been motivated by political considerations, as Sultan Muhammad al-Fatih wanted to win over the eastern Church (the Church of Constantinople), so as not to give it the opportunity to think of joining forces with the Church of Rome. He feared as well that the Greek Orthodox might migrate to nearby lands, especially given that the Muslims with him were a minority. However, after the occupation and annexation of Egypt to the Ottoman Sultanate, this system did not prevail there. A new law *(Qanun-name-i Masr)* was issued in 1525, shortly after its occupation. One of the articles of the law stripped the Coptic patriarch of his control over legacies,[15] which indicates that his mandate was different from that granted to his Greek Orthodox counterpart.

This seems to be quite logical, given the philosophy of the Ottoman state in administering conquered nations. The Ottomans brought together under their rule diverse races, nationalities, and countries. Consequently, it was not possible to fashion a unified system that would guarantee the exact same treatment of the various peoples of this vast empire. There are indications that the Ottomans approved most of the local laws and customs of conquered countries, although many of those laws and customs had been formulated by Christian kings who had preceded the Ottoman state. However, they nonetheless came into force under the Ottoman consuetudinary law.[16] Thus, the Ottomans continued to utilize the procedures and laws that the Mamluks laid down for the administration of Egypt. Accordingly, the Copts were dealt with in the same way they had been dealt with for a long time. Their legal treatment was based on two principles: first, the relations of the Islamic state with *ahl al-dhimma*, which was governed by *'aqd al-dhimma*; second, inherited customs and traditions concerning the organization of the Coptic community, the role of the popes, and the mandated powers they had acquired over the course of time.

Consequently, the Ottomans pursued the same policy as their predecessors in Egypt and made no changes whatsoever. Even the appointment of the pope remained a domestic matter in which the authority in Istanbul (the state capital) did not intervene. It was sufficient to have the approval of the Ottoman pasha in Egypt (the governor who represented the Ottoman sultan) to appoint the pope, after which a ruling would be issued by the *qadi al-qudah* (chief judge) in Egypt.[17]

However, this state of affairs was subjected to many changes that impacted both the structure of the community and the mandate granted to the pope, which we shall discuss further on. The Ottoman government's policy toward the Copts was maintained within the framework of a "religious community" headed and led by a patriarch, who was supported by the institution of the church. In fact, the Ottomans preferred to conduct business in relation to institutions or associations rather than individuals.[18]

It is noteworthy that this contractual relationship between the government and the Coptic Church *('aqd al-dhimma)* would emerge every now and then during the Ottoman period, especially in times of sedition and crises.

The Copts would also demand their rights from this same starting point. Many documents from this period show that the Copts presented their demands on the grounds that they were *ahl al-dhimma* and obligated to pay the *jizya*, the per-capita tax imposed upon them.

The following chapters will focus on the role of the popes in their leadership of the Coptic community by studying the linkage between the church organizational structure and prevalent patterns of authority. Of particular interest will be certain internal changes brought about in church structure as a result of an ongoing conflict between the clergy and the Coptic gentry for control of the community.

1

Exercising Authority: Patriarchs and Public Policy

(Pope John XIII to Pope Matthew III, 1484–1646)

Legislation and New Social Circumstances (Popes John XIII and Gabriel VII, 1484–1568)

Structure and Discipline under Pope John XIII (1484–1524)

The term of office of Pope John XIII (Yuhanna ibn Rizqallah ibn Girgis) (1484–1524) represents a transitional stage between two different periods, as he witnessed the waning of the Mamluk state and the rise of the Ottomans as rulers of Egypt. The Ottomans entered Egypt in 1517, and from that time Egypt was transformed from the capital of an empire to a mere province subject to the new seat of authority in Constantinople (Istanbul).

It is well known that the Ottomans did not introduce fundamental changes in the systems and customs of the peoples whom they occupied. Accordingly, the period of Pope John XIII shows how the Ottomans, during the early stages of their rule, retained the administrative practices of the societies under their power, with the exception of a few changes in the financial systems designed to facilitate the flow of wealth to the capital, Istanbul.

During this early period in which decisions were made in Istanbul, the governors in Egypt implemented the policies of the state. As the Coptic Church was recognized as a religious establishment or community under that rule, its leadership—the pope and his bishops—took on a liaison role in the community's dealings with the state.

The jurisdiction of the Coptic patriarchate during the time of Pope John XIII was rather extensive. In one of his letters, John speaks of himself as "in charge of the see of St. Mark in the great city of Alexandria and the city of Jerusalem, Egypt, the Ethiopian provinces and Nubia."[1] Notwithstanding, during his reign as pope, the church lost some of its previous areas of jurisdiction: the dioceses of Cyprus and Rhodes were lost. In the case of the latter, the influence of the Coptic Church was reduced to two Coptic monks who tended to the congregation there.[2] The see governing the Pentapolis in North Africa was another casualty of this period. Mentioning this see, Pope John states only: "Anba Kiriakūs, archbishop of the Five Cities (Pentapolis), who presently resides in his monastery in Shayhat mountain, is now called Sawiris."[3]

Given the fact that it was the patriarch and bishops who had the final word in the leadership of the community, the role of the Coptic scribes and bureaucrats—lay gentry often referred to as the *mubashirin*—was minimized considerably. Although there were Coptic notables who wielded great influence and authority, such as Sheikh Yunis al-Nasrani who was *mubashir* for the senior emir *(malik al-umara')*,[4] the church hierarchy remained in control of all diplomatic matters. As Pope John himself stated frankly in one of his letters to the people of Samanud: "It is not the Coptic notables who rule the church but it is the church which rules over everyone, and all rulings are not by the notables but by the bishops or head priests."[5]

The concept of *ta'ifa*—denomination, or confessional minority—was the framework that suited the nature of Ottoman rule in Egypt. The Ottomans recognized institutions and not individuals, with the natural consequence that the patriarch and his assembly of bishops were the legal representatives of the community before the government.

One of the expressions of the pope's control over all religious as well as non-religious affairs of the community during this period was his responsibility for collecting the *jizya* from the Copts on behalf of the government. In this context Pope John, for instance, sent a letter to the Copts of Lower Egypt urging them to pay the *jizya*, and to consider it a duty that does not contradict religious loyalties, and which was consistent with the Gospel injunction to "render unto Caesar the things that are Caesar's."[6] This was a heavy burden borne by the popes. An illustration of this occurred a century and a half later when the *diwan* (chancellery) of al-Jawali confiscated the inheritance left by Pope Mark VI (101st pope, 1646–56), because there was an outstanding sum due from the *jizya* set for the Copts. His possessions were sold to make the payment and one of the *mubashirin* provided the balance.[7] Pope Mark VI (see chapter two) was the last of the patriarchs to hold office before the occurrence of new circumstances that changed the organization of the community and its representation before the government.

At the beginning of the fifteenth century, the extent of the pope's authority, supported by the government, was made evident in the penalties meted out by Pope John XIII against members of his own community.

Confronted by a case of bigamy that took place in Tukh al-Nasara,[8] where a Coptic man married a Coptic woman while still legally married to his first wife, the pope cited Christian canons that forbid such behavior, then passed sentence on the man:

> No one shall share with him in prayer and mass, go to church with him or to his home, nor greet him or talk to him or give and take with him, share his food or anything else with him, because he has been excommunicated. For whosoever deviates from the canons of his religion is forbidden, and whosoever mixes with a forbidden person shall himself be forbidden. Let all the people know this: the men must shun 'Abid ibn Barsum, and the women must shun Rifqa bint Rufa'il as long as both have deviated from the canons of their religion.[9]

The viability and effectiveness of these penalties is linked, outwardly, to a religious rationale. Their practical application, however, hinged on the relationship between church and state. To a great extent, adherence to church penalties was largely motivated by fear of the legal and social consequences connected with violating such community-based canons designed to govern behavior.[10] The confident imposition of this penalty by the pope, at this early stage in the Ottoman period, attests to his active position as head of the community. Members of the Coptic community, in turn, seem to have been keen to respect these laws governing their membership, since those laws provided the natural context for their social protection from government intrusion.

The social value of such decrees as 'mechanisms' of marginalization may be questioned. Compliance with the penalties meted out was indeed very strict among the Copts, and they shunned all dealings with such culprits.[11] Such actions were a form of self-policing for Copts, who found themselves living in a society governed by legislation rooted in another religious tradition—that of the majority of the population. In this context, the pope had a wide-ranging mandate and an overwhelming influence over his community. It will become clear later on that the eighteenth-century patriarchs were unable to mete out any penalty for similar contraventions due to changes in the ethos and structure of the community.

Sexual Mores and Papal Responses

Toward the end of the Mamluk period, new cultural attitudes and sexual mores left their mark on various classes of society. Despite the religious façade presented by the sultans and emirs, there is evidence that the Mamluk leadership tolerated certain transgressive practices like prostitution.[12] Some of the rulers during this period had no aversion to this practice, allowing it publicly. The great affluence and economic prosperity witnessed during Mamluk times contributed to this situation, as wealthy citizens participated in the importation of slave girls to serve as concubines.

The Mamluk government's acknowledgment of prostitution in public policy extended to the imposition of taxes on income earned. While such taxes were abolished and prostitution was suppressed on an intermittent basis, there is evidence that indicates the practice continued until the end of this period.[13] Indeed, toward the end of Mamluk rule, when the state found itself in dire need of monetary sources, it retained and strengthened this type of taxation, as it brought great amounts of money into the state coffers.[14]

It was only natural that the Copts would be affected by these phenomena, just like other groups of society. The Copts, in particular, amassed great fortunes and many of them enjoyed a life of luxury and comfort.[15] They had female slaves in their homes, some of whom were Muslim women.[16] Pope John XIII addressed these problems head on, adapting and reapplying church canon law to rein in excesses among the members of the Coptic community. He put to good use the mandate granted to the popes by the holy councils by establishing a new legislative philosophy emanating from their stable bases, acknowledging the reality on the ground and facing it with courage. The pope demonstrated the church's awareness of the influence of these phenomena on Coptic society, and this led him to examine some of the canons and adapt them to the changes in society.

The Population Crisis and Coptic Marriage

Many studies have noted the stifling economic crisis of Egypt toward the end of the Mamluk period. Writings of fifteenth-century travelers and of modern historians and travelers report high death rates due to the plague that spread worldwide during that period. Some historians have estimated the loss of rural residents at 80 percent. The plague became known in the east as the Great Annihilation and in the west as the Black Death. It led to an economic crisis: a drastic shortage in labor and an inability to plant large areas of land. Some villages contained fertile agricultural land but no one to plant it.

This had a marked effect on the Copts, as it led to the destruction and desolation of a large number of monasteries, because the urban and rural populations around them had been wiped out.[17] The depletion of the Coptic community was one of the problems still facing the church in the sixteenth century. This problem became more pronounced in regard to the provisions of the canons concerning marriage, especially intermarriage between relatives, as church laws forbade intermarriage for any relations closer than third-generation cousins.

In the face of such a population decrease, it was natural for the few families left in the villages to band together. If the church's canonical restrictions were to be applied, problems would arise because of the presence of only one or two Coptic families in one village. The chances for marriage outside of those circles were effectively nil. As a result, many families ignored church statutes and arranged for the marriage of third-generation cousins, for the sake of survival.

Such patterns of such intermarriage are documented in the case of a family from Asyut. After the death of his wife, a Coptic man named Rizqallah wished to marry a relative who was a cousin of his deceased wife. However, he was opposed by Christians who claimed that the church canons forbade such a union.[18] It appears that such views were widespread because people depended on the written canons, without taking into consideration the immediate concerns of the Copts.

Pope John XIII faced this situation by exhorting the community to disregard the judgments passed by people, as the church alone with its legislative powers had the first and last word on such matters. He cited the text of the law from the collection of church canons compiled by the thirteenth-century author al-Safi ibn al-'Assal *(al-Majmu' al-safawi)* that dealt with this matter:

> The agreed laws of the Church Fathers at the Council of Nicea, and most of the Melkite laws which do not forbid third-generation intermarriage among the many things they forbid, allowed the heads of the clergy to deal with this matter in the best interest of the community and in a manner that does not contradict the legislation. The last chapter of the collection of canons compiled by al-Safi ibn al-'Assal reveals that they are allowed to do this. Seeing that they were a protected minority *(dhimma)* and *their numbers had dwindled in most of their countries*, to the extent that the young men and women found no marriage partners from among the fourth-generation cousins, which compromised their chastity to the extent that some of them may have renounced their faith, they were of the opinion that the common good warranted second-generation intermarriage.

He adds:

> Abba Mikha'il, Archbishop of Damietta, had also mentioned in his collection of laws that intermarriage between first cousins, paternal or maternal, was the custom among Copts before entering the faith, and when they became the disciples of the Evangelist Mark he did not deny them this, so they kept doing it. . . . Consequently, if the Church Fathers had allowed second-cousin intermarriage as we have explained above, because they considered it beneficial for their people after it had been allowed only after third-generation cousins. . . . We affirm to all those who speak in denial of this matter, that none of them has been empowered by God Almighty to speak of matters that do not concern them. These affairs are the concern of the bishops who are the teachers and fathers of the church, who must take into account what their people can sustain in the times in which they live.[19]

The number of times a person could get married also became an issue of contention during Pope John XIII's reign. Coptic canon law stipulated that a third marriage was permissible but undesirable, and that a fourth marriage was outright adultery.[20] When such a case was brought before Pope John XIII—he was asked about a man who had been married three times and each time his wife died, and who wanted to marry for the fourth time—the pope agreed to the union, and sent a message to the priests explaining his philosophy in approving this marriage, which was technically in violation of church canons. He wrote a relatively long six-page pastoral message, explaining:

> Then a group inquired about the case from the medicinal and not the canonical point of view (in the sense that there was a firm belief that a fourth marriage was unlawful) . . . as for the canonical laws, the Church Fathers said that the third marriage was a sign of seduction to a person with self-control and an unclean pitfall in the eyes of the church, and that it was greatly detested and there could be no lawful marriage after that. If the person in question can control himself, then that would be best, but if he is unable to do so and there is fear that he might fall into sin, then it is because of this fear that we have consented by the grace of God for one of the priests to perform the marriage. . . . We have allowed this because of the lack of patience and endurance. For the Holy Bible says that whosoever can endure let him endure, but if he lacks patience then he should marry, for it

> is better to marry than to burn in sin. The Church Fathers who laid down the above-mentioned laws said: "If we have deferred something, then pass the appropriate judgment. If something is still remaining, then it should be mentioned by the bishops. If we have passed up something, then God shall reveal it to him who is deserving and shall guide the church with him who is deserving until it reaches peaceful waters. Those who passed judgment concerning the contrition of sinners in times long past delegated to the leaders the power to facilitate it or to be severe toward it, as the case may be. . . . Patriarch Severus [Sawiris] said that necessity compels us, because of the hardness of the heart and the corruption of the times, to give license in certain matters and to be merciful to some people. . . . Thus it is now necessary that, because of the vast destruction, desolation, and the scarcity (of people) everywhere . . . I am permitting the leaders of the clergy throughout the ages to take into account the time and the age and to decide on matters, in a manner that would not detract from the basic principles, with an eye to the restoration and salvation of the spirit. They should manage their congregation according to what they (the congregation) can withstand in their age."[21]

In these examples, the patriarch devised novel methods to deal with the canons of the church. He sought for the spirit in which they were written, trying to renew them in a manner compatible with their philosophy, while adapting to new social exigencies.

The pope was also forced to mete out punishments to address and curb incidents of prostitution, concubinage, and homosexuality within the Coptic community. Some Copts were engaging publicly in prostitution, and many, especially the rich among them, took on concubines from among the slave population, as this phenomenon had become widespread and popular in Egypt. Some also went so far as to engage in polygamy. In such cases Pope John XIII meted out harsh penalties in two aspects. The first pertained to ritual participation in church worship: he excommunicated those involved in prostitution. The second involved the severing of social ties: he forbade all Christians to have anything to do with those sinners who persisted in their transgressions and would not repent.

One of the problems facing the church was not only prostitution itself, but also the practice of boasting about it in public. It became customary for men to exchange favors by exchanging prostitutes, or to cover up for each other, especially in the case of married men. Some men would even disguise themselves when they went to the well-known whorehouses in Cairo, or would have their attendants arrange clandestine meetings for them with the prostitutes. In such cases the pope imposed the above-mentioned religious and social penalties, and counseled men to marry according to the law.

> He who is not married should marry as has been ordained by Christian canons to preserve his uprightness. The apostolic Pope Athanasius said in the ninety-fourth part of his canons: If a young man is deserving of marriage and his parents do not get him married, then if he sins his sins shall fall more upon them.[22]

Concubinage[23] arose with the influx of slaves flowing into Egypt and the spreading fashion among the wealthy to own both black and white slave girls. It was quite common for rich Copts to acquire slave girls for their households. Indeed, there is consistent evidence for the Coptic practice of concubinage since the time the Arabs entered Egypt.[24] However, church opposition varied according to the period and according to the method of decision-making at the community level. During the time of Pope John XIII the position of the church was unwavering: he stood firmly against any violations of or deviations from the church canons on this matter.

It appears that Pope John was greatly disturbed when some Copts asked about the fate of children from concubinage according to Coptic Church canons. In one account, there is the story of a slave girl who became pregnant twice. The first time she gave birth to a girl who died, and the second time she gave birth to a boy. When asked, she acknowledged that the boy was sired by her married master.[25] It is interesting that certain people inquired about the church's opinion regarding this matter on the premise that "this matter was detrimental to the wife." Pope John's answer was stern and severe. He imposed the harshest penalty on violators: he forbade them from taking communion, and he also forbade any dealings with them by members of the Coptic community until they had returned to the church, renounced their sins, and were cleansed. In this, he took a strong position against a practice that he feared might become widespread, although he knew that he was up against the rich and influential in the Coptic community.[26]

Pope Gabriel VII (1525–68)

Pope John XIII's successor was Pope Gabriel (Ghubriyal) VII. Of him, one of the monks at the Monastery of St. Antony wrote, "He had a strong standing among his people and an extraordinary influence over all Christians."[27] There is plenty of information available about this patriarch and his family. His full name, as written in many official documents, was Ghubrial ibn

Yuhanna ibn Mihanna,[28] and before he was appointed pope he had a brother who was also a bishop (Bishop Mikha'il ibn Yuhanna ibn Mihanna).[29] He attended many occasions with Pope John XIII[30] and had been himself a renowned monk called Rafa'il from the Monastery of Our Lady of Suryan. The evidence suggests that he came from a wealthy family. Pope Gabriel himself endowed many pieces of land to the monasteries, including a large house in Cairo.[31] He also endowed a large area of land in 1557 to his two brothers living in Cairo, 'Anbar and Yusuf, and to their children.[32] These actions by the pope indicate the power, wealth, and influence his family had among the Coptic community.

During my search into the records of the Cairo shari'a courts, I discovered that Pope Gabriel continued to fight against polygamy with the same vehemence as his predecessor. He used the same procedure of imposing social penalties to punish offenders and to dissuade others from engaging in multiple marriages: according to his decree, those being penalized by the church were to be ostracized by the entire community. The power of this patriarch is evidenced by the community's strict adherence to this sentence and their fear of violating it. An example is found in the case of a family living in Misr al-Qadima (Old Cairo) who were in the habit of practicing polygamy. The natural place for them to solemnize their marriages was in the Islamic courts. Accordingly, I found marriage cases belonging to the family of Sadaqa ibn Shammakh ibn Manqura, indicating that his four children (two girls and two boys) were married in the shari'a courts.[33] When the entire family was penalized by the church, and the Coptic community was ordered to shun them completely, the extent of the Copts' compliance with the orders of Pope Gabriel is evident in the subsequent lack of interaction between this family and their Coptic neighbors. Although Sadaqa ibn Shammakh ibn Manqura's family was in the business of pressing and trading linseed oil, which was a very popular one, their dealings with the Coptic community were very limited indeed. There are accounts of twenty-eight transactions (financial, commercial, or personal), which can be broken down as follows: nineteen with Muslims; seven with Christians, who were then subject to the same penalties; and two with Christians whose positions are not identified. This means that the Coptic community shunned this family almost completely, even while other Copts were engaged in the same profession.

The same results obtain in the case of other Copts who resorted to Islamic shari'a courts regarding marriage and related matters during the time of this patriarch in Old Cairo. The following table shows the extent of this practice.[34]

Registration number	Time period	Number of cases	Cases involving Copts
86	April 5, 1544–March 28, 1545	528	7
87	March 2,1548–January 30, 1549	553	2
88	February 24, 1551–December 29, 1551	678	7
89	January 18, 1552–April 5, 1553	785	7
90	November 1, 1561–September 17, 1562	549	5
91	January 17, 1564–November 29, 1564	354	4
92	July 24, 1566–March 4, 1567	364	3
Total		3,811	35

Despite the population density of Copts in Old Cairo, the percentage of those who resorted to Islamic courts for marriage and related matters was, in the end, less than one percent. And these documented cases are confined to a very small number of families—only three in total. Thus, Pope Gabriel's policy of ostracizing church members who sought multiple marriages through the Islamic courts seems to have dissuaded the vast majority of the Coptic population from engaging in these practices.

Relations with the Church of Rome (Popes John XIV and Gabriel VIII, 1571–1603)

The reigns of Popes John XIV and Gabriel VIII (like that of their predecessors and namesakes John XIII and Gabriel VII) gave rise to new circumstances and challenges for the Coptic community. The most important development was brought about by the Church of Rome in its efforts to bring the Coptic Church under its banner. The reaction of the Coptic patriarchs to these efforts—and the conformity or disagreement of the Coptic population regarding the church's official stance—had a very powerful impact on the way that John XIV and Gabriel VIII discharged their duties of office. The political and administrative situation prevailing in Egypt at the time also helped bring matters to a head.

Pope John XIV (1571–85)

In the early sixteenth century, the Church of Rome was confronted by two challenges simultaneously. The first was the danger posed by the Turks and their penetration into the Christian world. Their occupation of new territories, formerly under Byzantine control, was seen as a threat to Roman church hegemony.[35] The second was posed by the reform movement led by Martin Luther in Europe. One of the many measures taken by the Church of Rome in reaction to these challenges was an ecumenical effort to unite the Christian world, including the Coptic Church.

A century earlier, the Turkish danger had motivated the convening of the Council of Florence in 1442, which had been organized on the initiative of the Byzantine emperor for the sake of Christian unity. A representative of the Coptic Church had attended. This council was unable to put its resolutions into effect.[36]

The latter half of the sixteenth century, however, saw a series of attempts by the Catholic Church to draw the Coptic Church into an anti-Reformist movement. The first of these attempts had come in 1561 during the tenure of the Coptic pope Gabriel VII. The pace of this dialogue quickened during the time of the succeeding popes. Letters were exchanged, and this correspondence has been published and analyzed in an important study by Buri.[37] Later official letters between the Roman and Coptic papacies, up through the early eighteenth century, have been published by Antoine Rabbath[38] and Jean-Pierre Trossen.[39] However, the rush of messages exchanged at the end of the sixteenth century is especially noteworthy.[40] Of central concern to this point is the position of the Coptic patriarchs with regard to this correspondence and its impact on the status of the Copts.

In his reply to a message from Pope Gregory XIII of Rome, one notes the sincerity of Pope John XIV (1571–85), his desire to unite the Christian world, and his praise of the measures taken by the Church of Rome to this end. While he mentions doctrinal differences, he describes them as "stubborn opinions" to which the churches should not be too much attached.[41] When Gregory sent a Roman delegation to Cairo to negotiate with the Coptic patriarch, matters ran smoothly as the Coptic patriarch agreed to proclaim officially a formula of faith. Pope John held a meeting that brought together some of his bishops, and all were initially open to the idea of unification, but later a number of them decided to stand in opposition to the proposal.[42] The delegation made another attempt with the Coptic pope, and it appears that he had come to a unilateral decision to sign a treaty of agreement with the papal delegation, but he died suddenly before he could sign it.[43]

It is noteworthy that Pope John XIV restricted the discussion of union with the Church of Rome to the clergy. The decision whether to approve or oppose such a union belonged solely to the bishops. No discussion with the Ottoman government ensued, despite the fact that an ecclesiastical agreement with Rome would have had larger political implications with respect to the jurisdiction of the sultanate. It seems, however, that the patriarch was oblivious to these risks and viewed the prospect of ecumenical rapprochement as an "in-house" matter. During John's reign as pope in the last quarter of the sixteenth century, he and his clergy still retained sole and uncontested control of the church's leadership.

Pope Gabriel VIII (1587–1603)

After John XIV's death, the Roman papacy once again renewed its efforts at unification with the Coptic Church, and additional messages were exchanged between the two sides. John's successor, Gabriel VIII, appears to have favored unification. Indeed, some sources say that he actually signed a decree of unification with the Catholic Church in January 1597.[44]

Pope Gabriel VIII's desire for unification with the Church of Rome led him to take a bold step at the urging of the Roman pontiff Pope Sixtus V: he agreed to begin applying the Gregorian calendar to church life in Egypt. This controversial decision immediately ignited a vehement rebellion against Gabriel. Over the course of his reign, he would be dismissed and then later reinstated. This reaction against the pope's act reveals a growing degree of political awareness among the Coptic gentry at the end of the sixteenth and the beginning of the seventeenth centuries.

Details of this incident are in the records of the shari'a courts. It began in the Bab 'Ali Court in Cairo, which was the highest court in Egypt at the time and was headed by a Turkish judge appointed by the capital of the Ottoman Empire in Istanbul. This judge held sway over all the courts in Egypt. In reaction to Gabriel's decision regarding the Gregorian calendar, some of the Coptic gentry in Lower Egypt submitted a query to the muftis requesting a fatwa, or formal legal opinion, on the position of the Coptic patriarch vis-à-vis Islamic law if he were to violate the principles and canons of their church.

The phrasing of the query is revealing. It asked, "What do you say about the head of one of the Christian communities who deliberately causes his community to violate the dictates of their church with regard to fasting and feasts? If their case is submitted to the ruler *(wali al-amr)*, would he force the members of this community to obey their leader, thereby going against their church, or would he order that leader to allow them to follow the dictates of their church?"[45] The wording of the question predetermines the answer, as it presupposes that the most important function of the patriarch is the preservation of his canons and his church system, in accordance with the *tawqi'* that defines the scope of his authority.

The answer given accorded with the wishes of the requesters. The court decided that, from the point of view of shari'a, the patriarch had no right to change the calendar, and that he was not entitled to force others to violate the church system. The Copts' act of resorting to a fatwa indicates an awareness of the efficacy of the court's decision and its impact on issues that might be brought to court in the future. It also shows that the Coptic gentry of Lower Egypt knew that this matter was governed by the jurisprudential technicalities used to determine the status of Christian communities within the framework of the Islamic state, and that the final word was that of the Ottoman ruler *(wali al-amr)*.[46]

The matter did not end there, however. On the basis of this sentence, Coptic dissenters obtained similar judgments from the courts of Mahalla al-Kubra and Diwan 'Ali. They then headed to the Court of Alexandria and brought an additional action against the patriarch. This time they sought to demonstrate the patriarch's desire to contradict their ancient books in the matter of determining the date of Easter. They used the same arguments to accuse him of contravening their ancient customs and insisting on a weak basis of calculation, one deemed inaccurate according to the opinion of Muslim astronomers. Their question to the muftis this time rested on a dangerous issue: Was the patriarch authorized to act in contravention of Muslim rulings? The answer given prevented the patriarch from implementing the Christian ruling and obligated him to abide by the ruling of the Muslim astronomers.[47]

Analysis of the discourse used in opposition to this patriarchal policy shows that the notables' arguments did not contain any reference to the history of hostility between Copts and the Church of Rome, nor to any change in loyalty to another authority outside the realm of the Ottoman sultanate. This means that no one knew about the unification efforts that provided the larger context for the proposed change in calendar. In fact, the Coptic pope was misleading the Roman Church. He had told the Copts nothing. At the least, if these notables had known about this proposed unification, it would have provided them a stronger argument for motivating the Ottoman state against the patriarch.

As far as Pope Gabriel VIII is concerned, what was at stake in these conversations with Rome? Among the many letters sent by the Coptic patriarch to the Roman pontiff, one frequently finds requests for monetary assistance. The Coptic patriarch laments the bad economic conditions in Egypt, refers to his many financial responsibilities as head of the church, and appeals to the pope of Rome for financial support. There are hints in this correspondence that the Catholic pope had previously promised and sent amounts of money at regular intervals.

One Coptic manuscript recounts this conflict in very different terms from our other sources. According to this text, Pope Gabriel was the one who brought in the Muslim astronomers, and their opinion was not to abide by the proposed revision. On the next page of the manuscript, we are then told that certain Lower Egyptian gentry sought this order and that they spent large sums of money to prove the soundness of this calendar calculation (it is not clear which calculation they mean, the western or the Coptic). These gentry accordingly laid down a timetable to determine Easter and obtained an edict from Constantinople to apply it.[48] The confused account that this text gives reminds us of the need to use caution when reading and interpreting the historical sources.

In any case, the rebellion against the pope's decision was based in Lower Egypt. In contrast, the Coptic notables of Cairo seem to have sided with the patriarch, or at least did not actively oppose his directives. This limited exertion of power by the Coptic gentry in Lower Egypt under Gabriel VIII would portend a more widespread rebellion against the next pope (which will be discussed further on). Unfortunately, we do not have many details about the position of the Copts in other areas of Egypt. There is evidence that, at the end of the sixteenth century, Lower Egypt churches were under the influence of the monks of Wadi Natrun, and that this may have contributed to controversies that erupted between Copts and their bishops in some areas. We have ample information about the power and influence of monks at the monasteries of Baramus and St. Macarius in particular. A century earlier, Pope John XIII (1484–1525) had drawn attention to the role that monks played in setting the people in Lower Egypt against their bishops.[49] These conditions may have still obtained in the late sixteenth century when the Copts in Lower Egypt began to be emboldened in their opposition to the church hierarchy. However, this matter requires further, in-depth research into the social causes and outcomes of these conflicts. The sources available at present do not provide us with a conclusive explanation for this series of events.

Although the gentry of Lower Egypt compelled the patriarch to bow to their wishes regarding the calculation of the date of Easter, such problems did not deter Pope Gabriel VIII from his goals in other areas, nor did they limit his capacity to make decisions that affected the traditional foundations of the Coptic Church's heritage, such as his continued issuing of orders to amend certain fasts and abolish others.[50] Nor did Gabriel's death in 1603 mark an end to the Catholic Church's efforts at reunification with the Coptic community. To the contrary, the Church of Rome pursued its aim relentlessly until it realized a major breakthrough a century and a half later, when one of the bishops of the Coptic Church (Bishop Antunius of Jirja) converted to Catholicism in 1758. This event, however, would elicit a much less accommodating response from the Coptic pope at that time, Pope Mark VII (1745–69), who initiated a series of harsh polemical attacks against the Catholic Church and its beliefs.[51]

A Period of Turbulence: Stirrings of Internal Conflict (Pope Mark V to Pope Matthew III, 1603–46)

The first half of the seventeenth century witnessed important changes in Egypt's political and administrative system. The centralization of authority of the Ottoman state began to break down, and the military began to gain more influence at the expense of state authority. There were decentralizing trends at work in the Coptic Church as well: stirrings of an internal conflict within the church would result in major changes in the composition of the community and its centers of power.

Pope Mark V (1603–19)

According to Coptic sources, the Coptic gentry of Lower Egypt continued to rebel against papal leadership during the reign of Pope Mark V (1603–19), and these tensions seem to have spread to Cairo as well. The church sources from the period deliberately focused on the Copts of Lower Egypt in an effort to make it appear that this was a conflict between Lower Egypt dissenters and the Cairo faithful. However, we find that the Cairo Copts were involved in the dispute, for some of them sided with the patriarch while others were against him.

There are conflicting reports about the causes of this dissension. One of the manuscripts makes brief mention of the matter: "This pope was afflicted by many hardships caused by the people of Lower Egypt because of fasting and marriages, and the rulers of Egypt imprisoned him in the tower of Alexandria." The author of the manuscript then passes a general judgment on Pope Mark V, saying that he loved money and wine.[52] This alleged love for wine was included in the text of the legal petition that a certain Fadlallah al-Dimirdashi submitted—on behalf of the Lower Egyptian gentry—to the wali of Egypt, enumerating the accusations against the pope, saying, "He sits on a high chair and orders the people to bow before him and offer him incense as though he were a god, he forbids meat and milk and allows wine."[53] It is evident that the wording of this petition is deceptive, as the plaintiff writes about Christian fasting in a manner designed to make it objectionable to the Muslim ruler. He further presents the rituals involved in honoring the patriarch in a manner implying that the head of the Coptic Church had assumed for himself manifestations of power and influence that should have been accorded only to the wali. In the end, the plaintiff's rhetoric was effective and he got what he wanted: the wali imprisoned Pope Mark for over a year and moved to replace him with another patriarch.[54]

It is worth mentioning that the wali who removed the patriarch had embarked on a movement of reform since coming into office. The reforms involved his putting an end to many forms of oppression imposed by the senior military personnel against the Egyptian people. The wali made a point of responding to most of the grievances submitted to him, and took resolute decisions in many matters affecting the interests of the people.[55] Thus, his decision to remove the pope may have come within the context of correcting perceived wrongs for Egyptians in general. In this way, his response to a request made by a member of the Coptic community followed suit: it put an end to reported acts of oppression exercised by the influential leader of a large minority religious community.

Some modern historians have reported that the main reason for the rebellion of the Coptic gentry of Lower Egypt against the patriarch was their desire to practice polygamy, and that they were joined by the bishop of Damietta. The first to put forward this thesis was a British historian who does not identify her sources.[56] However, most historians since have followed her lead.[57] Whatever the reasons for the origin of this conflict, its outcome and its impact on the Coptic community can be deduced from various sources.

The outcome of the complaint lodged by the gentry of Lower Egypt was that the wali decided to depose the patriarch and appoint another one named John, whose given name had been Girgis ibn Butrus. Once in power, this new pope began to remove the aides of the deposed Pope Mark V and to replace them with new aides, who were to be responsible for the management of the *waqfs*. In particular, he appointed Mu'allim Mikha'il ibn Rafa'il as his deputy for the administration of these *waqfs*.[58]

A conflict ensued, which took place in the district of Qasr al-Sham' in Old Cairo. It should be noted that the entire population of Qasr al- Sham' was comprised of Copts, most of whom were tenants of church *waqfs*, as the majority of the houses and utilities belonged to the *waqfs* of Old Cairo. Accordingly, this district was affected by the change in church leadership in two ways. First, as Copts, the residents owed allegiance to their church leadership. Second, as tenants of church houses, they had a direct legal relationship with the church administration: for example, the administrator of the *waqf* had to approve the length of their rental contracts. Consequently, the change of administrator could either benefit or harm their economic interests, and such changes could have an impact on their opinions regarding the exercise of church leadership.

The problems began with the family members of Pope Mark V: the interloper pope, John, raised a complaint against the brother and father of his ousted predecessor, accusing them of seizing patriarchate *waqf* possessions unlawfully. The wali referred the matter to the Misr al-Qadima Court, and the patriarch's father and brother were actually arrested. The document notably refers to Pope Mark as "the former Christian patriarch."[59]

John's deputy was relentness in his pursuit of residents of Qasr al- Sham' who remained loyal to Pope Mark V. The Christians in this district seem to have been divided into two factions: one faction sided with the deposed pope, while the other faction was opposed to him and supported the interloper. Many cases were heard by the Misr al-Qadima court concerning these divided loyalties, most of which ended in favor of John's deputy. These decisions seemed to mark a recognition of the new leadership as a fait accompli. The residents of Misr al-Qadima were compelled to accept the measures imposed by Mu'allim Mikha'il as deputy for the newly recognized pope.[60] Between the two factions, there were ongoing tensions, to the extent that some residents secured court decisions evicting other Christians from Qasr al- Sham', on the grounds that their presence was detrimental to the residents of the district.[61]

This conflict intensified after the return of Pope Mark V from his exile. It appears that the patriarch was reinstated after the tenure of Wali Muhammad Pasha Qul Qaran ended on August 28, 1611. There were clashes between the supporters of the two rival claimants to the papal throne. After Mark V's reinstatement, many of the Qasr al- Sham' Christians supported his decision to remove the deputy appointed by John and to appoint somebody else in his place.[62] The deputy stood firm against these actions, protesting that he had in his possession official documents from an official patriarch (that is, the interloper patriarch), documents that upheld his legal right to serve as *waqf* administrator.[63] However, the majority of the Coptic residents of Qasr al- Sham' supported Mark V in this matter and he served out his term until his death in 1619.[64]

Pope John XV (1619–28)

Pope Mark V's successor was named Pope John XV. The sources hardly mention this John except for a few lines that describe his uprightness, justice, and impartial decisions. It is noted, however, that he died of poisoning. The story goes that during a tour of Upper Egypt he spent the night in the home of one of the notables of Abnub, who happened to have a concubine (or perhaps more than one) in his household. When the pope reprimanded him, the notable served him poisoned food and he died.[65] This incident is a further indication of the growing tension between the pope and this class of Coptic notables.

The response of the pope on the occasion of his visit to the notable's home makes sense when one considers that if he were to have ignored this violation of canon law, it would have been construed as a form of tacit approval by a local community that would have been all too aware of his presence in town. It is noteworthy then that the sources in question use the term "reprimanded" to qualify the pope's reaction, a term that does not imply an actual penalty. Registers of shari'a courts during the time of Pope John XV reveal numerous cases of concubinage among the Copts, and in the legacy of a Coptic man, there is mention of his white slave Qamar bint 'Abdallah, and her son Bahiri whom he had fathered, as well as the slave Rommana bint 'Abdallah the Ethiopian, also designated as the mother of one of his children.[66] There are many other such cases, but there is no evidence for a generally applied penalty intended to remedy the then-widespread phenomenon of concubinage.

Pope John XV personally assumed the responsibility of running the *waqfs* and financial matters, without delegating this authority to any of the gentry. He assigned the administration of the *waqfs* of inhabited monasteries to the heads of those monasteries, who were chosen from among the monks. This also applied to the convents of nuns, as they were likewise the legal administrators of their *waqfs*. So we find that Sister Irani bint Yuhanna ibn Mikha'il, mother superior of Dayr Harit Zuwayla, Mariam bint Yusuf ibn Yuhanna, mother superior of Dayr al-Banat in Misr al-Qadima, and Rifqa bint Ma'tuk ibn Mansur, mother superior of the Convent of Ifrusiya, all rented out the property of their convents.[67] This consolidation and centralization of authority by the pope in matters pertaining to the administration of *waqfs* could have been intended to prevent problems associated with changing the *waqf* administrator with each transition in papal leadership. Pope John XV therefore insisted that the administration of the *waqfs* should remain in the hands of the heads of the monasteries, who were largely unscathed by these growing tensions between the priesthood and the laity.

Finally, his actions could also be understood as an attempt to curb the growing influence of the notables, out of fear that they might assume more administrative control over the affairs of the community.

Pope Matthew III (1628–46)

The choice of Hegumen Tadrus al-Tukhi, head of the Monastery of St. Macarius, as the next pope was a wise one for many reasons. Al-Tukhi, who came to be known as Matthew III (1628–46), had been in good standing during the time of the previous pope, and he had had many dealings with the gentry of Cairo and Lower Egypt, according to evidence found in the documents of the shari'a courts.[68] He had also obtained practical administrative experience from traveling between Cairo and his monastery in Wadi al-Natrun to finalize the financial affairs of the monastery. This experience was the outcome of Pope John XV's policy of assigning the task of administering monastery *waqfs* to the heads of monasteries.

The wisdom of Pope Matthew III was apparent from the first day he took office. In an unusual action, he registered a deed at the Bab 'Ali Court that contained the Ottoman pasha's approval of his appointment as the new patriarch. The deed stated that he alone was responsible for the *waqfs* of all the churches and monasteries in Upper and Lower Egypt.[69] Scholars of Ottoman documents know that the appointment of a *taqrir al-nuzur* (*waqf* administrator) was issued only at the request of the appointee. This means that Pope Matthew III himself requested this *taqrir*, which safeguarded his full rights to manage the affairs of the *waqfs* of the churches and monasteries.

The rest of Matthew III's tenure was largely a period of peace and quiet.[70] This peace, however, was a precursor of storms that shook the foundations of the community and led to its reorganization after the death of this wise and knowledgeable patriarch.

2

Contesting Authority: Patriarchs and Coptic Notables

(Pope Mark VI to Pope Mark VIII, 1646–1798)

At this point, we are confronted by problems that are practical and scientific at one and the same time. In a book (and a series) dedicated to the history of the patriarchs and their leadership role in the Coptic community, any deviation from this focus might be considered an unwarranted digression. However, beginning from the middle of the seventeenth century, there occurred a real and tangible shift in the leadership of the community, away from the Coptic popes and toward the *arakhina* (distinguished notables). The patriarchs retained their leadership in name only, while the power of the notables in the life of the church came to be acknowledged and accepted by all. The government administration began to regard the notables as the actual motivators and decision-makers for the community and dealt with them as such. And in general, the Copts themselves seem to have been content with this arrangement. The church—at all levels—accepted the notables' new leadership role.

If our sole goal were to focus exclusively on the patriarchs for our study of the Coptic Church's history from the latter half of the seventeenth century through the end of the eighteenth, the end result would be only a few lines to sum up this era—despite the fact that it is a period replete with social-historical interest. Accordingly, I have decided to document this period from a variety of angles, which from my point of view are more useful for placing these historical developments in their proper context and for understanding the many ways in which these changes in leadership impacted life within the Coptic community.

Pashas and Patriarchs

The end of the sixteenth and the beginning of the seventeenth century had witnessed a series of global shifts and internal upheavals that led to the weakening of Ottoman state structures, especially the ranks of the military.[1] These circumstances left their mark on all provinces within the empire, including Egypt, and one result was a widespread decentralization of authority. The seat of authority at the imperial capital granted a wider mandate to the pasha (governor) in Egypt, who served as the sultan's official representative there. One of his new prerogatives was the appointment of key officials without consulting Istanbul. For instance, the pasha was entitled to appoint the *daftardar* and the *ruznamji*, two of the highest administrative posts: the *daftardar* was the chief financial official, and the *ruznamji* was the chief administrative official.

However, the authority of the pasha himself was merely formal, and by the period under consideration here it had declined considerably in relation to other centers of power in Egypt. As of the beginning of the seventeenth century, there was a real shift in authority toward the *ujaq*s (military officials), who were competing with the Mamluk houses in the struggle for power. The balance then tipped in favor of the Mamluks, who reasserted their power once again in the middle of the eighteenth century.[2]

This shift in power into the hands of the distinguished emirs and *ujaq*s enabled them to gain control over most of the wealth of Egypt. They took over the most important urban and rural estates during the seventeenth and the first half of the eighteenth centuries, and sought to increase their sources of income by various means at the expense of the state treasury and the taxpayers.[3]

This change in the political model of Egyptian rule in the seventeenth and eighteenth centuries had another important effect, which was the change in the concept of institution, for it also was transformed into an empty form with no real substance. This applied to state institutions and structures as well; the military establishment itself produced strong personalities who overstepped the role designed for them by the state, accumulating power and authority that enabled them to make enormous personal gains. In these circumstances, the military establishment was penetrated by individuals who were not in the least bit connected to the military, to the extent that the practical notion of the military was lost. This also happened in other areas of the Ottoman state.[4]

Similar patterns in the accumulation and distribution of power were noticeable in the Coptic community. Church government became more localized, as personal influence and special interests became the order of the day. Consequently, dealings within the Coptic community increasingly relied on the patronage of influential persons and not necessarily on the canonically established clerical hierarchy. In this way, the situation of the Coptic community was, to a large extent, a reflection of the larger political landscape. The pope continued to serve as the official representative of the community in name only, while true power rested more and more in the hands of influential notables. As influence was linked to wealth, to a large degree, the Coptic *mubashirin* became responsible for the affairs of the community vis-à-vis the government administration, while the patriarchs and their councils of bishops virtually disappeared from government correspondence.

This shift within the community toward the senior *mubashirin* came as a result of an internal conflict that traced its roots to the start of the seventeenth century. The biography of Pope Mark VI (1646–56) sums up the conditions prevailing in the period prior to his rule, and at the same time also serves as a key indicator of what was on the horizon in the coming 150 years until the end of the eighteenth century, when the patriarch became like the Ottoman pasha, an authority in name only, while the real power was in the hands of a new ruling class.

The book of the lives of the patriarchs contains a fleeting observation describing the beginning of Pope Mark VI's tenure in office: "At the beginning of the period of Pope Mark there occurred a rivalry between him and Mu'allim Bishara, which resulted in intensification of the boycott between them and strong hostility."[5] This sentence gives a hint of the vehement conflict that was stirring the pope and the senior *mubashirin* who were gaining power. The writer goes on to describe the patriarch, saying, "He forcefully took great wealth from the people; he was full of wrath and all the bishops, priests and laypeople were aggravated by him."[6]

The documentary record, however, belies this report. The actual record of the inheritance left by this patriarch reveals that he had no possessions except his few clothes and personal belongings, which amounted to 7,078 para, a very modest sum.[7] This means that the patriarch possessed no wealth. In fact, at his death, his estate owed money to Diwan al-Jawali.

In light of this, we can therefore reassess the accusations made against the patriarch by his biographer as the beginning of the notables' infiltration into the religious institution, and perhaps a corresponding shift of sentiment in favor of this rising lay class. In the end, the patriarch's estate was confiscated by Diwan al-Jawali and it was sold at auction in the presence of this Mu'allim Bishara.[8] It was not common practice for the Copts to allow the estate of their patriarch to be auctioned off in such a public manner. The confiscation was a strong and clear message to the church hierarchy that the notables were on the rise and were taking charge. After Mark VI's death, even the nomination and appointment of patriarchs fell into the hands of the gentry, and they took authority in all matters related to community life.

The Role of the Distinguished Notables in the Lives of Copts

The circumstances surrounding the death of Pope Mark VI and the auctioning of his estate represent a dividing line in the history of both the church leadership and the community. After this, the notables were meticulous in maintaining control over the selection and burial of subsequent popes. Thus, after the death of the next patriarch, Pope Matthew IV (1660–75), the notables outdid themselves in shrouding him for burial, and Mu'allim Bishara bore the greatest share of the expenses for his funeral ceremony.

The Arabic term *arakhina* was widely used to designate this wealthy class of Coptic lay elite. The *arakhina* had long played an important role on behalf of their community whenever the opportunity presented itself. They had a high profile in the state financial and administrative apparatus, often working with the distinguished emirs and persons of influence. Until the middle of the seventeenth century, they acted as assistants to the patriarch in the discharge of his duties. However, from that point onward, the notables acquired numerous additional assets that placed them in a particular position of eminence within their community. The result was an important cultural transformation in the history of the Copts.

This class of lay Copts inherited the highest-ranking posts in the state's financial and administrative apparatus: they were often employed in the service of high-ranking *ujaq*s and emirs, which brought them close to the decision-makers in Egyptian government and society. Once the *ujaq*s and emirs assumed the reins of power, they began to entrench and expand their personal fortunes at the expense of state resources. It was only natural that the interests of this ruling class should coincide and become cemented with the interests of the Coptic *mubashirin*, and that the *arakhina* should seek to benefit from the influence of their employers in order to further the interests of their community.

This is not the place to list all the names of the *arakhina* and their posts during this period. Suffice it to say that Copts were found virtually everywhere in the service of men of influence. The *mubashir* to the *katkhuda ta'ifa mustahfazan* was always a Copt, this *katkhuda* being the highest-ranking position in Egypt from the second half of the seventeenth century until the first half of the eighteenth. This post of *mubashir* to the *katkhuda* was held by the following persons:

1. Mu'allim Girgis Mansur al-Tukhi, who served under Ibrahim Katkhuda Mustahfazan;[9]
2. Mu'allim Yusuf Makramallah, who served under Ahmed Agha Katkhuda Mustahfazan;[10]

3. Mu'allim Lutfallah Abu Yusuf, who served under Amir Kujak Muhammad Katkhuda Mustahfazan;[11]
4. Mu'allim Girgis Yusuf al-Suruji, who served under 'Uthman Katkhuda Mustahfazan.[12]

One of the highest-ranking posts attained by a Copt was the position of *mubashir* to Diwan al-Ruznama, the most important financial administrative organ at the time. The most prominent persons to assume this post were Mu'allim Yuhanna Abu Masri[13] and Mu'allim Rizqallah al-Badawi.[14] One could go on and on in listing the names of those who served as *mubashirin* for the most influential people in Egypt.[15]

Religious and Economic Ties

Contemporary sources mention the good relations maintained by the *arakhina* with Islamic religious leaders during this period. Copts were, moreover, engaged in the service of the most prestigious and politically connected families in Egypt, as in the case of Mu'allim Butrus wild Yusuf, *mubashir* for the household of one Sadatina bani al-Siddiq.[16] There was also a Copt in the service of the *qadi al-qudah*, the most important figure in the Islamic legal system.[17] The Coptic gentry were likewise on good terms with many of the religious scholars *('ulama)* at al-Azhar University. A case in point was one of the most prominent sheikhs of al-Azhar in the middle of the eighteenth century, Skeikh 'Abdallah al-Shabrawi,[18] who had many dealings with wealthy and influential Copts. Such dealings went a long way toward facilitating business that required shari'a approval and the settling of problems related to application of Islamic law. For example, because of his good relations with the *faqih*s (those who rendered legal opinions), Mu'allim Rizq succeeded in changing the content of a decree (fatwa) that had convicted a Christian of insulting a prominent Muslim merchant and sentenced him to death by burning.[19] Such relationships also had a bearing on the ability of certain Coptic personalities to rise to social prominence: in these circles, there was a marked diminishment of religious and community prejudices.

The economic fortunes of the *mubashirin* swelled during this period. This is evident from the huge inheritances they left behind, some of which have surfaced in the registers of the court of al-Qisma al-'Arabiya.[20] Their wealth is also clear from the huge size of the financial transactions made by the *arakhina* in this period, including their vast expenditures on churches, monasteries, and other projects within the community. The amassing of these Coptic fortunes was linked to the fortunes amassed by the Muslim emirs. Indeed, a certain percentage of the emirs' wealth lined the pockets of *mubashirin*. However, further research is required to determine how the *mubashirin* sources of income were invested and enlarged. It is clear, however, that they dedicated a great deal of their wealth to serving the interests of their own community.

The Selection and Succession of Coptic Lay Leaders

As for the Coptic Church, the clergy largely acquiesced to the leadership of the *arakhina* and left the running of community affairs to them, while the common Coptic layperson regarded them as a source of refuge and protection in times of trouble. This does not mean that there was always complete agreement among the notables. Internal conflicts sometimes manifested themselves, as a result of attempts made by some to have their sons inherit their power and influence within the community, or to divide their spheres of influence. In some cases, conversion to Islam by certain families of distinguished notables led to devastating feuds.[21]

As a way of adjudicating authority in a peaceable manner, the *mubashirin* established among themselves a custom similar to the system of the *sheikh al-balad*, in which the emirs would elect one of their own as the first among equals. Thus, it became a common practice among the Copts to elect one of the *arakhina* to be the leader of their compatriots, even if others within the group maintained a similar level of power and influence. This selection was not done by nomination and voting, but was performed through the granting of a title that authorized that person to serve as a spokesperson for the community before the government. This matter is quite clear in the church sources. We can easily trace the succession of *arakhina* community leaders in the eighteenth century as follows.

At the beginning of the eighteenth century, the head of the community was Mu'allim Yuhanna Abu Masri, who was called "senior *mubashir* and head of the *arakhina*."[22] Also designated as "*mubashir* of the bountiful treasury,"[23] he became a high-ranking employee in Diwan al-Ruznama.[24]

Mu'allim Girgis Abu Mansur al-Tukhi succeeded him as "head scribe"[25] and "head *arkhan*" (the singular form of *arakhina*).[26] He was employed in the service of Amir Murad Katkhuda Mustahfazan,[27] and died in 1718.

After him came Mu'allim Lutfallah Abu Yusuf, *mubashir* for Amir Muhammad Kadak Katkhuda Mustahfazan.[28] In the Coptic Synaxarion he was given the title of "Head of the *Arakhina*,"[29] and it was said of him, "There was no one in his time who could rival his wealth." He died in 1720.[30]

Next in line was Mu'allim Girgis Yusuf al-Suruji, *mubashir* for Amir 'Uthman Katkhuda Mustahfazan.[31] He spent a huge amount of money on the restoration and renovation of churches and monasteries and followed the same pattern as Mu'allim Lutfallah Yusuf in his attention to the affairs of the community. He is described in Coptic sources as "bestower of all his wealth, zeal, toil, and labor on the martyrs and saints; solicitous to the restoration of the churches and monasteries just as much as the Emperor Constantine."[32] He died in 1737.[33]

Next came Mu'allim Nayruz Abu Nawwar, whom al-Jabarti called "Head of the Copts." His most important post, which spread his influence considerably, was his employment in the service of Amir Ridwan Katkhuda 'Azaban.[34] He was given a special title by the patriarch: "the legal *nazir* [overseer] over all the Jacobite Christian *waqfs* in Egypt and so forth."[35] He died in 1759.[36]

Following him was Mu'allim Rizq, *mubashir* for the *ruznama*, who played an important role in this period. He had been a friend of Mu'allim Nayruz and assumed his powers when the latter died. He died in 1770.

Mu'allim Rizq passed on the leadership to Mu'allim Ibrahim al-Gawhari, who became perhaps the most renowned Copt during this period of history. Upon his death on May 31, 1795, al-Jabarti wrote the following obituary:

> The *dhimmi* Mu'allim Ibrahim al-Gawhari, head of the Coptic scribes in Egypt, has died. In this state of Egypt he has attained greatness, a resounding word, an exalted reputation, and fame for a long period of time, not attained by any of his kind, to our knowledge. He was consulted in all matters great and small, even regarding the accounts of the *ruznama* and *miri*, all revenues and expenditures, and all scribes and treasurers were at his beck and call.[37]

Coptic sources went so far as to call Mu'allim Ibrahim al-Gawhari "Sultan of the Copts."[38]

His brother, Mu'allim Girgis al-Gawhari, succeeded him until the end of the century. The biographies of the two brothers are always linked, for they worked in tandem on many of the projects they pursued for the benefit of the community. In his obituary, written in 1810, al-Jabarti said, "When his brother died, he succeeded him in the presidency of the *mubashirin* and scribes. He controlled all matters in all the provinces of Egypt; his word was effective and he was greatly venerated."[39]

Elections and the Erosion of Papal Authority

One other indication of the leadership role of the Coptic *arakhina* during this period was a newly adopted method for the election of popes. The selection of the pope had traditionally been done through the collaboration of the bishops and the notables. This was the case throughout the early

Ottoman period, starting with the selection of Pope Gabriel VII (1525–68) and ending with Pope Matthew III (1628–46).[40] However, when it came to the selection of Pope Mark VI (1646–56), the entire matter fell into the hands of the *arakhina* alone. The person who nominated and selected the patriarch without the participation of the bishops was Mu'allim Bishara, who was head of the *arakhina* at the time.[41]

Likewise, it was the *arakhina* alone who selected the next patriarch, Pope Matthew IV (1660–75). For the selection of the pope who succeeded him, Pope John XVI (1676–1718), the prominent notables went to St. Anthony's Monastery in the Eastern Desert to choose the patriarch from among the monks of the monastery, again without consulting any of the clerical hierarchy.[42] As for Pope Peter VI (1718–26), he too was nominated, selected, and appointed by the most renowned Coptic notable at the time, Mu'allim Lutfallah Abu Yusuf.[43]

Although Coptic sources are not forthcoming about the procedure for selecting the patriarchs after this last-mentioned patriarch until the end of the eighteenth century, it seems reasonable to assume that the role of the *arakhina* continued unabated in such matters, as it had by then become an established precedent.

In contrast to church practice prior to the middle of the seventeenth century, when the patriarch had been the legal representative of the community and his council of bishops participated with him in deciding all matters concerning the entire community,[44] in the eighteenth century all matters were decided by the notables, to the extent that they sometimes intervened in areas that had traditionally been the exclusive preserve of the episcopal hierarchy. Thus, when the king of Ethiopia requested the appointment of an archbishop for his country, Pope Peter VI informed Mu'allim Lutfallah Abu Yusuf, who in turn nominated and selected the Ethiopian archbishop who was to be appointed.[45]

The Coptic Church's financial management and sources of income rested in the hands of these same notables as well. Indeed, local priests depended largely on their good relations with the notables for maintaining their livelihood.[46] The story about the church of Abu al-Sayfayn in Harit Zuwayla gives evidence of how the priests' loyalty to the *arakhina* transcended their loyalty to their patriarch and bishops. According to one account, Mu'allim Ibrahim al-Gawhari asked one of the priests to hurry up the church service so he could catch up with the *diwan*. The priest answered bravely, "The *mu'allim* who is in heaven is One and the church belongs to God and not to one individual, so if this does not please him then let him build another [church] for himself."[47] This story demonstrates that the priests typically acquiesced to the requests of the notables, to the extent that when one of the priests dared answer back it was a story to be retold.

The official role of the *arakhina* as representatives of the Coptic community in relations with the Ottoman state is vividly illustrated in one incident that took place over the government's taxation policies. In 1734, orders came from Istanbul to amend the *jizya* system, dividing it into three brackets, according to the resources of the taxpayer. The Coptic reaction to this decree is given in our sources: one thousand people gathered for a public demonstration.[48] The mixed crowd was comprised of craftsmen, poor people, and a group of notables including Mu'allim Rizqallah al-Badawi. However, on their way to the Citadel to discuss this matter with the pasha, they were stopped by an army battalion, perhaps joined by some citizens. Ahmad Shalabi reports that two of the Copts were killed, but a report in a Coptic manuscript source says that no one was killed but there were injuries. In the end, despite this resistance, Mu'allim Rizqallah al-Badawi[49] and a number of notables succeeded in meeting the pasha and discussing the government's decision to increase the *jizya*.[50]

This incident warrants our attention, insofar as it highlights a recognizable cast of players in this social drama—the pasha, Mamluk emirs, the military, Muslim sheikhs, Egyptian common people, Coptic notables, Coptic common people. This mix of leadership roles and demographic groups provides us with a glimpse of the complex political and social conditions prevailing in Egypt during this period. At the same time, however, the event is significant for what it indicates about the boldness of the Copts under the leadership of Mu'allim Rizqallah al-Badawi and other *arakhina*. It is clear that they were unwilling to acquiesce quietly to a government decision that would harm them, especially when the decision was linked to an issue so fundamental to the Copts' relationship to the Islamic concept of the state.

Finally, there is further evidence for the disempowerment of the Coptic clerical hierarchy in the area of church discipline. The patriarch himself was unable to punish men who divorced their wives in shari'a courts "for no legal cause."[51] He could only offer a reprimand if members of the *arakhina* class married their daughters to prominent Muslims or to non-Coptic Christians. Blame was not cast on the act of intermarriage itself, but on the fact that priests were forced to perform the wedding ceremony.[52] Concubinage also continued, largely unchecked, among the Coptic elite until the nineteenth century.[53] Resistance to this practice had always been considered a badge of honor for patriarchs of previous generations. However, none of the eighteenth-century popes issued any condemnation of it despite its prevalence. It would appear that the church was forced to turn a blind eye to such matters so as not to clash with the most influential of the lay notables. In this respect, we can contrast this situation with the church mechanisms in place at the beginning of the sixteenth century.[54]

Even as church sources during this period criticized the conduct and ineffectiveness of certain patriarchs, especially pious members of the *arakhina* class were being singled out for their saintliness. Some of their number were even included in the Coptic Synaxarion, an official book containing biographies of saints remembered during the Coptic Mass. This had not always been (nor would it always be) the case. In the eleventh century, the *History of the Patriarchs* had taken a critical stance toward such wealthy lay Copts, describing how "they slandered, and were arrogant and proud" and how "they and all Christians throughout Egypt became overbearing and haughty . . . and their concern for worldly affairs superseded all else."[55] And later, at the beginning of the nineteenth century, this same class would be judged just as harshly when their star had begun to be eclipsed by that of non-Orthodox Egyptian and Syrian *mubashirin*. The Copts would regard it as a sign of God's wrath upon them: thus, Pope Peter VII (Butrus al-Gawli, 1809–53) wrote a message "in answer to those who claim that God has destroyed the Coptic community before the rulers [i.e., the *arakhina*] who are presently in charge, because of His wrath against them."[56] However, for a period of almost 150 years, from the mid-seventeenth century to the end of the eighteenth, these Coptic lay notables were viewed as virtually beyond reproof and their leadership role was welcomed and blessed by the church.

Ritual Life and Church Restoration

Ritual Life

Coptic religious festivals were occasions for expressing the social status attained by the Coptic community during this period. Examples of several types of these festivals follow.

The first was the consecration of a new patriarch. From the middle of the seventeenth century, these rites—which involved the recitation of long and varied readings—took on a more public aspect. Church sources, in discussing the festivities held for the consecration of Pope Matthew IV (1660), say, "It was a famous day in Egypt."[57] The same was said of the consecration of the next pope in 1676.[58] This was not merely rhetorical hyperbole. The consecration ceremony of Pope Peter VI in 1718, which was carried out in its entirety by Mu'allim Lutfallah Abu Yusuf, then head of the Coptic *mubashirin*, was attended by "many foreigners, Greeks, Armenians, and the military."[59]

A second Coptic religious festival that attained a wider public profile was Holy Saturday, the evening immediately prior to Easter Sunday. It appears that this festival became a national occasion celebrated by all Egyptians. One of the Muslim sheikhs, who could find no place to record his objections to the exaggerated celebrations, wrote a few verses on the wall of a palace next to the mosque of Yashbak al-Dawadar:

> No more grief, for I am living in a land in which the good traits of the virtuous are defects;
> He who is faulty is perfect because he has great wealth, and he who is perfect is lacking because of his poor means;
> The days still go on to give prominence to the lying defective person, and to obscure the virtuous person of good repute;
> As Holy Saturday is being acclaimed and celebrated by all, Laylat al-Qadr is being obscured.[60]

A third such public rite involved communal acts of pilgrimage, either to local saints' shrines or to more far-flung destinations like Jerusalem. Sources tell us of a large caravan in 1709, prepared and funded by Mu'allim Girgis Abu Mansur al-Tukhi; attended by some invited bishops, this excursion was joined by groups of pilgrims from Upper and Lower Egypt who assembled at Salhiya, and from there headed out on the road to Jerusalem.[61] There were regular passings of Coptic pilgrimage caravans going to Jerusalem throughout most of the eighteenth century.[62] Not all of these endeavors were successful, however. Al-Jabarti records the attempt made by the Coptic community leader Mu'allim Nayruz Nawwar to organize a grand festival to accompany a caravan of Copts headed to Jerusalem in 1752. This episode demonstrates efforts of the Copts to emulate the Muslim celebration of the *hajj* season to the Hijaz. However, an attack on the pilgrimage caravan ended up preventing the celebration of the festival.[63]

A fourth such festival in which the Coptic Church became audible (if not visible) to the larger public was the preparation of the chrism or *mayrun* (a consecrated oil that completes one of the seven mysteries or sacraments of the church). The rites associated with this festival extended over a number of days and were accompanied by chants, hymns, and readings. The rite required the participants to circle around inside the church in a prescribed procession, while their expressions of joy resounded in the districts neighboring the church. This had long been a task reserved for the Coptic patriarchs, who would invite the bishops to attend this important event. However, the preparation of *mayrun* had been neglected in Egypt for almost two and a half centuries—from 1461 to 1703—until one of the lay notables, Mu'allim Girgis Abu Mansur al-Tukhi, took the initiative of preparing it. Manuscript 839/128 from the Coptic Museum relates the details of this important liturgical event, as well as the enormous amount of money paid by this notable to buy the ingredients. He even sought the help of one of his influential Muslim friends to bring the balsam ointment from the Hijaz when he went on pilgrimage there. His Muslim friend was willing only to assume the cost of purchasing the ingredient after his return. He also consulted with Sheikh 'Abd al-Rahim al-Sharif, the sheikh of Suq al-Fahamin, to learn the types of aromatic spices required for making the *mayrun*. After it was prepared, a matter which entailed hosting six bishops at the notable's expense, he presented each of them with a full clerical outfit and a new set of vessels and cloths for the altar.

Before the end of the century, a new batch of *mayrun* was prepared, this time financed by Mu'allim Ibrahim al-Gawhari in 1786. On this occasion, he invited all the bishops to attend, and they all did, with the exception of the bishop of Qusqam, because he was sick, and the bishop of the Church of Jerusalem, because he was in Jerusalem. A contemporary chronicler describes what he witnessed, saying, "No one can possibly describe the joy and splendor in all matters throughout the entire period of the preparation of the *mayrun* as what happened to the Coptic community. They were the envy of all the communities and of the Muslims, and I believe that there never was and never will be anything like it."[64]

The notables' role in renewing the *mayrun* rite is an indication not only of their great wealth, but also of their rivalry to spend money on the affairs of the community and to maintain their social stature in the wider society. Indeed, in addition to calling on the assistance of Muslim friends to help facilitate their acts of ritual patronage on behalf of the Coptic Church, the Coptic *arakhina* were also keen to attend Islamic ritual festivals and *mawlids* as a show of courtesy and as an expression of their conviction that such public celebrations were joyous occasions shared by all Egyptians.[65] These diplomatic appearances not only kept the Coptic community in the public eye, but also reinforced the notables' right to represent their community in the eyes of their Muslim neighbors.[66]

Church and Monastery Restoration

Church restoration and renovation has long been a very sensitive matter in Egyptian society, a potential source of disturbances and sedition. This matter is governed by *fiqh* texts, which did not allow the building of new churches under any circumstances and placed restrictions on activities of restoration and renovation.[67] However, such laws have not always been consistently applied in practice. As a case in point, Musa ibn 'Isa, the wali over Egypt in in the eighth century (787), allowed Christians to rebuild their churches that his predecessor had destroyed. He did so upon consultation with the two renowned Egyptian *faqih*s, al-Layth ibn Sa'ad and 'Abdallah ibn Luhay'a. However, this position was not widely accepted in the fifteenth century, as we find that ibn Taghri Bardi comments on this matter: "It is one of the unacceptable acts of Musa ibn 'Isa."[68] On the other hand, in the eighteenth century, there seems to have been a loosening of restrictions, with successive fatwas allowing church restoration and renovation with the approval of the Ottoman rulers.[69]

Notwithstanding, church restoration was executed cautiously and was fraught with difficulties, which explains the relative lack of references to church renovations or restorations in our sources before the middle of the seventeenth century. Beginning then and throughout the eighteenth century, however, circumstances changed and most of the churches and monasteries underwent a large-scale facelift, to the extent that there is now not one historic church or monastery that does not show signs of the eighteenth-century renovation movement. This cannot be explained away by the extensive wealth of Copts alone, as there had always been very wealthy Copts. Rather, the conditions of the era presented the notables with this opportunity, and they seized it fully. The churches and monasteries renovated in this period cannot all be listed here, but there is no doubt that this renovation effort was applied to all Cairo churches without exception and to most churches in the provinces. Similarly, all the monasteries still inhabited at that time were also renovated and restored, and new buildings were constructed. A case in point is the Monastery of St. Paul in the mountains by the Red Sea. After having been abandoned for 119 years, it was revived in 1701, its dilapidated walls rebuilt, and its church renovated.[70] Then in 1732 a new church was built, funded by Mu'allim Girgis Yusuf al-Suruji, who invited the patriarch and notables to attend the consecration, arranging for a caravan to the monastery at his own expense.[71] Then again, in 1778, Mu'allim Ibrahim al-Gawhari built another church in the same monastery, which he named after St. Abu al-Sayfayn.[72]

The Coptic notables competed in their restoration and renovation of churches and monasteries throughout Egypt, endowing them with numerous large *waqf*s.[73] What were the circumstances that allowed for this large restoration movement and how were the shari'a laws adapted to implement it? These decisions were made on a domestic level: it would appear that the local emirs did not give much thought to the reaction of the Ottoman sultanate or seek its approval for what they were doing. The notables depended very much on the authority of the emirs, and on their good relations with the prominent *'ulama* and *faqih*s, to facilitate matters.

It appears that some *arakhina* felt that matters were going in their favor, and did not consider it necessary to secure permission in advance. In the late seventeenth century, Mu'allim Yuhanna Abu Masri and Mu'allim Girgis Abu Mansur al-Tukhi carried out unauthorized renovation and construction work that was completed without permission and without any repercussions.[74] However, at the beginning of the eighteenth century, when Mu'allim Lutfallah Abu Yusuf tried to restore two churches at the same time and add new buildings to the properties, someone reported him for these activities, and the matter reached the Ottoman pasha. High-ranking personalities (so called by the Coptic source) who loved this *mu'allim* intervened, and they reached a settlement with the pasha: Mu'allim Lutfallah had to pay a fine of forty purses from his own treasury.[75] Eventually, the incident was smoothed over without any additional fuss. However, the case of Mu'allim Lutfallah made the *arakhina* aware that they should act cautiously, which drove them to resort to a legal course involving one of two procedures.

The Church of Babylon al-Daraj in Old Cairo will illustrate the first procedure. The Copt Girgis Sidarus—who was a *mubashir* in the service of Amir Yusuf Bek Mir al-Liwa, and a *qa'immaqam* (an administrative officer in charge of a district)—submitted a request to his employer, Amir Yusuf, in which he asked permission to renovate the church. (In the document, the church is actually referred to as a *dayr*, or monastery). He wrote, "There appeared cracks in the walls which might cause them to collapse suddenly, thereby placing passers-by at risk." The emir then referred the request to the chief judge, who assigned a *waqf* appraiser to examine the monastery and give his views on the petition. The appraisal agreed with the opinion of the applicant, and as a result he gained the approval of the judge and received permission to renovate.[76] The same procedure was followed for other churches (also referred to in the documents as monasteries), among which were the Church of the Virgin al-Damshiriya in Old Cairo[77] and the Church of the Virgin Qasriyat al-Rihan in Old Cairo.[78]

As for the second procedure, the *nazir* (notable or church administrator) would submit a question to the *'ulama* (board of legal scholars), from whom he would obtain a fatwa allowing him to renovate. He would then submit it to the judge, who would issue a legal document granting him this right. This procedure was used many times by Mu'allim Ibrahim al-Gawhari.[79]

The following is the text of a question and answer concerning the renovation and restoration of one such church in Alexandria. The petition submitted read as follows:

> What do you say concerning a monastery, which is a meeting place for the monks of the Coptic Christians, whose walls are cracked and weakened and which is about to collapse, according to expert opinion; and all those taking shelter in it fear for their lives from thieves, as they have no other shelter. The case being such, would the ruling class [*wulat al-umur*] grant permission to renovate and restore what has been destroyed or not? Or how would this be resolved? Please answer and may you be rewarded.

The Hanafi mufti replied:

> Thanks be to God, deserving of all thanks. Yes, whereas the walls of the monastery are cracked and that it is about to collapse, the ruling class—may God recompense them and us—can grant permission to the monks to restore that which has been ruined in their old monastery and rebuild the parts which have been destroyed.

He then went on to quote the imams of the Hanafi school of law, and granted the church administrator permission to renovate in the form of a legal document.[80] What is certain is that both the mufti and the *qadi* were fully aware that the place was not a monastery at all but a church, and that there were no monks in it, but that this was simply a formality that had to be observed.[81]

Coptic sources ascribe this era of church restoration to a measure adopted by Pope John XVI (number 103, 1676–1718) regarding church administrators, claiming that this patriarch appointed the *mubashirin* notables to be administrators for the churches after this same post had been given to artisans and craftsmen.[82] However, this historical judgment is misleading: here one sees the inability of earlier Coptic historians to comprehend fully the complexity of the situation on the ground. With an eye toward reconstructing these patterns more accurately, I have made a list of all the church administrators prior to the period of this patriarch. It was surprising to find that the administrators were from among the class of *mubashirin* notables, with the exception of three convents in Cairo—Harit al-Rum, Harit Zuwayla, and Misr al-Qadima—whose administrators were Yusuf Shenuda the tailor, ʻAtallah Saʻad (no profession mentioned), and Yuhanna Yusuf the lumber merchant, respectively.[83] In the eighteenth century, there were church administrators not from the *mubashirin*, such as Gabriel the tailor, son of Quzman, who was *nazir* for the church of Qum Ashfin.[84] In addition, some priests served as *nazir*s in the eighteenth century: one example is the priest Hanna who was *nazir* for the church of Abu Sarga in

Old Cairo.[85] These findings indicate that the matter is linked to the circumstances prevailing during the period and not to specific personalities.

Books, Education, and Art

This renaissance in the restoration of churches and monasteries was accompanied by another very important movement of educational and cultural reform. The *arakhina* invested significant funds in these areas. Here we need to exercise considerable caution, however, as the sources are very sparing in their information about Coptic educational institutions and their cultural circumstances throughout the Ottoman period. This lack of information in the sources is related to matters of *fiqh* that govern the drafting of shari'a documents.[86]

What is clear is that during the eighteenth century numerous books were transcribed, most of them at the expense of the notables, who in turn donated them to the churches and monasteries or kept copies for themselves. An indication of the large volume of books transcribed, and the corresponding popularity of reading among certain social circles,[87] can be found in catalogues of Coptic Arabic manuscripts; indeed, around 50 percent of surviving Coptic Arabic manuscripts were transcribed in the eighteenth century.[88] The demand for such books gave rise to a thriving business for scribes.

Scribal activities were not limited to the capital, Cairo. The copying of books took place all over Egypt. To demonstrate the popularity of books in areas far removed from the influence of the capital, the following list presents some of the known scribes from Upper Egypt.

1. Marqurius from Minyat Abu Fis (1703): manuscript 322/11 (Biblical), Coptic Museum
2. Priest Marqurius Mikha'il of Asyut, children's tutor (1715): manuscript 816/344 (Liturgy), Patriarchate (1722); manuscript 482/325 (Theology), Coptic Patriarchate Library
3. Yusuf Ya'qub al-Malawani (1740): manuscript 34/3 (Biblical), Coptic Museum
4. Girgis al-Jizawi ibn Sa'adallah al-Nahal (1749): manuscript 225/155 (Liturgy), Coptic Museum
5. Girgis ibn Bulus—Biba al-Kubra (1785): manuscript 251/22 (Liturgy), Coptic Museum
6. Nassim Abadir al-Abutiji (1779): manuscript 1105 (Miscellaneous), Coptic Patriarchate
7. 'Abd al-Massih Yusuf al-Buqi of Asyut (eighteenth century): manuscript 1072/1 (Miscellaneous), Coptic Patriarchate

The names of many other transcribers are recorded from elsewhere in Egypt. In reviewing this evidence, it is noteworthy that the production of texts shifted from the institutional church hierarchy to professionalized groups outside the clerical leadership—groups that made book production a source of income.[89]

A careful study of the subjects transcribed tells us something about the cultural values at work in the Coptic Church during this period. One figure who attracted attention was St. John Chrysostom (347–407), a fourth/fifth-century theologian and preacher of wide renown. The discovery of more of his works led Mu'allim Ibrahim al-Gawhari to dedicate a translator to translate his writings from Greek into Arabic.[90] Books were also translated from the Amharic language to complete the biographies of the saints,[91] as well as from Syriac.[92] Finally, numerous panegyrics were composed for various saints during the eighteenth century. Many of these panegyrics are still recited today in the Coptic Church. The composition of these texts, which was financed by the *arakhina*, have not had their fair share of study to date. In addition, our knowledge of eighteenth-century book production is hampered by the fact that churches and monasteries only typically commissioned books on religious themes. It is more difficult to reconstruct the other kinds of books that educated Copts may have been reading.[93]

With regard to institutions of learning, the only ones we know about so far are the *kuttab* (elementary schools). The documents do not contain information about Coptic institutions of learning on account of shari'a law, although it is likely that education for eighteenth-century Copts was not simply a private matter. An important document on this topic is still a puzzle: in a deed from the court of Damietta, dated to 1781, there was a registration of what was termed "Coptic Christian College in Khatt Suq al-Laban close to the shrine of al-Sada al-Arba'in—in the port of Damietta."[94] However, we cannot be sure that the term 'college' in this context was related to an institution of higher learning, and we have very little information to date about the curricula, subjects, or teaching staff which would allow us to draw definitive conclusions. Given the fact that a similarly named Islamic institution has been discovered in documents from the period, it is possible that something of a cultural and educational awakening was taking place in Egypt in the eighteenth century.[95]

The restoration of churches and the transcription of manuscripts are also connected to another important subject—art, including manuscript illumination and icon painting. A great number of seventeenth-and eighteenth-century manuscripts abound with exquisite decorative motifs,[96] in addition to colored illustrations related to the particular subjects of the books.[97] In addition, any student of Coptic art will find that the historic churches are full of icons dating back to the eighteenth century. Again, the notables played an important role in the commissioning of such icons; they spent lavish amounts of money and gave icons as gifts to churches and monasteries. The commissioning of such art of course implies the presence of Coptic artists who painted as a profession, the most famous among them being Ibrahim Sim'an al-Nasikh (d. 1783).[98] Other known names from the artists' guild of the time are Surial ibn al-Qiss Abu al-Mina, an Egyptian icon painter,[99] al-Qiss Manqarius Girgis, and al-Qiss Kyrillos. The most famous non-Egyptian artists active in the production of icons for Coptic churches were Yuhanna the Armenian and Girgis the Greek.[100] The presence of such non-Egyptian artists also confirms the laicizing trends in the culture of that period, and how the visual environments of churches were shaped by persons other than the clergy.[101]

Secular Bishops

Another noteworthy development that contributed to such laicizing trends during this period was the rise of bishops who were not recruited from the monastic ranks, but instead from among notables whose wives had died and who had not remarried. Although the Bible nowhere stipulates that a bishop should be celibate, the thirteenth-century Coptic expert in canon law Safi ibn al-'Assal records the Coptic Church's decision to select bishops from among the cadre of monks.[102] However, in the eighteenth century, it is evident that this tradition no longer held in all circumstances.

Documents from the period mention, for example, the name of Mu'allim Girgis, the son of Buqtur al-Manfaluti and the *mubashir* to Amir 'Abd al-Rahman Agha Aghat Ta'ifat Mustahfazan.[103] According to a deed, Mu'allim Girgis bought a house in Harit al-Rum in 1769. In the margin of the same deed, another transaction is added: fourteen years later, in 1783, a certain Mu'allim Ibrahim al-Gawhari sold the property in his capacity as deputy for "*al-dhimmi* Girgis the bishop, now called Yusuf."[104] Sometime in the interim, this lay Coptic notable from Upper Egypt had been ordained a bishop. Indeed, at the time that he sold the house he had been serving as a bishop for at least five years: another manuscript in the Coptic Patriarchate Archives, dated November 1, 1778, mentions "*al-dhimmi* Yusuf, Bishop of Jerusalem."[105]

Bishop Yusuf al-Sohagi also belongs to the same caste of influential laymen who became bishops. We do not know his secular name, but he is mentioned in the Patriarchate Archives as "Mu'allim Yusuf, the Christian bishop, son of Gabriel, the Upper Egyptian from Sohag."[106] And when he died in the year 1772, his full name was mentioned as "*al-dhimmi* Yusuf the bishop, son of *al-dhimmi* Gabriel, the Upper Egyptian from Sohag." We learn details about his family—that they were heirs to his estate, which consisted of a house that he had bought decades earlier, in 1738, before being consecrated a bishop. From his estate we learn that he had been married and had one child, a daughter, prior to his ordination. His wife had died and his heirs were limited to his daughter Mukhtara and his two nephews: one was named "*al-dhimmi* Girgis, son of *al-dhimmi* Qudsi, son of *al-dhimmi* Gabriel al-Sohagi"; the other is referred to as "*al-dhimmi* Gabriel the priest, son of *al-dhimmi* 'Abd al-Sayyid, son of *al-dhimmi* Gabriel al-Sohagi."[107]

Bishop Bishara al-Khanani is a third bishop whose wife had died. At the time of his death, his estate was divided among his natural heirs: "With the passing away of *al-dhimmi* Bishara the bishop, son of 'Abd Rabb al-Sayyid al-Khanani, his inheritance goes to his children: *al-dhimmi* As'ad, *al-dhimmi* Banub, *al-dhimmiya* Ward."[108] Bishop Athanasius, son of 'Abd al-Massih al-Ghamrawi, was another active bishop who probably falls into this same category: his name is mentioned often in documents and manuscripts, although we do not have much information about him.[109]

Naturally, the above-mentioned figures are not the only secular bishops who lived during this period. There are many indications of others, such as "Mu'allim Gadallah, son of Mu'allim Buqtur, the Christian bishop."[110] Another bishop had been a priest before taking the bishop's robe: "Mu'allim Makram, Christian priest, who is presently a bishop, son of Mu'allim Bishara."[111] It is impossible to provide a complete list of Coptic bishops who did not come from the monastic ranks, partly because the Coptic sources have only sparse information about them, but also because the shari'a court documents prove unhelpful in this area.[112] And yet, although we do not know the exact number of secular bishops or their ratio to monastic bishops, we can infer that the phenomenon was fairly widespread and robust. It took place even as Coptic monasteries themselves were undergoing a major movement of restoration during this period. The rise of the secular bishop was therefore not due to a lack of qualified monastic candidates; rather, it was part and parcel of the newly assertive role that Coptic notables were playing in the organizational life of the church.

What conclusions might we draw then regarding this new practice of filling bishoprics with *arakhina*? First, it confirms the destabilization of the church hierarchy during this period, as the episcopal ranks were 'infiltrated' by individuals who did not hold the usual monastic pedigree. Second, it reveals one more way that the class of notables or *mubashirin* succeeded, to a large degree, in assuming control by rising to the highest ranks of clerical leadership.

Ibrahim al-Gawhari: Last of the Coptic Sultans

Part One of this volume concludes with Ibrahim al-Gawhari, one of the most brilliant personalities in the history of the Copts. There is scarcely a Coptic source that does not glorify him, and the church ranks him among its saints. Upon his death, a famous bishop of this period (Yusab, bishop of Jirja and Akhmim, d. 1826) delivered his eulogy and described him as "a great *arkhan*, devoted, a saint."[113] His biography came to be included in the Coptic Synaxarion, alongside the early Christian saints and martyrs of Egypt, and his life story was thereby narrated to children as a role model for the true Christian.

Ibrahim al-Gawhari seems to have been more fortunate than many of the notables who preceded him. His biography was written by two important historians or authors from the period. He is first mentioned by 'Abd al-Rahman al-Jabarti, the most famous historian of the Ottoman period, whose book remained the sole source of information on that long period until quite recently. Later, he appears in an account written by a renowned Coptic bishop of the Ottoman period, and it appears that this bishop's report was the direct cause for Ibrahim al-Gawhari's inclusion in the Synaxarion. This literary information is supplemented by the various mementos that Ibrahim al-Gawhari left in a number of churches and monastery collections. As a notable who spent liberally and lavishly on the renovation of churches and monasteries, Mu'allim Ibrahim was the last link in a chain of great *arakhina*.

My purpose here is not to rewrite this man's personal biography. Other Copts have already done that.[114] Instead, I want to reflect on his role as a man who stood at a point of transition in the Coptic Church. Although his brother Mu'allim Girgis al-Gawhari took up where he left off in terms of charitable work for the church, the political and social circumstances of the time did not allow him to play the same role as his brother. Barely three years after Ibrahim al-Gawhari's death came the French Expedition (1798), at which time Egypt passed through a major upheaval in its balance of power, which tipped in favor of the French. The early reign of Muhammad 'Ali that followed was also a period of instability, which posed difficulties for Mu'allim Girgis' leadership. Consequently, Ibrahim al-Gawhari is generally considered to be the last prominent notable to provide strong leadership for the Coptic community and, as a result, Coptic writers often refer to him as the "Sultan of the Copts."

When a Coptic intellectual of the early twentieth century came to write a book on nineteenth-century "paragons" or "geniuses" among the Coptic community,[115] he was surprised to find that he could not identify a single Coptic layperson from the first half of the nineteenth century who qualified.

As a result, for the period from 1796 to 1852, he concentrated his attention on two patriarchs and a prominent senior bishop.[116] For an example of outstanding lay leadership, he was forced to return to the late eighteenth century and the legendary figure of Ibrahim al-Gawhari.[117]

Thus, the transition from the eighteenth to the nineteenth century marked the end of the age of the Coptic *arakhina*. Over the next decades, the clergy would resume control of church affairs. The rule of Muhammad 'Ali would see the re-emergence of traditional lines of authority within the Coptic community. The pope would reclaim his role as the functional head and legal representative of the church, while the role of the notables receded. Muhammad 'Ali's policies, especially his increased administrative dependence on Levantine Christians or Catholic Copts, contributed to the disappearing role of the senior *mubashirin*. As the gentry's influence and patronage waned, the larger Coptic populace soon began to recognize the situation and pushed their clergy—the pope, along with his bishops and priests—to take on the leadership roles played by the *arakhina* during the previous 150 years of the church's history.[118]

Part Two

The Modern Coptic Papacy

(1798–2011)

Nelly van Doorn-Harder

Introduction

Few Copts today have a visual image of Pope Mark VIII (1797–1809). While portraits of the popes after him have become part of their frame of reference, Mark VIII remains invisible and unfamiliar, as do most of his predecessors. His reign fell at the junction of two major historical time periods. It was just into its first year when Napoleon Bonaparte invaded Egypt in 1798. He did not enter a stagnant country, as used to be the widely held assumption, but one in the midst of transformation, and his occupation hailed a new era in Egypt's history. In Napoleon's wake came profound changes in technology, education, print, transportation, and trade, and new forms of administration and law. Throughout the nineteenth century, Egypt changed from a traditional society into a modern one organized on new principles with new centers of power; from a province of the Ottoman Empire, it became a modern independent nation. At times in sync with the surrounding society, at times at a different pace, the Coptic Church equally transformed its hierarchies, structures, methods, and expectations. An ancient, regional institution became an international church with a worldwide membership.

Ten popes ruled during the two centuries covered in this part of the book. They represent the 108th to the 117th popes claiming succession to St. Mark. Among them were three whose reigns spanned more than three decades: Peter VII (1809–52), Cyril V (1874–1927), and the current Pope Shenouda III (1971–); combined, they held the office for over 130 years. Three of the ten are considered great reformers: Cyril IV (1854–61), Cyril VI (1959–71), and Shenouda III. These popes lived through turbulent times and had to negotiate ever-changing conditions, opportunities, and mindsets within Egyptian society. The four political revolutions they witnessed (the 'Urabi revolt of 1881–82 that initiated seventy years of direct and indirect British rule and involvement, the 1919 nationalist revolution, the 1952 coup that ousted the monarchy, and the January 25 movement that forced Hosni Mubarak to step down in 2011) had a profound impact on the Coptic community, as they had on the rest of Egypt.

Societal change greatly affected the role, authority, and agency of these popes. They had to battle external and internal forces that threatened to weaken the Coptic community. Some, for example Cyril V, were at loggerheads with certain segments of their own community—members whose background and education gave them sufficient confidence to question papal authority. This struggle concerning the popes' power and authority will be an oft-revisited theme in Part Two of this book.

The historical and social processes of the past two centuries have not only made the Copts and their popes visible beyond the borders of Egypt, they also spurred the Coptic community to discover its own roots, heritage, and culture. Especially during the past forty years, the Copts have transitioned from a community largely unknown to the world to confident partners in the ecumenical scene of global Christianity.

The current numbers show vitality undreamt of during Napoleon's occupation. At the time of this writing, over one hundred bishops help administer a church that consists of around 9 percent of the Egyptian population of over 83 million; nearly a million Copts live in sixteen dioceses outside Egypt.[1] In 1960, 206 monks were living in nine monasteries; by the year 2001 over 1,200 monks populated twenty-one monasteries.[2] Reminiscent of the earliest Christian centuries, women have started to play influential roles in what is considered to be a true cultural and spiritual renaissance. More than seven hundred nuns live the monastic life in seven convents, while thousands of women have dedicated themselves to the church as *mukarrasat* (deaconesses).

Over the past two centuries, even the faceless figure of Mark VIII has taken on visibility in the portraits of his successors—portraits that range from incidental stylized icons to those of Pope Shenouda III, whose every move is captured in images. As the pictures of influential popes have become familiar, all Copts have come to share mental images of these leaders, even the less famous ones. Copts know that the indistinct portrait of the gently smiling pope on the shroud covering his coffin in the old cathedral in Ezbekiya is that of Peter VII (1810–52). They even think he rests there because he built the cathedral, although it was his predecessor who started its first building stage. There is a vague sense of remembrance at the somewhat surprised expression of Cyril V (1874–1927), the staunch patriot who is known for his arch-conservatism and resistance to change; the current renewal of the church started during his reign with the activities of highly educated members of the Coptic laity.[3]

Gazing from the covers of his biographies, the stern and penetrating look of the famous reforming Pope Cyril IV (1854–61) encourages Copts to action. One century later, the iconic visage of another great reforming pope, Cyril VI (1959–71), with a glimmer in his eyes, challenges them to follow his rigorous ascetic and intense spiritual practices. Of the many pictures capturing Pope Shenouda III, the most famous ones show him as a hermit monk in the desert, or dressed in full papal regalia, wearing his crown while smiling widely. His image is on or inside nearly every Coptic book and other media produced during his reign. It conveys a sense of nearness and belonging even though during the past two centuries the spatial distance between the pope and his flock has grown.

The image of a friendly pope belies the long battle Shenouda III and the other popes of the nineteenth and twentieth centuries waged in order to restore their authority as sole rulers of the Coptic Orthodox Church. They wrestled for their ecclesial power with Coptic notables, laity, dissenters, foreign missionaries and emissaries, and on and off with the Egyptian government. While Pope Mark VIII headed a church largely controlled by a few highly respected Coptic notables, due to changes in Egypt's government his successor Peter VII regained his traditional authority as the rightful head of the Coptic community. His immediate successors had to accommodate themselves to a flock that no longer lived in the state of *ahl al-dhimma,* under which they had enjoyed fewer rights than their Egyptian Muslim neighbors. They had been emancipated, attaining a position that in principle was equal, one that allowed them to seek new rights on the national scene.

The nineteenth century was a period of great change, not only for Egypt but for the entire world. When it ended, the seemingly invincible Spanish, Portuguese, and Ottoman empires had begun to crumble, while Great Britain had taken control of one-quarter of the world's population and one-third of the land area. The use of electricity, steel, and petroleum had triggered industrial revolutions that made Germany, Japan, and the United States into influential powers. Egypt's international profile also expanded as the country gradually gained independence from the Ottoman Empire and as it became incorporated into the world economy, especially through the export of cotton. Concurrently, it was influenced by western ideas with increasing numbers of Europeans and Americans settling in the country. Economic and social changes offered opportunities to groups and individuals; new elites arose, and by the end of the century the relationships between the individual and society had changed.[4]

Conventionally, Napoleon's arrival in Egypt in 1798 is taken as the point that marks the beginning of a new era of colonialism that extended into the final decades of the nineteenth century, and even into the early decades of the twentieth. When this era ended depends on one's particular perspective. From the Egyptian nationalist point of view, some writers place the end in 1882 at the 'Urabi revolt, which expressed Egyptian discontent with foreign influence and ushered in British colonial control. Others place it in 1914 at the onset of the First World War that led to the 1919 revolution for independence.

But how can we identify moments in Coptic history that represent a radical break with the past? I begin with the year 1798, but does this make sense in view of the pope who was ruling at that time? The social context, issues, and challenges that Pope Mark VIII (1797–1809) dealt with in fact resemble those of his predecessor, Pope John XVIII (1769–96). Could the truly defining year be sometime during the 1820s, when Protestant missionaries whose activities were to challenge Coptic teaching and identity arrived in Egypt? Or should we choose the year 1854, when Pope Cyril IV, in reaction to the work of these foreign Christians, launched a reformation of the church and community? Other dates that stand out are 1856, when the Ottoman government lifted the special status for non-Muslims living under Islamic law, that of *ahl al-dhimma*, *dhimmi*s, or 'protected people'. And every Copt knows 1874, when al-Majlis al-Milli (the Coptic Community Council) was inaugurated, a time Copts have referred to as the "awakening."

The year 1918 stands out as the year the famous Coptic layman Habib Girgis proposed a comprehensive project to teach Coptic youth and children about the Bible, which is now known as the Mashru' Madaris al-Ahad (the Sunday School Movement). This initiative marks a new phase in Coptic Church history in which lay Copts became involved in its spiritual activities and the foundation was laid for a new type of Coptic leadership. Around the same time, Copts joined Egypt's political movement for independence and became involved in the nationalist Wafd party, which was launched in 1919. Joining the nationalist movement represented a new stage in the development of a modern Coptic self-image—one that saw them reclaim their identity as specifically Egyptian Christians, the cultural descendants of the pharaohs.

The Sunday School initiative not only represented a formative moment in the reform movement of lay Copts that changed the course and mindset of the entire community; it also indicated a new stage in the long contest for power between the laity and the popes. The rift grew between the popes, educated in traditional institutions, and laypeople, whose ideas about the position and role of the Coptic Church in Egyptian society were shaped by western-inspired institutions.

The personality and ruling style of the last pope of the nineteenth century, Cyril V (1874–1927), epitomize the profound dichotomies facing both the Coptic community and Egyptian society in the transitory period at the turn of the century. Cyril was a traditional man who struggled with the reality that by the beginning of the new century, in spite of his own ecclesiastical power and charisma, lay Copts were transforming the church's paradigms for the twentieth and twenty-first centuries. During his rule the impact of these activities had become so noticeable that the launching of the Sunday School Movement has become a more important date in Coptic history than the day this pope passed away.

What are our sources for studying the history of the Coptic popes in the nineteenth and twentieth centuries? While many primary sources remain unexplored, the body of information about Egypt during this period is growing. The monumental work of P.J. Vatikiotis, *The History of Modern Egypt: From Muhammad Ali to Mubarak*, narrates the country's history up to the time of Pope Shenouda III. Detailed studies such as Khaled Fahmy's *All the Pasha's Men* have reconstructed the history of the national movement, the motives of rulers such as Muhammad 'Ali Pasha, and how the "small people," the farmer army conscripts, experienced sweeping changes in society.

However, in most studies of the period neither the Copts nor their popes play significant roles. The reports and memoirs of travelers and missionaries to Egypt provide interesting but often biased information.[5]

'Abd al-Rahman al-Jabarti (1754–1822), who taught at al-Azhar University, chronicled Egypt's history until his death and mentions the Copts mainly when adversity befalls them or where he considers their behavior immoral or offensive.[6] Doris Behrens-Abouseif is one of the few who has detailed Coptic life in the nineteenth century using the Arabic sources available to her at the time of writing.[7] Among Coptic authors, Iris Habib al-Masri stands out with a nine-volume history of the Coptic Church, of which the last five volumes cover the nineteenth and twentieth centuries. A noticeable feature of this work is that the author follows the reigns of the Coptic popes in presenting her account, which becomes progressively more detailed as she covers the twentieth century.[8] Yet we still lack in-depth studies of the nineteenth century based on sermons, archives, and material produced by the popes themselves before the time of Pope Cyril VI (1959–71). For this time period, the research done by Magdi Guirguis and Paul Sedra stands out, as it relies on new original sources and attempts to deconstruct many oft-repeated stereotypes. Instead, they furnish insights into the religious, political, and cultural struggles faced by the community and its popes.[9]

For the turn of the century, we have detailed descriptions of Coptic participation in politics by Behrens-Abouseif and by B.L. Carter. At that time, Pope Cyril V was battling for the authority of the church with reform-minded lay Copts, a struggle that has been detailed in an exceptional article by Samir Seikaly.[10] The closer we come to the 1920s, the less we hear of the by-then-failing pope. Following his death in 1927, the Coptic Church was guided by three less memorable popes while turmoil ruled, both within and outside the church.

For the twentieth century, the various decisions of the Holy Synods remain a crucial source of information.[11] Vivian Ibrahim's *The Copts of Egypt: Challenges of Modernisation and Identity* provides new material and insights for the formative period between 1882 and 1954.[12] Wolfram Reiss has provided us with an in-depth study on the development of the Sunday School Movement.[13] About the reigns of the two most recent popes, Cyril VI and Shenouda III, there is an abundance of material written by the Copts themselves. Of course, in this context we need to mention the writings of the long-time observer of the Copts, Otto Meinardus, who knew both popes in person. Moreover, a new generation of Coptic scholars such as Mariz Tadros and Anthony Shenoda has started to produce research on the contemporary church.[14] French historian Brigitte Voile has placed the accounts of the many miraculous occurrences that happened during the reign of the saintly Pope Cyril VI in a socio-political framework.[15] As we draw nearer to the time of Pope Shenouda III (1971–), the available material becomes overwhelming. Not only does this pope produce numerous writings himself, but already during his lifetime several books and dissertations about his reign have been published.[16]

But up to the second half of the twentieth century, there is a paucity of material that moves beyond anecdotal and/or mythical lore and reveals the thoughts, words, motivations, and actions of the popes themselves. My goal in the second half of this volume is to lift the tips of the veil, so to speak, in presenting a study about the history of the Coptic papacy from 1798 to the present.

3

Preparing for Reformation

(Pope Mark VIII, 1797–1809; Pope Peter VII, 1809–52)

Transforming Society: Pope Mark VIII

When Mark VIII became the 106th pope in 1797, he could not foresee the enormous turmoil and transformations that were about to take place. Although Egypt was experiencing political chaos at the end of the eighteenth century, the Coptic community was thriving, protected by powerful lay leaders such as Girgis al-Gawhari (d. 1810), who had replaced his brother Ibrahim as director of taxes and finance. Copts worked in public service as financiers, tax collectors, and scribes. The administrators seem to have written Arabic in Coptic script, which they taught their children. Using what seemed to be secret codes, they kept their skills within the family and passed positions on to their offspring. Besides working in administration and as farmers, the majority of weavers, blacksmiths, and carpenters were Copts.[1] Few Copts worked in trade, a potentially lucrative field that was monopolized by Syrian Catholics.

Just before the French invasion, times were far from quiet; a virtual social revolution was already influencing the traditional ruling institutions, hierarchies, and systems of patronage. Military discipline had deteriorated, with free-born Anatolian and Balkan soldiers replacing the traditional slave conscripts in the Mamluk and Ottoman units. Infighting among the Mamluk ruling families had disrupted income from trade and tax collection, while disease and insufficient Nile floods caused shortages of food and labor, resulting in great economic inequality.[2]

The French pushed the social disquiet even further and triggered what Egyptian historian al-Jabarti described as "a series of great misfortunes" and "general devastation."[3] In this time when "the common meaning of life was corrupted," Christians found themselves in double jeopardy since the invaders were Christian.[4] Coptic historian Ya'qub Nakhla Rufayla wrote that when the news of the approaching French armies spread in Cairo, "chaos ruled, the number of robbers multiplied, streets were cut off in the city, the inhabitants of Cairo became agitated and attacked the houses of Coptic, Syrian, French, and Greek Orthodox Christians under the pretext of searching for weapons."[5]

The Copts found themselves at a loss in the new situation. Napoleon had no intention of giving Christians special preference; at the same time, Muslim suspicions about their alleged collaboration with the French triggered riots against them.[6] After the French army left in 1801, Cairo and Egypt descended into a three-year period of sheer civil war, with the Ottoman regiments and the Mamluk households fighting to regain control of the city and its agricultural surroundings.[7] Mobs burned down the Coptic papal headquarters in Harit al-Rum—destroying the precious *mayrun* (holy oil) that had been consecrated just a few years earlier. Mark VIII was forced to build a new papal residence and cathedral in great haste.[8] The complex was built in Ezbekiya with an endowment left by the powerful notable Ibrahim al-Gawhari, who before his death had already secured the necessary decree from the Sublime Porte to build the new church.[9]

Pastoral Concerns

To alleviate the suffering of his community, Pope Mark issued regular encyclicals in which he urged his flock to repent.[10] In his view, the Copts shared the blame for the unspeakable events that had transpired. His writings reveal not only the vices of some of the Copts—corruption was rampant among those handling money—but also the reality that many Copts were poor. Four years after the French left he wrote:

> "They have all gone astray; they are all corrupt; there is none that does good, no, not one." . . . Are we starting a life of repentance or not? . . . Do we resolve to fast, pray, and show compassion and charity to our brothers the poor, or not? Are we ready to keep the Commandments? . . . We have done what does not please His Righteousness which has brought these trials on us while we still have not returned from our disgraceful behavior.[11]

Like his predecessor, Pope John XVIII (1769–96), Mark VIII used a particular genre of writing from the Ottoman period called *adraj* (decrees or letters). These letters were meant to admonish the Coptic community against immoral conduct, to explain theology in practical terms accessible to the laity, and to warn against foreign missionaries, who at this period were the Roman Catholics.[12]

The immorality Mark mentions in his letter can refer to several forms of behavior. Both he and his predecessor were distressed by the vice of public drinking and intoxication, especially by priests. Sometimes worshipers brought alcohol into the church to feast after the service. Most offensive were priests who were intoxicated in public or even during the liturgical prayers.[13] The contemporary historian al-Jabarti observed incidences of Coptic revelry with alcohol, especially during the French occupation. He described the excessive parties local Christians (Copts, Syrians, and Greeks) held in August 1799 on the occasion of the Festival of the Nile. Feeling protected by the French presence, they openly drank alcohol, uttered blasphemies, and insulted and mocked the Muslims.[14] Naturally, conspicuous drinking by the community, and especially by priests, concerned the pope not only on account of the public embarrassment and negative image this behavior would convey to the Muslims, but also for its possible repercussions.

Furthermore, there was the ongoing controversy of mixed marriages between Copts and Catholics, which Coptic clergy considered to be an act of immorality since, in the clergy's mind, it undermined the core of Coptic life, the family. But Pope Mark's remarks can also refer to the various practices that the Copts had adopted from the surrounding Muslim society mentioned in Part One, such as divorce, polygamy, and black magic. All the vices mentioned here—public intoxication, intermarriage, and practices forbidden by the church—undermined the pope's authority. Yet at this time he could not prevent the rich notables from engaging in whatever they thought might benefit their social networks, wealth, and prestige. Forbidding such practices would affect the church's income, as it relied on the donations of the wealthy. When we consider these habits, we can understand Mark's anxiety that his community was being punished because its members trespassed God's sacred laws.

Not yet having access to the printed word, Mark had to rely on the bishops to spread his message via sermons. To aid him, he could use the services of the famous Bishop Yusab (1735–1826), whom in 1791 Pope John had consecrated Bishop of Akhmim—one of the centers of Catholic missionary activity. Bishop Yusab was a learned theologian whose special mission it was to point out to his flock the heresies they had fallen into, Roman Catholic or otherwise.[15] Pope Mark tried to educate and guide the community, and in spite of the chaos surrounding him, he continued to consecrate bishops and priests. In the same context, we hear about a particularly memorable consecration in 1808, that of Bishop Macarius, the Ethiopian archbishop.

Worried about the state of their church, which he heard had adopted some "heretical beliefs," Mark provided the Ethiopian delegation with books and sermons that would "strengthen them in the orthodox faith."[16]

The Coptic Notables

Three Coptic notables gained fame during this period: Girgis al-Gawhari (the brother of the famous Ibrahim al-Gawhari), Mu'allim Ya'qub Hanna, and Mu'allim Malati. Girgis al-Gawhari, who had replaced his brother as the head of administrators and clerks, contacted Napoleon personally in order to plead the Coptic case, to no avail. Yet he maintained his high government position in finance during the French invasion and kept it under Muhammad 'Ali until he fell from grace, accused of being too lenient in collecting taxes.[17] Hanna, a tax collector from Mallawi, gained wealth by arranging the provisions for the French army. Convinced that Egyptians should be trained in defending themselves against Mamluks and Ottomans, he asked the French for permission to form a Coptic legion in their army, consisting of two thousand men. The pope and the majority of the Copts did not approve of this initiative, as they foresaw negative repercussions from Muslims, but Hanna went on to earn his place in history as the first Coptic army commander in centuries.[18] Naturally, when the French left he had to flee, which he did on a British battleship. His ultimate motives seem to have been to seek Egypt's independence from the Ottoman Empire—a thought born a century too early. The notable Mu'allim Malati, who had held the position of chief judge during the time of Napoleon, is especially remembered for the fate that befell him after the French left: he was beheaded by the returning local rulers.[19]

Although Napoleon's stay had been short and disruptive, it had left innovative ideas about the army, learning, and science. It even inspired some Egyptians to reconsider their country's position as a province of the Ottoman Empire. In the power vacuum left by the French, a revolutionary coalition emerged that brought to power the commander of the Albanian contingent of the Ottoman troops, Muhammad 'Ali (1805–48), whose reign had an enormous impact on the status and opportunities of the Coptic community. By the second half of the nineteenth century, his reshaping of society led to opportunities in education and work unthinkable in the eighteenth century. Although the time of the notables was not yet over, the era of individual Copts who used the new avenues for upward mobility had come.

Muhammad 'Ali's New Egypt

In 1805, Muhammad 'Ali became viceroy of Egypt by Ottoman decree. He was a foreigner who did not speak Arabic. Although closely connected with the Sublime Porte in Istanbul, his gaze was directed toward the west, whence he sought expertise and knowledge. In outlook he remained autocratic. To protect his position and property he built up a large army and navy, first relying on a new military elite from the Balkans and Anatolia and, by the 1820s, recruiting Egyptians as well. To maintain the army he relied on direct tax collection and specially grown crops, introducing new crops such as long-staple cotton for export to satisfy a growing market in Europe. To support the new economic activities and supply the army, he introduced the newest technologies of the time; he built factories, canals, roads, and improved communications. The army needed "medical and veterinary staff, a commissariat, uniforms and weapons, and so on all the way to military cartographers and a band."[20] Initially relying on foreign expertise, especially the French, Muhammad 'Ali opened professional schools to train local specialists.[21] He created a strong and centralized state and ruled the country like an army general as if it were his personal estate, monopolizing private property, commerce, and industry and "forcing taxes out of the people with the help of the *courbash* (the rhino whip)."[22]

The ultimate building blocks of these socioeconomic and political foundations of the modern Egyptian state were the farmers. Muhammad 'Ali privatized the land to increase production and maximize the flow of revenue to the capital. Through this policy farmers lost their independence or fell into debt, because peasant land was taxed at a higher rate than the large estates, thus forcing them to work in corvée service or as day laborers.[23]

Muhammad 'Ali's new bureaucratic reforms had a great impact on the role of Pope Peter VII (also called Butrus al-Gawli, 1809–52), who ruled concurrently with the pasha. Following the *ahl al-dhimma* system, the Coptic popes traditionally had been the official representatives of their community vis-à-vis the ruler. As explained in Part One, by the seventeenth century this role had gradually been taken over by powerful and wealthy lay notables. With the new political regime, several sources of their wealth were abruptly cut off. In 1811, Muhammad 'Ali had massacred the ruling Mamluk families whose money the Coptic notables had managed and who had lent support in dealing with the rulers. The pasha had also broken the power of leading Muslim sheikhs, fearing they might incite revolts against his rule, thus eliminating another traditional source of support. Decline in wealth and support networks, however, was not the only reason the notables lost their positions of influence. Following his own centralized system of governing, Muhammad 'Ali preferred to deal with representatives of institutions rather than with groups of individuals.[24] Due to this policy, the pope regained his power vis-à-vis the government as official representative of the Coptic community.

Initially, the Copts regretted the loss of their prestigious representatives, especially since at the beginning of his reign Muhammad 'Ali did not favor the Copts, but recruited the services of foreign Christians such as the French and Armenians (one of his ministers, Artin Bey Chakrian, was an Armenian Christian).[25] These foreigners had the advantage of knowing the European markets, which became especially important when Egypt started to export cotton crops. But the ruler still had to rely on Copts as land surveyors and scribes who helped him reorganize the chaotic tax system left behind by the Mamluk princes and kept the accounts for the budget. Handling the money came with its own problems: corruption was rampant and Copts were not always above the temptation to line their own pockets.

Setting Boundaries: Pope Peter VII (Butrus al-Gawli, 1809–52)

Pope Peter VII, who hailed from the Monastery of St. Anthony, faced the complex task of accommodating the new government, reassuring his own fearful community, negotiating foreign Christians, and grooming bishops and priests to replace the lay administrators. Around the time he came to power in 1809, the last prominent Coptic notable, Girgis al-Gawhari, passed away. This moment embodied several of the challenges that lay ahead. Girgis al-Gawhari had been a man of such great influence and power that al-Jabarti mentions him, specially commenting on his generosity: "He was high-minded and generous, and when Ramadan approached he distributed gifts of honey candles, sugar, rice, clothing and coffee to all the eminent personalities."[26] He died shortly after falling from grace and his government position was taken by a Levantine Catholic, Ghali Sergius.

The demise of such a powerful leader caused great stress within the Coptic community, which felt insecure under the new ruler and threatened by other Christian groups who were benefiting from their decline in influence. To calm fears and craft a response to the Catholics, Pope Peter wrote a treatise called "To Those Who Say that God Has Defeated the Coptic Community before the Ruler of the Times in His Anger."[27] During his reign, he seems to have made wise use of this experience when dealing with representatives of foreign churches. He could still rely on the notables, since they did not disappear overnight—they were simply less powerful. We find regular mention of Peter conferring with them, for example about building new churches in Jerusalem.[28]

Pope Peter VII came from the village of Gawli in the Asyut district and was the first patriarch to be consecrated in the new church in Ezbekiya. He is not remembered as one of the pioneers of the Coptic Church revival, but according to what has reached us through his sermons and in reports about his reign, he was a true scholar, specializing in theology and church history.[29] Moreover, he was famous for his piety. Described as "God-fearing, caring, and ascetic, he lived a simple lifestyle. He loved the good, spoke sparingly, was venerable and dignified, spending his days devoted to study. He never sat on anything but the ground, wore only [garments made of] coarse wool, and slept on a straw mat. He seldom angered and if he spoke it was with politeness and decorum."[30] According to the annals, his prayers were so powerful that they helped the water level of the Nile rise after the prayers of others—Muslims, Jews, Catholics, Syrians, and French—had failed.[31]

Equaling Peter in holiness was al-Anba Sarabamun, the bishop of al-Munufiya and al-Beheira, whose remains now rest below those of Peter in St. Mark's Cathedral in Ezbekiya. A well-known story with several versions has Bishop Sarabamun drive out an evil spirit from one of Muhammad 'Ali Pasha's daughters.[32] After she had recovered, the pasha offered the bishop four thousand gold coins, of which he only took a few to distribute among the guards.[33]

Although Pope Peter VII might not have been aware of his contribution to reforming the Coptic Church, in retrospect he made several crucial decisions that would influence the church's position and strength for years to come. His monastic virtues must have helped him navigate the internal and external challenges that came with the pasha's new policies to open Egypt up to the world. Representatives from other churches and missionaries entered the country, trying to influence the Coptic faithful. At the same time, the reach of the Coptic Church began to expand beyond Egypt's borders. Thus Peter's role became reminiscent of that of the Coptic leaders in the early centuries who had been forced to defend the theological and sociological boundaries of their church vis-à-vis competing powers.[34]

International Church Relations

On the international level, the Russian Orthodox Church twice invited Peter to place his church under Russian protection, an invitation that he politely refused. This patriotic stand impressed the pasha. The Russian envoy was equally impressed by Peter's humble conduct.[35] According to some sources, "neither the magnitude nor the height of the pyramids, the obelisks and their inscriptions, nor the numerous ancient monuments, their engravings and art" had impressed the Russian envoy as much as had the behavior of this pope.[36]

Instead of losing independence under the protectorate of another Orthodox church, Peter's papal realm of influence expanded when in 1821

Muhammad ʿAli conquered Sudan and annexed Syria, Palestine, and the Hijaz, the western part of present-day Saudi Arabia with the Muslim holy cities of Mecca and Medina. Although by 1839 the Ottoman and colonial forces had frustrated the pasha's attempts to extend his power, Peter's consecration of Anba Domadius as the first bishop to Sudan, where "over time Christianity had nearly died out," was lasting.[37] Another positive outcome for the Coptic Church of Muhammad ʿAli's expeditions was that in 1818 it obtained the permissions required to rebuild churches and monasteries in Jerusalem.[38] One final noteworthy international development was the consecration of a new bishop for Ethiopia.[39]

Encounters with other churches inside Egypt had mixed results. During a painful episode the Catholic Church convinced Muhammad ʿAli to unite the Church of Egypt with the Church of Rome. Starting in the fifteenth century, the Catholic popes had made several attempts to persuade the Coptic popes to agree to such a union, which could, of course, only be acceptable to Rome if the Copts were prepared to renounce what the Catholics considered to be 'heretical' beliefs and submit to its teachings. In particular, Copts would also have to accept the decisions taken at the Council of Chalcedon (451).[40] In 1822 the Catholics almost succeeded. In January of that year, the pasha forced his highest Coptic civil servants, the head of finances Muʿallim Ghali, his brother Francis, and his son Basilios, to join the Catholic Church. Six months later, when Muʿallim Ghali was murdered by one of the pasha's men, this 'union' fell apart, but the high-profile conversions meant the informal beginning of the Coptic Catholic Church. Yet it was not until 1895 that a Coptic Catholic patriarch was ordained and this church gained formal status in Egypt.[41]

By the mid-1820s, Egypt's increasing openness to the western world also brought in Protestant missionaries who had seen their activities in other parts of the Ottoman Empire blocked by the Sultan.[42] According to the *Missionary Register* of 1829, the first ones, sent by the English Church Missionary Society (CMS), described the Copts as "poor (except for a few rich laymen), sometimes numerous, generally ignorant and superstitious."[43] In 1826, CMS missionaries started to open schools, and by 1833 there were two schools for boys and one for girls.[44] In his seminal study about the influence of the CMS missionaries, Coptic historian Paul Sedra explains that they did not come to convert Copts to Anglicanism, but to recapture "an 'uncorrupted' Christianity" in order to "resurrect the wondrous 'primitive Church,' faithful to the teachings of the Scriptures."[45] To reach this goal, CMS schools had to convey an order of life based on the Scriptures, which was expressed in the values of "industry and discipline."[46]

Pope Peter VII was aware of and interested in the educational models used in the CMS schools and had close contacts with its principal missionary, John Lieder, who remained in Cairo from 1825 until his death in 1865.[47] The reports Lieder sent back to England relate that the pope, accompanied by several priests and laymen, attended the inaugural public exam of the schools. He was "much pleased with the instruction of the children, but especially with the order in which it [the exam] is conducted." In "the first school for female education he ever saw," he was fascinated by the girls' exams, hearing them read parts of the New Testament, "a thing formerly unheard of in Egypt."[48]

In 1840, the missionaries suggested that Pope Peter open a seminary to train clergy. Being a learned man himself and in need of an educated clergy who could fill the position of the nobles, the pope accepted the initiative, and the seminary opened in 1843 after three years of debate. Students were recommended by the pope, and in the first year he ordained three as deacons. Before their education proper could begin in 1845, all the students had to learn Arabic, Coptic, and English first, as they were illiterate.[49] The project ended in 1848 when the Church Missionary Society decided it was not viable because the students were not really interested in studying theology.[50]

Education and Emancipation

The missionary schools were just a fraction of the educational opportunities that opened up during the reign of Muhammad 'Ali. Between 1811 and 1836, sixty-seven schools were established. In principle these were to provide for the needs of the military by training medical doctors, agricultural and mechanical engineers, and language specialists. For the Copts, education would serve as an important vehicle for upward mobility, although initially they did not benefit from these governmental schools since these were primarily intended to strengthen the army. In fact, during the first decades not only the Copts, but most Egyptians, were still missing out on educational opportunities. The students as well as the teachers of these schools were mostly foreign, and Egyptian students a minority.[51]

When the government launched its educational system, its purpose was to serve the army and Coptic students were not allowed to attend. They were *ahl al-dhimma*, *dhimmi*s, or "protected people," non-Muslims living under Islamic law. Since the *dhimma* status had not yet been lifted, Copts could not join the army. They were officially restricted from access to the highest administrative posts and had to pay the *jizya* (a special poll tax), and their testimony was not accepted in courts of law. The underlying principle of these rules was that non-Muslims could not be in any position superior to Muslims. Hence they were forbidden to ride horses or carry weapons and had to follow certain dress codes concerning the color of their robes and turbans. The *ahl al-dhimma* system was based on segregation, minimizing contacts between different religious groups, but granted certain religious communities (or *millets*, as they were called in the Ottoman Empire) a degree of autonomy concerning religious and personal-status affairs.

Because they did not have access to the new schools, Copts did not become part of the new intelligentsia until later in the century; in 1846, the majority of doctors, engineers, and technicians trained in the new schools were Muslim, while 47 percent of the Copts worked as servants and clerks.[52] Not being Muslims themselves, the French had suspended the status of *dhimmi* in Egypt, but several years after they left, in 1817, these measures had been reinstituted to satisfy public Muslim demands. In spite of the *ahl al-dhimma* status, Muhammad 'Ali was lenient toward the Copts and other Christians; in 1819 limitations on the building of churches were eased, while it also became permissible to ring church bells and wear crosses openly.[53]

In 1839, starting with the decree called the Hatt-i Sherif of Gülhane, the Ottoman authorities launched several attempts to reorganize and reform the empire's social and military structures. The goal of these so-called Tanzimat reforms was to compete better with the European powers and stem segregationist and nationalist movements within the empire. Especially in mostly Christian regions, Christians had started to bypass the Ottoman legal system by appealing to several protective legal and fiscal rights negotiated by western powers. These rights were called "capitulations." As a result, the empire was losing legal control over several of its minority groups.

The Hatt-i Humayun decree, issued in 1856, specifically addressed the position of non-Muslims and promised legal equality for Muslims and non-Muslims. As a result, the *dhimmi* status was lifted and religious minorities were granted cultural and political rights in return for their loyalty to the empire.[54] In Egypt, Khedive Sa'id (1854–63) abolished the *jizya* in 1855, while in 1866, under Khedive Isma'il (1863–79), Copts gained equality in political affairs, which meant they could be elected to government bodies such as the Majlis Shurat al-Qawanin (the Advisory Council of Laws).

As soon as it was introduced, the newfound freedom also came with setbacks; new rights were paired with new obligations. For some of the Christian and Jewish religious leaders, removal of the *dhimma* status entailed loss of income, since traditionally they had been in charge of adjudicating personal-status issues related to inheritance, adoption, and marriage.[55]

On the national level, Muhammad 'Ali relied on a draft for Egyptians to strengthen the army. To replace the Turkish soldiers with local recruits, his successors had to cast the net ever wider, encountering strong resistance from groups such as the Bedouins who refused to become conscripts.[56] Muslims had previously envied the Copts for being excused from the draft, but by 1856 Copts were officially conscripted into the army as well. Especially during the era of Pope Cyril IV, the pope whose reign features in the next chapter (1854–61), the draft became problematic in some areas with a large Coptic population. For example, at the time the new status was introduced the majority of able Coptic males in the town of Asyut were drafted, leaving their families without support.[57] The pope's intervention was required in order to solve the matter.

This situation, however, was exceptional, and under normal circumstances the popes encouraged male Copts to join the army. Thus when in 1832 Muhammad 'Ali ordered the recruitment of five thousand Copts to provide services to the army, there had been no papal objection.[58] The issue of drafting Coptic soldiers must have been something of a public matter, since one of the few recorded quotes from Pope Cyril IV concerned Coptic participation in the army: "Some say that I asked the Pasha to exempt our Coptic sons from military service. God forbid that I would be such a coward, not valuing my country, or slandering its dearest sons by depriving them from the love of the country, or not inclining them to serve and defend it truly. That was not what I asked for nor what I ask for."[59]

Although the Copts were the ones who had been restricted by the *dhimma* position, before the end of the nineteenth century neither Copts nor Muslims could imagine an independent Egypt with its own government. Both groups would be emancipated after they gained access to education and printed material; both were galvanized by anti-foreign, nationalist sentiments; and both took part in constructing a new Egypt.

4

Educating Egypt

(Pope Cyril (Kyrillos) IV, 1854–61; Pope Demetrius II, 1862–70)

Cyril IV: The Reforming Pope

Copts have considered the initiatives taken by Pope Cyril IV so formative in the life of their church that in 1912 and 1961 they commemorated the fiftieth and hundredth anniversaries of his passing away with ceremonies at the patriarchate in Cairo.[1] On the occasion of the hundredth anniversary, a theological college was launched and an encyclical issued that mandated Mass to be celebrated in all the churches of Egypt.[2]

Throughout his short reign, Cyril IV was among the strongest advocates of the newly emerging rights and pushed for Coptic participation in the army and local government councils, and for Coptic access to the professional schools of medicine and engineering.[3] Release from the *dhimma* status not only brought new opportunities for work and education, but also instilled a sense of empowerment and confidence in the Copts and pride that they had an important role to play in Egypt's development. The new status was confirmed by significant symbolic moments such as carrying the cross during the public rally that accompanied Cyril's return from a visit to Ethiopia in 1861.

Cyril IV is known as 'Abu al-Islah'—the father of reform. He himself had been educated at a traditional religious elementary school called *kuttab,* where he was taught reading, writing, arithmetic, and Christian doctrines and prayers. He was born in 1816 near Akhmim in Upper Egypt and—like Peter VII—he had been a monk, under the name of Dawud, at the Monastery of St. Anthony, where at the age of twenty-four he had become the abbot. In his capacity as Abbot Dawud, he understood the need for monks to be educated and had tried to instill in them a spirit of learning by organizing classes and founding a library in the monastery.[4] He also understood the need for Egyptians to be educated and had opened a school for the boys of the surrounding families in the monastery's branch in Bush. These initiatives were not just academic. Cyril was up against powerful forces, as superstition and the use of magic were still rampant among the Copts. At the time of his own election, it had been a bishop who objected to his candidacy, referring to predictions by sorcerers who saw an ominous fate for the Egyptian rulers if Dawud were to be elected to the papal throne.[5]

As historians Samir Seikaly and Paul Sedra have discussed, when Cyril ascended the papal throne, he did not envision a comprehensive plan for reform. But for the Copts, who had just started to benefit from the government's new schools and the developing print industry, times were changing rapidly, and Cyril was a keen observer. The observations of the foreign missionaries concerning the Coptic Church alerted him to its dismal state, especially its clergy who were uneducated and often forced to sell their religious services.[6] Contact with the west also opened his eyes to the plight of women and their need for education. Sedra has argued that in his reforms, Cyril not only followed the concerns raised by Evangelical missionaries, but he also applied their methods by imposing certain rules, discipline, and order.[7] Targeting the church's leadership first, he set out to reorganize the papal administration and improve the clergy's level of theological knowledge.

Administrative Reforms

Cyril ordered a review of the church's revenues and expenditures and created a new *diwan* (unit) that oversaw the *waqfs* (religious endowments), correspondence, and religious work.[8] This administration was quite comprehensive and was adopted in more or less the same form by his successors. Among other things, it tried to keep track of donations, church buildings, monasteries, pilgrimages, and gifts donated via vows, as well as help to the poor, to Ethiopian monks, and to clergy.[9]

Cyril tried to elevate the educational level of the priests by summoning those living in and around Cairo to weekly meetings for theological reading and discussions. He enforced discipline in churches concerning the use of sacred music, the vestments of the presiding clergy, and bans on public intoxication.[10] The Coptic printing press that he had imported from Austria in 1859 produced Biblical literature and texts such as liturgies, hymnals, synaxaria, and lectionaries that were distributed to local churches free of charge.

Priests were responsible for performing the church's sacraments and rituals; they prayed for those who had died and oversaw the *tula'* (the various funerary rites and rituals to commemorate the dead).[11] Since the thirteenth century, they had been forced to cobble together an income made up of incidental services, weekly offerings, *al-'ushur* (tithes), *al-nudhur* (votive offerings), and the *ma'lum* (gifts in kind from the parishioners such as grains, fruit, and honey).[12] In order to prevent corruption and excesses, Cyril IV tried to reform the system by providing salaries for the priests, so that they did not need to depend on the charity of parishioners. Furthermore, he arranged for the deacons to be instructed in Coptic chanting, language, and church dogma.[13] This reform did not last long; his successor Demetrius II annulled the new rules. The system of the priests' salaries was not changed until 1971, when Pope Shenouda III placed them under the control of the church administration.[14]

Educational Reform

To create a space for the Copts in the wider Egyptian society, Cyril jump-started education for the Coptic population. Adjacent to the patriarchal residence, he opened a school where Copts could learn the necessary skills and languages required to join the rapidly developing society (Arabic, Italian, English, French, and Turkish). The Madrasat al-Aqbat al-Kubra (Patriarchal School) replaced the traditional *kuttab.* It provided higher education and produced a new generation of Coptic elite who gained wealth and influence by entering government service under Khedive Isma'il. The schools also gave Copts access to the various new jobs and institutions evolving from Egypt's contacts with Europe. When railways and postal services opened, the schools' alumni found ample job opportunities, as they did in banks and businesses. Government positions allowed Copts to acquire vast areas of land, with the result that by 1891 Coptic families in Upper Egypt were the fourth-largest landowners, after the state, the family of Muhammad 'Ali, and high officials.[15]

The Patriarchal School was so successful that Cyril opened another one in the Coptic stronghold, the neighborhood of Harit al-Saq'in. Although controversial at the time, among his memorable feats seems to have been the opening of the first Egyptian school for girls.[16] Apart from providing opportunities for upward mobility, the schools also taught the Coptic language for the first time in centuries. Not catering to the military, these schools were exempt from following the traditional, strict rules and discipline applied at national institutions and thus could develop modern methods of teaching and learning.[17] In order to overcome the initial suspicions of Copts who were reluctant to send their children to the schools, Cyril maintained a small office on their premises and chose new deacons from among the graduates.[18] Enrollment was not restricted to Copts only; the schools attracted many Muslim students as well.

Part of Cyril's greatness lies in his understanding of the need for the Copts to redefine their social identity, since they now were a newly empowered community of 'citizens'—no longer 'protected' subjects—with their own church, language, and educational systems.[19] Whether he realized it or not, the Coptic community was just one of many parts of Egyptian society that were experiencing a kind of emancipation. Muhammad 'Ali had tried to preserve the pharaonic heritage for Egypt by taking steps to prevent artifacts from being carried away to fill European museums. Khedive Sa'id (1854–63) tried to curb Turkish dominance in Egypt by fostering national sentiments—expressed, for example, in patriotic songs he commissioned his poets to write.[20] Understanding the importance of the written word, Cyril imported a printing press, thus allowing the Copts to participate in producing journals and newspapers.[21] The emphasis on relearning the Coptic language became an important symbol marking the community's Egyptian identity during this period. The cathedral in Ezbekiya, erected in haste by Pope Mark VIII, was replaced by an imposing, solid building, fit to be the center of a vibrant religious community. In an attempt to rid the community of the danger of adoring saints rather than God, and also to convey Coptic modernity, Cyril is also said to have banned icons from the new cathedral, burning the ones that had adorned the former building.[22]

International Relations

Apart from being an effective church leader, Cyril IV developed into a shrewd politician. He had gained international experience when in 1851 Pope Peter VII sent him on a mission to Ethiopia to solve problems concerning doctrinal issues with the church there. The trip took one year and four months and, upon his return on July 13, 1852, he found that the pope had passed away that April. Several reform-minded Copts considered him the best candidate to succeed Peter, but more conservative members of the Coptic community forced the postponement of his election. In order to test his aptitude for the office, Cyril was first ordained Metropolitan of Cairo before ascending the papal throne in 1854.

Cyril's stay in Ethiopia had made the new pasha, 'Abbas I (1848–54), suspicious of his relationship with the Ethiopian emperor. Lacking the visionary powers of his grandfather Muhammad 'Ali, the reactionary 'Abbas tried to reverse the modernizing trends by closing schools and expelling foreign professionals. Perhaps in fear not only of Cyril's political capabilities but also of his educational ideas, 'Abbas had tried to thwart his election and later fired high-placed Coptic officials in revenge for their choice of pope.[23]

In September 1856, the new khedive Sa'id asked Cyril to visit Ethiopia for a second time to address a potential border conflict between the two countries. Upon Cyril's arrival, the Ethiopian emperor Theodorus II received him cordially. However, when the news arrived that Sa'id was gathering military strength to invade Ethiopia, the emperor imprisoned the pope. He escaped execution thanks to the intervention of the emperor's mother, and on February 13, 1858 returned to Cairo, where he was welcomed by joyful crowds of Copts who carried the cross openly in the streets.[24]

Besides the Copts, several other Christian communities had lived in the Ottoman Empire. During the time of Muhammad 'Ali in particular, many had moved to Egypt to lend their skills to the burgeoning economy. Armenian Orthodox had originally settled in Egypt during the Byzantine era and their community had grown rapidly during the rule of Muhammad 'Ali, who appointed them to high government positions. There were also Syrian and Greek Orthodox Christians living in Egypt.[25] From the accounts of travelers who observed the antipathy of the Copts toward other Christian denominations, we know that the relations between the Copts and these communities were not always smooth.

Cyril realized that in the new Egypt the Copts needed to have good relationships with these churches, and started to strengthen the ecumenical bonds with the Anglican Church and the other Orthodox churches inside and outside Egypt. For his part, Khedive Sa'id saw these international relationships as a possible threat to national interests.[26] Coptic allegiance potentially differed from that of the majority. For example, during the Crimean wars (1853–56), Copts backed the Orthodox Russians while Muslims supported the Ottomans. Early in January 1861 Cyril happened to be in a meeting with the patriarchs of the Greek Orthodox and the Armenian–Gregorian churches when the khedive summoned him to the palace. Already upon arrival the pope was unwell and shortly afterward, in January 1861, he passed away.

Foreign observers at the time found the circumstances of Cyril's sudden passing obscure, even suspicious, indirectly blaming Sa'id for the pope's death and suspecting it to be a move against the pope and, by extension, against the Christians.[27] Doris Behrens-Abouseif, however, has argued that throughout his reign, Sa'id consistently acted in a tolerant manner toward the Copts. Among others, he appointed a Coptic governor, sent Coptic students to Europe, and backed their mission against foreign encroachment. Shocked by anti-Christian pogroms in Jedda, he even threatened the Muslim leaders in Cairo that they "would lose their heads" if they encouraged or even tolerated similar behavior toward the Copts.[28] But Cyril was a strong and brilliant leader who had ambitions beyond his pastoral duties and at times ignored the reality that the khedive was his superior. Not only did his successor suddenly have a large vacuum to fill, he also had to keep a low profile and maintain good relations with Egypt's rulers. It took two years of debate and sparring before Pope Demetrius II was deemed the right person to fulfill these demands and was elected to St. Mark's throne.

Keeping the Faith: Pope Demetrius II (1862–70)

Mixed Memories

Western observers did not look favorably upon Demetrius II, who had been the abbot of the Monastery of St. Macarius, and the Coptic understanding of his achievements is mixed. English reports portray him as a "brute" who persecuted the converts who left the Orthodox Church for Protestant denominations.[29] This perception is probably due in part to the unfavorable reports left by foreign missionaries, on account of Demetrius' efforts to withstand the encroachment of western missions on the Coptic Church. The Copts, naturally, highlight these efforts.[30]

As for the Coptic memory of Demetrius II, some historians have not quite known how to place this leader who had to fill the large shoes of Cyril IV, the Father of Reform, whose energetic personality was compared to that of the reactionary Demetrius as the lightness of a clear sky is contrasted to "darkness" and a "black cloud." Many describe his reign as "a time of inactivity."[31] Demetrius did in fact cancel several of the reform initiatives his predecessor had introduced, such as the central payment of priests, but left other measures intact. He continued Cyril's administrative system, which provides us with more information about his dealings with the clergy and churches than we have from his predecessors. He clashed with reform-minded bishops. For example, following Cyril's opposition to superstition, the Bishop of Fayyum and Bahnasa, Anba Isaac, tried to ban celebrations for the *mawlid* of St. George in opposition to folk beliefs and excessive practices of piety. In the end, Anba Isaac failed. Such a measure would have harmed the priests' annual income, and Demetrius responded by throwing the priests back on the charity of the believers, defending the celebration of the *mawlid* as a "tradition that had been practiced since early times."[32] It might be precisely this guarding of tradition that has led other Copts to remember him as a pious man who continued the educational efforts of his predecessor by opening sixteen new schools. While some were also closed, by 1878 there were twenty-five Coptic schools in total.

Western Missions

Like his predecessor, Pope Demetrius inherited an equally complex political situation and unique challenges: due to the influence of American missions his church's creed, its institutions, and his own authority were being questioned.[33] The CMS missionaries, who had entered Egypt during the 1820s, had aimed at changing Coptic mindsets, not at conversion. When in 1854 the American Mission moved into Egypt, however, the situation changed. The Americans, as Heather Sharkey explains in her book about their mission in Egypt, set up schools, supported a larger role for women in the church, encouraged Copts to read the Bible in Arabic, and trained laypersons to play decisive roles in all levels of church hierarchy.[34] As a result of these activities, the number of their followers grew rapidly.

At first not understanding the potential harm of schools and evangelizing activities, the Muslim government backed Protestant initiatives to educate Egyptians. These initiatives proved to be a far greater cultural challenge than the earlier attempts by the Russian Orthodox and Catholic Churches to annex the Coptic community. The Protestant educational services came with Bible studies and preachers who changed Coptic attitudes and minds, threatening the church from within. The missionary Andrew Watson (1834–1916) commented on the moment when Demetrius realized that he and most of the Coptic clergy had grossly underestimated the influence of the missionary activities: "The Patriarch shortly after his election made a tour in person throughout lower Egypt, and even there he had seen enough to convince him that his new-born dignity would not be worth much to him long, unless his people were brought into stricter obedience to the faith delivered to them by their ancestors."[35]

In his capacity as pope, Demetrius saw it as his prime duty to defend his church. But before I elaborate on his efforts to halt the Protestant tides, some background is required on the foreign missionary presence in Egypt before the American Protestants arrived.

Foreign Missions before 1854

The history of the Catholic presence in Egypt can be traced back to 1219, when St. Francis of Assisi met with the Ayyubid sultan al-Kamil at the Crusaders' siege of Damietta. In 1623 the Capuchins arrived, and in 1687 the Franciscans. From 1699, this mission operated under a special Austrian–Hungarian treaty of religious protection. Until the First World War, the entire Catholic community in Egypt could appeal to this arrangement, although technically those who were Egyptians remained under Egyptian jurisdiction.

By the end of the eighteenth century, Pope John XVIII (1769–96) had started to feel the pressure of Copts converting to Catholicism. Not only did the problem of mixed marriages arise, conversion also affected the Copts financially, since converts who associated with Catholic Syrians threatened the Coptic monopoly on the financial sector.[36]

In spite of a presence spanning almost three centuries, it was not until 1895 that the Vatican appointed a Coptic Catholic patriarch to shepherd the five thousand Egyptian Catholics. Until that year, the Coptic Orthodox clergy had successfully blocked the establishment of a Catholic clerical hierarchy. Coptic Catholic services were in Coptic and Arabic, followed the Coptic liturgy and hymnal, and were confusing to the average Copt, who could not tell the difference between a Catholic and a Coptic service.[37] To be sure his flock would not be attracted by the Catholic services, Cyril V issued several encyclical writings to warn his bishops, priests, and lay Copts.[38]

During the nineteenth century, the Protestant presence in Egypt grew rapidly. Between 1824 and 1864, Lutherans from Basel set up educational missions, while in 1819–20 the first Anglican, William Jowett, visited Egypt on behalf of his church with the goal of converting the Muslims and developing friendly networks among the Coptic clergy. Pope Peter VII provided him with a letter of recommendation that allowed access to bishops and monasteries.[39] However, the negative reports on the state of the Coptic Church that these visitors sent home insulted the pope and raised suspicions about their true motives. Yet Peter still recognized the value of their initiative to educate Coptic clergy and lay leaders and backed the efforts to open a seminary. Although the institute's existence was short-lived, the idea that clergy needed education had been planted and had taken root.

The American Mission

The pressure from Protestant churches became keenly felt when in 1854 the American Mission moved into Egypt. During the reign of Demetrius, they started to open schools in the Coptic strongholds of Asyut and Minya. These schools were attractive to Copts because of their superior curriculum in comparison with local educational offerings. By 1878 the Protestants had opened more than thirty-five schools, and in 1899 they formed the American Presbyterian Synod of the Nile, which in 1926 would become the Evangelical Coptic Church.[40] This education changed some Copts' opinions about their own church, opening their eyes to its shortcomings. Young men were no longer just vaguely dissatisfied with the conservative and poorly educated clergy and some of the church's archaic customs; they started to attack them, and some joined the Protestant churches. In particular, the Protestant insistence that each individual should endeavor to understand the Scriptures eroded the authority of the Coptic clergy, and it made some Copts doubt the doctrines of their church. Watson wrote that "a desire to read the Bible and controversial books became quite general. The Scriptures were searched by some for the confirmation of their Church doctrines, and read by many for knowledge of God and His truth, which they contain."[41]

At this time, the foundation was laid for the recurring conflicts between the Coptic clergy and laity that would last until deep into the twentieth century. Watson provides several anecdotes that tell of a loss of respect for the Coptic pope caused by such missionary activities. When Pope Demetrius witnessed the son of a Copt who had joined the Protestant church reading the new Bible translation provided by the missionaries, he chided him, "Why do you read such a book as that? Don't you know that the Americans have corrupted the Word of God and made it teach heresy?" Rather than being intimidated, the young man replied, "How do you know that it teaches heresy? Where are the Bibles that you have caused to be printed for your people? Bring us a copy and we shall compare it with that printed by the Americans."[42] To add insult to injury, the pope found out that his own brother was an avid reader of the new translation.[43]

Apart from such academic and theological attractions, for Copts in the countryside joining the Protestant churches also meant escaping various forms of extortion practiced by local clergy desperately in need of income. During the reign of Isma'il (1863–79), the government demanded twenty-one separate taxes from farmers; simultaneously those same farmers were being squeezed by the priests. Thus, joining the Protestant church became a possible escape from one of two oppressive regimes.[44]

The tensions between the Copts and the foreign churches put the reigning pasha Isma'il in a dilemma. On the one hand, the British and U.S. consuls pressured him not to interfere with the Protestant missions; on the other hand, he supported the pope's attempt to ward off foreign intrusions. To stress his support for the pope, he donated fifteen hundred feddans (over 1,500 acres) to the Coptic Church to build its own schools and in 1867 opened the state schools to non-Muslims.[45] Moreover, Isma'il lent the pope a boat to visit the Coptic communities living upriver along the Nile. On March 11, 1867, Demetrius began one such trip during Lent, a holy time when no Coptic pope had ever traveled. The timing was highly symbolic. So was his entrance into Asyut, where a crowd awaited him with a donkey on which he rode into the town, like Jesus into Jerusalem. Watson describes the event in passing while detailing how the pope tried to combat western missionary work. But the story is significant since it testifies to the great love and respect the majority of the Copts, who were poor and uneducated, had for their pope:

> Seated on a donkey and preceded by priests and boys bearing crosses, flags, palm branches, lighted candles, and burning censers, beating on cymbals and chanting in Coptic as they went along, "Hosanna to the Son of David, blessed is He that cometh in the name of the Lord," the procession moved slowly along from the river up to the town, the gathering crowd increasing in length and density every minute.[46]

During the trip, Demetrius issued public statements concerning the dangers of the new theologies; he had Coptic leaders who had joined the Protestants beaten by soldiers or put in prison, and forbade Copts to sell land to the newcomers to prevent them from building new churches.[47] Coptic men and women who had become evangelists for the new denomination were treated especially harshly.[48] But the attraction of the vibrant new churches could not be stopped: in 1865 the church had sixty-nine members, by 1875 it claimed 596, and by 1897 its recorded membership was 5,355. The church's staff grew as well: by 1880 the Protestant community had six Egyptian priests and 161 church workers, with women outnumbering men by fifteen to nine.[49] In 1882 the Anglicans returned with the goal of building additional churches.

Transmitting the Faith

Cyril IV had understood the importance of educating the clergy as well as the laity. To guide the church in a time of change, its leaders not only needed to receive a solid general education, but also needed to study Orthodox theology. To Demetrius, knowledge of the church's dogmas seemed crucial in order to counter Protestant ideas. It was during his reign that the priest Philotheos Ibrahim Baghdadi (1837–1904), the dean of St. Mark's Cathedral, became famous for his sermons and public expositions on the Orthodox faith that could last for over three hours.[50] Traveling up and down Egypt, he organized Coptic versions of revival meetings. For example, in 1883, before continuing to Aswan, he visited Asyut to lead "45 days and nights of religious celebrations," in churches overflowing with Copts filling the windows and niches.[51] Father Philotheos' writings about Coptic dogma and the church laws on personal status, and his refutation of Roman Catholic teachings, convey deep concern with the correct teaching of Coptic theology.[52] Warning the Coptic believers, as Iris Habib al-Masri has pointed out, also contributed toward building Coptic confidence, since he "opened their [the Copts'] eyes to the richness of their faith and heritage which far surpassed anything the western churches could offer."[53]

Egypt's Belle Epoque

Most accounts of the nineteenth century focus on the newfound opportunities for careers, education, and landownership, and seldom pay attention to the other side of the ledger. Because they lived in a strictly stratified society, for the majority of Egyptians daily life did not change that radically. Most of the Copts were poor, described as "ignorant" and "superstitious" by foreign visitors and missionaries.[54] They shared in the fate of the Egyptian farmer, whose energies were sapped by government demands for labor and production.

The farmers and workmen formed the building blocks of what is now considered to be Egypt's golden era, or 'Belle Époque,' which started during Sa'id's reign. His successor Isma'il envisioned a transformation of Egypt according to European models. To reach this goal he rebuilt part of Cairo into a replica of Paris, set up an efficient postal system, and opened schools, even for the children of farmers. In 1873, the number of students in Egyptian schools had risen to ninety thousand, compared to six thousand in Muhammad 'Ali's time.[55] In his book on the period, Trevor Mostyn points to what he calls the "contradictions in the character of Isma'il": "He set up schools to fight illiteracy, but flogged the taxes out of the *fellaheen* who attended them. He used the *courbash* and forced-labour to build his new Egypt, but sent expeditions to Sudan . . . to put down the slave trade."[56]

Isma'il's most famous feat was building the Suez Canal, which brought benefit to many. Now foreign ships could take a shortcut when transporting their goods between Asia and Europe. Thousands of pilgrims making the Hajj to Mecca would follow in their wake. But for Egyptians the opening of the canal led to bankruptcy and British occupation.

While their rulers lived lavishly, farmers and workers were confined, regulated, and supervised—first by Muhammad 'Ali's regime, and after the 1840s by the ruling landowner class. Such poorly educated classes were the majority of Demetrius' flock. Some of them entered the education track toward upward mobility, but the majority remained illiterate—as the parents of the reforming Pope Cyril IV had been—and the gap between rich and poor, between the educated and the uneducated, widened, especially within the church.

The Orientalist Gaze

Demetrius had a keen sense of the double prejudice toward his church. To westerners, the Coptic Church was part of the mysterious Orient. Although it belonged to a wider Christian community in the east, it remained largely unknown to western observers. Recent studies on the so-called "Orientalist gaze" have analyzed the cultural lens through which westerners observed countries such as Egypt. In *Colonising Egypt,* Timothy Mitchell describes how Europeans did not quite know what to make of this country that was organized radically differently from their own.[57] When they gained control, colonizing powers reorganized it according to their own principles. Egypt and similar 'exotic' countries were mostly imagined from pictures; every visitor had seen the pyramids long before setting foot in the country.

The Copts had no place in this visual image and were sought out only by certain visitors. These visitors—mostly church delegates and missionaries—came with a specific agenda and their own sets of prejudices. Alastair Hamilton's book *The Copts and the West* documents many examples of Catholic delegates who, without knowing a word of Arabic, spent their time in Egypt writing attacks on the Copts. They came with such rigid mindsets that it never occurred to them to learn more about Coptic faith and practices.[58] Demetrius sensed the danger of the double gaze of western Christians toward his church that envisioned it simultaneously as an alien country and an alien form of Christianity. Naturally, Demetrius felt a need to protect the identity and quality of his community.

Of the few western visitors who were interested in Egypt's Christians, the majority had trouble placing them in their own theological frame of reference. Egypt was the land where the Holy Family had taken refuge and it had been the cradle of Christian thinking. Names of early church leaders such as Clement, Origen, and Athanasius of Alexandria belonged to the worldwide Christian heritage. Yet this great legacy seemed to be lost to the Copts of the nineteenth century, who worshiped in seemingly unremarkable, poorly lit churches.[59] Jesuit Michel Jullien expressed this sense of bewilderment laced with contempt in 1889: "They had no idea of mental prayer, hardly ever took communion, and were deaf to the exhortations of the missionaries. Their hearts were as empty, cold and dilapidated as their churches. But such was the result of schism [from the Roman Catholic Church]."[60]

While Protestants stressed the diligent study of the Bible, hard work, education, and reason, the Copts prayed seven times a day, valued long litanies of praise, and withdrew into the desert to meditate on the Biblical text. Western forms of orthodoxy, based on preaching the Word, clashed with the orthopraxy of praising God for the sake of worship; western 'reason' met Coptic 'superstition.' Demetrius was as confused by the Protestants as they were by him. He could not understand why they had abolished all fasting while even Muslims practiced it. At the same time, British Lady Lucie Duff Gordon considered him a rude, money-hungry individual out to persecute converts to Protestant churches. Writing during the 1860s, she was sure that the missionaries could not fail and confidently asserted: "They are backed by the government, and they know that the Europeans will always side with them."[61] It is to Demetrius' credit that in spite of these obstacles he continued to resist the forces that could have destroyed the Coptic Church. Although battered, it survived, and so do the Copts' fond memories of this pope.

A Devout and Brilliant Shepherd

Demetrius II is remembered not only for his conservatism, but also as a saintly man. Copts fondly relate how he built schools, was received by joyous crowds when going down the Nile, and impressed the Turkish sultan during a reception at Pasha Isma'il's palace. Unlike other dignitaries, Demetrius did not want to kiss the hem of the sultan's garment. He kissed the left side of his breast instead, while quoting the first part of Proverbs 21:1: "The king's heart is a stream of water in the hand of the Lord."[62] He left the second part of the verse unstated: "He turns it wherever he will." Clarifying his refusal to kiss the sultan's garment, he explained that by kissing the sultan's breast he was in fact kissing his hand. The sultan was highly pleased, while without stating the obvious, Demetrius expressed the view that in the end God would decide matters, not the sultan.

Demetrius was also active in the face of cultural and religious challenges. In response to the Protestant initiatives, Demetrius opened a modern Coptic school in Asyut, appointing an alumnus of one of the foreign mission schools as its principal.[63] But in spite of his efforts, the point of no return had been reached. He died in 1870, and by then Protestant schools had ushered in a new awareness among lay Copts that burst to the surface after his death. In 1874, when a new pope was finally elected, the Coptic leadership class had changed: they no longer consisted of the wealthy only. Due to the new educational opportunities available to them, a new Coptic intellectual elite had begun to emerge. During the reign of Sa'id Pasha (1854–63), the first four Copts had been sent for study to Europe. These laymen had their own vision of the role and position of the pope, their church, and their community.

By the end of Demetrius' tenure as pope, turmoil was in the air both inside and outside the church. Demetrius ruled during the time of Khedive Isma'il who, inspired by a visit to the 1867 World Exhibition in Paris, had decided to replicate its opera house and its magnificent boulevards and parks in Cairo. But by the time of Demetrius' accession, the seeds of the economic problems that led to the khedive's downfall and to the takeover of Egypt by the British (1882) were already being sown.

Between 1863 and 1876, when Isma'il declared virtual bankruptcy, Egypt's debt grew an average of £7 million per year. In order to become part of the world economy, Sa'id and Isma'il had developed the country's infrastructure, putting in place communication and transport systems such as the telegraph, post, railroads, and canals. Their efforts were financed with foreign money, creating huge debts and causing large numbers of foreigners to enter the country.[64] The crown of Isma'il's work had been on November 17, 1869, when he held a costly extravaganza to celebrate the opening of the Suez Canal with the French empress Eugénie as guest of honor. Being part of the clerical elite, Demetrius had attended "the greatest festival that Egypt had seen since the days of the Ptolemies" in person.[65] Yet, when he passed away one year later, the economic climate had already turned gloomy and resentment against foreign encroachment was growing.

During the reign of Pope Demetrius II, several transformations had started to affect all areas of social, cultural, and political life—transformations that were of lasting importance to the Coptic community. The activities of the missionaries not only allowed for social upward mobility, but also encouraged criticism of the church's doctrines, practices, and clergy. Emancipation from the *dhimma* status and access to new forms of education allowed Copts to undertake new professions and enter higher social strata.[66] These developments triggered intense challenges to the authority the popes wielded over their community.

Until the second half of the twentieth century, the Coptic Church witnessed an ongoing conflict between the pope and the laity. By 1954, Copts would have so little respect left for Pope Yusab II that they removed him from office. We see the pendulum swinging back with Pope Cyril VI (1959–71) and Pope Shenouda III. During their reigns, the conflicts between the popes and the laity would be contained, channeled, and transformed. The next section will deal with the tenure of Pope Cyril V, a period of such rapid educational, social, and cultural development within the church that Coptic lay leaders spoke of it as a time of "awakening." However, Pope Cyril V had a different perception of these developments: in his eyes they posed a very real threat to the future of the Coptic community.

5

Redefining Authority

(Pope Cyril (Kyrillos) V, 1874–1927)

A Man of Two Centuries

In 2001, *Al-Ahram Weekly* looked back on the long reign of Pope Cyril V, reminding its readers of the intense interest Egyptians once had in the role and person of this formidable figure:

> On August 9, 1927, *Al-Ahram* announced the death of Pope Kyrollos V, the 112th patriarch, in the succession of St. Mark "who abolished paganism and raised the banner of Christianity in the Nile Valley and the Roman colonies in North Africa." The passing of this religious authority continued to absorb *Al-Ahram* for much of the remainder of the year, for the simple reason that the Coptic pope was an extraordinary man who had lived through an extraordinary period of upheaval and transition.[1]

This was indeed a time of extraordinary growth and progress, which (despite certain setbacks) the Copts describe as the golden age of their history. In tandem with the developments in society, the Coptic Church was going through changes that were unimaginable even three decades earlier.

The verdict on the rule of Cyril V varies depending on the position and interests of the observer. At the time of his death, *al-Ahram* evaluated his reign from a nationalist, Egyptian vantage point, praising him for his patriotism, piety, and selflessness. From the turbulence of the nineteenth century, Cyril's leadership guided the church into the tumult of the twentieth century. During his papacy he witnessed two revolutions (1881 and 1919), and during his long lifetime he lived under nine rulers whose titles evolved from pasha to khedive to king (namely, Muhammad 'Ali, Ibrahim, 'Abbas, Sa'id, Isma'il, Tawfiq, 'Abbas II, Husayn Kamil, and King Fuad), plus the British occupation.

Transitions within the church had started even before Cyril's election. Pope Demetrius had passed away the year after the opening of the Suez Canal. During an interregnum of four years, Metropolitan Markus of al-Beheira administered the affairs of the church with the help of five Coptic notables, one of whom was the historian Ya'qub Nakhla Rufayla. To assist the future pope in the administration of community affairs, in 1874 this group established a church community council called al-Majlis al-Milli. The council consisted of twelve elected and twelve substitute members and was to be chaired by the pope. Much of what has been written about the reign of Pope Cyril V revolves around the ensuing struggle between him and the council members.[2]

In fact, between 1854 and the 1952 revolution, new movements of Coptic reform arose approximately once a decade. All but the first one (which had been initiated by Pope Cyril IV) were led by laypeople, and most of these met with fierce resistance from the pope and the clergy. At the time, however, conservatism was not the exclusive domain of Coptic religious leaders. The traditional legal scholars at al-Azhar University were as averse to change as the Coptic clergy, as they challenged each and every suggestion brought in by reform-minded Muslim leaders. "Coptic reform," Donald Reid has observed, "had its own internal dynamic, but it was also in tune with the wider rhythms of Egyptian national and Ottoman imperial reform."[3]

Communal and Church Reform: Contesting Papal Authority

The Community Council

The conventional wisdom has been that during the last quarter of the nineteenth century the Coptic community went through a period of 'awakening', or *al-nahda* (renaissance). Having previously been confined to certain professions, thanks to the new schooling systems Copts could join the ranks of teachers, journalists, physicians, lawyers, and government employees. The historian and reformer Rufayla himself had benefited from these new opportunities; he studied Arabic, Coptic, English, and Italian in a school founded by Cyril IV. After working as a teacher he became a journalist, and in 1877 co-founded the Coptic newspaper *al-Watan*.[4] For Rufayla and other educated Copts of his generation, 'awakening' not only meant becoming educated, it also involved active and thoughtful participation in the church. These Copts no longer blindly followed their priests and bishops; they became part of a new lay leadership who helped administer and direct the church and community. These laypersons were well-educated notables who had reached high positions in society and in the state administration.

Among their most illustrious members was Butrus Ghali Pasha (1846–1910), who served as Egypt's first Coptic prime minister (1908–10). These lay Copts acted on their concern for the welfare of the church and its members, especially those who were poor.[5]

Writing toward the end of the century, the historian Rufayla discerned three key stages of lay involvement in the 'awakening' process that took place between 1874 and 1892. In his analysis, the formation of the Church Community Council in 1874 was *al-nahda al-ula* (the first awakening). The second landmark event was the official institution of Coptic charitable organizations in 1881, while the third awakening occurred in 1892 when the council held its elections.

The original committee of five laypeople who oversaw the church's financial affairs drew up reform programs that allowed laypeople—who were by now far better educated than the clergy—to hold supervising roles in ecclesiastical affairs. The members of the resulting Church Community Council would advise the pope on Coptic financial and civil affairs (issues relating to personal status such as marriage, divorce, and inheritance), and supervise churches, schools, and the *waqfs* (religious endowments or charitable donations). The financial state of the church was in disarray and the council's goal was to administer its funds properly, to use them for the construction of more and better schools, and to alleviate the suffering of the poor. Its members were to be elected every five years. Together with the Holy Synod, the church's supreme ecclesiastical authority, the council would also be involved in electing a new pope. In each diocese similar councils were formed under the presidency of the local bishops. The involvement of the laity in church affairs could not be taken for granted, however. To justify the new governance structure, reference was made to Coptic canon law and the writings of the thirteenth-century Coptic jurist Ibn al-'Assal, according to which laymen with specialized knowledge were allowed to provide advice to the clerical hierarchy.[6]

The council was officially recognized by khedivial decree in 1874 and again in 1883, when the number of its members was reduced to twelve. This allowed for its constitution to be registered and also provided it with jurisdictional powers to apply the church laws pertaining to personal-status affairs. Under the governing system of that era, non-Muslim minorities had the right to apply these laws within their own communities. When the council's constitution was accepted on May 14, 1883, it gave its lay members powers in civil affairs traditionally belonging to the clergy. The decree marked two new developments in Coptic history: it legitimized the role of the laity in church affairs and it showed a new tendency to appeal to the government for arbitration in Coptic conflicts that used to be solved within the community.

Upon becoming pope, two of Cyril's first official actions had been to confirm the Majlis al-Milli and to establish a Coptic school for girls in the governorate of Sharqiya.[7] However, not long after his enthronement he refused to cooperate with the council, as he viewed it as undermining his papal authority and against the tradition of the church. He rejected it for nearly a decade, refusing to attend its meetings and sending protests against its existence to the khedive. Since the pope was the council's ex-officio chair, his opposition rendered it inactive. But his stubbornness met with formidable opponents: the council members were prosperous, well-educated landowners and professionals. Seven council members were beys and one of them, Butrus Ghali, was the first Copt ever to achieve the rank of pasha.[8] Although the ruling khedives sympathized with Cyril's position and understood that his authority was being undermined, highly-placed lay Copts often convinced them of the necessity to accept their agendas. Egypt's rulers also preferred to negotiate with well-educated Copts rather than facing clergymen, who had the reputation of being ignorant and incapable of serving the needs of the community.

In 1883, after vicious fights, the council members were reinstated, only to be dismissed again in 1884. In 1883, shortly after the 'Urabi Revolt, during which the pope had taken sides against Khedive Tawfiq (1879–92), the Egyptian government amended the charter of the council, allowing for new members to be elected. Cyril protested with a letter he delivered to the prime minister in person: "There is no need for the Council which some members of the congregation seek to create. . . . When we assumed the patriarchy our experience with the Council led us to the conclusion that it is useless and can serve no purpose whatsoever and we, therefore, dispensed with it."[9] In his response, the khedive made it clear that he had no desire to support the pope.

> We were surprised by your Excellency's letter in which you appealed against the implementation of the royal decree. On the basis of excuses that were inappropriate for your Excellency to voice you argued against a request to create a council to reform the affairs of the church, a request submitted by notables of that community, greeted favorably by the government and approved by His Royal Majesty the Khedive.[10]

The letter ended with the decree that the council's elections should be held without delay.

Although he complied with the khedive's orders, Pope Cyril successfully obstructed the council's work up until the year 1892. In 1891, he presented Khedive Tawfiq once again with an encyclical in which he denounced the council, stating that it acted against the church's tradition and doctrine. The council ignored his opinion and elected new members in 1892. The return of the council was such an impressive event that in the eyes of the historian Rufayla it represented the third "awakening."[11] Each of these critical moments involved various forms of khedivial intervention, politicizing the conflict between the clergy and the reform-minded laity on several levels.

Cyril declared this election illegal and Butros Ghali Pasha submitted a complaint to the government stating that the pope had "violated the laws of the church, breached its charter and brought harm to the congregation, whose misfortune it is that its council elected him to head the church."[12] The khedive accepted the new council, its complaints, and its petition to remove the pope as its chair and relieved him of his duties, replacing him with another member of the clergy.[13] Of course, the pope protested vehemently. Trying to regain his primacy, he sought the intervention of foreign powers and excommunicated the bishop appointed to replace him, Bishop Athanasius of Sanabu.[14] He found neither sympathy among the western powers nor effective support from other Orthodox churches.

On September 1, 1892, the situation escalated with a khedivial decree ordering Cyril to withdraw to the Monastery of al-Baramus. Metropolitan John of Alexandria, who had tried to prevent this attack on the pope's dignity, was summarily confined to the Monastery of St. Paul.[15] The fact that the decree, issued by the new khedive 'Abbas II, was backed by the British consul-general Baring and the Egyptian prime minister Mustafa Fahmi, shows the extent to which politics were involved in church affairs. Cyril's departure from Cairo on September 2 satisfied the council members but shocked the majority of Coptic believers.

The period without a pope proved disastrous. Cyril's replacement, Athanasius, lived in a state of excommunication, churches remained empty, and the clergy refused to celebrate the Eucharist or to preside over rituals of marriage and baptism. In the end both council members and the government implored the pope to return. Church bells rang when on February 4, 1893, nearly six months after his departure, Pope Cyril re-entered Cairo. He returned to his residence in a triumphant procession. "Never within memory has Cairo been the scene of such a thrilling popular ovation as greeted the Patriarch when he returned. The crowds held up the city. The people wept for joy, and sang the praises of the exile."[16]

The conflict had taught both the pope and the laity important lessons. The pope finally gave in to some of the laypeoples' wishes. He accepted that the clergy should have a solid education, backed the opening of new schools by Coptic individuals and charitable organizations, and allowed the seminary to be reopened. The reform-minded Copts understood the importance of the pope's office; his authority and symbolic power were a source of solace for the poor and uneducated Copts who still constituted the majority of church members.

Waqf Endowments and Their Pious Custodians

The goals of the Copts advocating reform were to raise the educational level of their clergy and improve care for the poor. They also fought against rampant corruption within the church, demanding accountability for its income and expenditures. An ever-recurring issue of contention was the income from the *waqfs*, the endowments of lands that mostly benefited the monasteries. Not only the pope but also the heads of the monasteries refused to allow these moneys to be overseen by the council, and in 1927 *waqf*-related cases were taken to court.[17] The revenues from the *waqf* endowments were at the heart of this battle, since they provided the monasteries with incomes far surpassing the needs of the monks. In 1926, for example, around one hundred monks inhabiting seven monasteries had access to LE300,000 in revenues from five thousand to nine thousand feddans of land. Nobody understood how that money was spent, since the monks lived in dire poverty. The salaries of priests were not paid from these revenues either. While some priests were forced to beg to supplement their income, and monks were dirt poor, in the fiscal year of 1919–20 the Monastery of al-Muharraq "earned LE1.5 million in cotton sales, a sum which seemingly disappeared."[18]

Apart from the financial battles, at the heart of the disagreements between Cyril and the council were interpretations about his role and authority as supreme ruler of the Coptic Church. He "had determined now to fight again solely for unquestioning supremacy."[19] The council, inspired by the presbyterial structure of the Protestant churches, was run democratically.[20] In 1878, Khedive Tawfiq had recognized the Protestant church as an official denomination. Cyril harbored deep suspicion against the Protestant missionaries, who scorned Coptic rituals and lured parishioners away from the church. He considered the reform-minded Copts to be agents of foreign powers ready to take over his church.

Furthermore, Pope Cyril adhered to the century-old model of his predecessors who, molded by living in the *dhimmi* status, had kept a low profile. The reformers wanted to use the massive amount of funds to benefit the community, especially the impoverished schools that were in an ongoing struggle for church funds. They blamed the clergy for the backward state of the Coptic community that practiced habits such as loud wailing at burials, "premature and senile marriages, the exclusion and veiling of women, belief in amulets," as well as "excessive drinking, smoking, and gambling."[21]

Thus this clash was not just between the modernizing and the traditional mindsets; in many ways Pope Cyril V's personality embodied the changes the church and society were going through. He lived during a great part of the nineteenth century (1824–1927) and was the longest-ruling pope in Coptic history. During his fifty-three years as pope he represented the traditional model of the monastic soul that seeks God in solitude. He had been a deacon since the age of twelve, and his love for seclusion had drawn him to the small and poor Monastery of Baramus when he was nineteen years old. There he stood out for his ascetic zeal and concern for the Coptic language, which he expressed in copying ancient manuscripts. This activity earned him the nickname of Hanna al-Nasikh, or Hanna the Scribe (Hanna had been his given name prior to his ordination). Born in Beni Soueif and educated by an older brother, he had never attended an official school and his strict discipline originated from his own spiritual regime. Having served on the papal staff since 1855 during the time of Pope Demetrius, he knew the workings of the office. Cyril was considered "ascetic, charitable, and a good pastor."[22] He cared deeply about the well-being of the faith and his flock, especially as he saw devout Copts being lured away by other denominations.

While keeping up his efforts to obstruct the Community Council, Cyril did understand that ignoring the complaints of reform-minded Copts would be detrimental to the community. In 1896 he sent out an encyclical admonishing the clergy to abide by the rules of their religious vocations, instructing them to remain in their parishes and minister to the needs of their congregations.[23] He "enjoined them to teach and preach, perform religious services, and administer communion; they were further admonished to console the bereaved and show charity to the needy."[24] At the time there were no requirements concerning the formal education of the pope or his bishops. This gap in academic knowledge slowly developed into a clash between the clergy and reform-minded Copts. The reformers had little patience with the pope, whom they considered to be an embodiment of the old school that hindered the church's progress. Convinced of the validity of their struggle, they were willing to battle him for the direction the church should be taking.

Communal and Educational Reform

The Charitable Societies and Press

By 1881, dissatisfied laity had found new ways to consolidate forces in anticipation of the pope's obstruction of the upcoming elections of the Majlis al-Milli members. In part also inspired by Pope Cyril's strong support of charitable activities, they started to create voluntary associations that attended to certain needs within society. The first one, al-Jam'iyat al-Khayriya al-Qibtiya al-Kubra (the Great Benevolent Coptic Society), was launched to serve the poor and developed into a large organization that ran educational and health projects.[25] To serve the needs of the 80 percent of the Coptic population that was illiterate, in 1891 the Jam'iyat al-Tawfiq (the Tawfiq Society, or the Reconciliation Society), was founded to pursue educational and cultural endeavors through the establishment of public libraries and the publication of books.[26] These inspired several other societies during the following decades. Rufayla identified the founding of such societies as the "second awakening." The Tawfiq Society, in particular, with its publications and schools run by highly effective teachers educating Christian as well as Muslim students, exerted great influence well into the twentieth century.[27]

Societies mushroomed all over Egypt, in Tanta, Cairo, Mansura, Qalyub, Damanhur, Suez, Beni Soueif, Fayoum, Minya, and Asyut. They were not only philanthropic, taking care of the poor and supervising Coptic education, but also served as the voice of the laity, strengthening its position and providing a platform for the pope's opponents.[28]

In 1895, the reformers opened another venue to air their ideas and launched the *Misr* newspaper to counter the pro-clerical *al-Watan* paper that had appeared since 1877. *Misr*'s audience was well educated and the paper's support came from printing announcements concerning the Community Council, the patriarchate, Coptic societies, and the government. Both papers became important voices for the Coptic community and advanced the public's knowledge on internal Coptic matters, Coptic history and culture, religious practices, and the various disagreements within the church body. Relaying the pope's opinion during the authority crisis of 1893, *al-Watan* accused foreign powers of wanting to dispose of their leader.[29] *Misr* combined reformist ideas with support for the British occupation; it defended the Copts from attacks by the Muslim press, and until the mid-1940s was a strong champion of Coptic political rights.[30] But when in 1905 mismanagement of the church's income became intolerable, both newspapers demanded that the Community Council be reinstated.

In 1906 a new council was elected, consisting mostly of lawyers. They formed several subcommittees that respectively attended to the work of the patriarchate, legal affairs, the schools, and the poor.[31] By 1908 they clashed with the pope, who accused the council members of making decisions without his consent and wasting the church's money. On October 29, 1909, Cyril dissolved the council. In 1912, the council's constitution was revised once again and Pope Cyril regained some of his prerogatives. The issue of religious endowments was addressed, and control over them was divided between the council and the ecclesiastical hierarchy, which supervised all but the most profitable endowments, especially those at the monasteries.[32] After a long battle, in 1927, the year of Cyril's death, another revision to the constitution restored several of the laity's rights.[33] The battles between the council and the popes did not end here, however, but continued far into the twentieth century. Despite these struggles, the issue that clergy and laity agreed upon was that Copts needed better education, and that children and youth especially needed to learn more about their faith and their church.

The Coptic Seminary

In view of the need to improve the clergy's educational level, the council had opened a theological seminary in 1875. Cyril closed the seminary a few months later, together with a school for girls. It was many years before he allowed the seminary to reopen, on November 29, 1893. This event was a milestone in the history of the Coptic Church. For the first time since the famous Catechetical School of Alexandria was active in late antiquity, the Egyptian church had a center for higher Christian learning again. To further the education of priests as well as the monks, three branch seminaries opened, in Alexandria, in Bush, and at the Monastery of al-Muharraq. Two distinguished Coptic scholars served as the seminary's first deans: Yusuf Manqarius (d. 1918), followed by the charismatic educator Habib Girgis, who had been an instructor since 1898 and led the seminary until his death in 1951.

At the Cairo Seminary, the famous scholar-priest Philotheus (1837–1904), who had preached against the Protestant proselytizing missions during the time of Pope Demetrius, taught Coptic language and theology to what a Coptic historian called "the class of divines from whom the prelates and patriarchs were selected."[34] To expand their knowledge of Greek, he also sent seven monks to the Theological College in Athens.[35] Philotheus continued the work of his predecessors to teach the Copts their own heritage and provided the schools with educational material by publishing religious literature.

The alumni of the seminary and schools started to produce a body of Coptic religious literature. Between 1877 and 1907, seven religious periodicals were launched that contributed to a growing awareness among the Copts of their own religious roots and teachings.[36] At the same time the number of clergy increased: by 1894, Pope Cyril had consecrated nineteen new bishops and metropolitans.

The Sunday School Movement

Graduates of the seminary had a profound influence on the life of the Coptic Church and community. Not only did the educational level of priests improve, but due to the tireless efforts of Habib Girgis, who is considered one of the most influential theologians and preachers of his time, its alumni also became involved in teaching youth and children.

Girgis' vision was to revive the Coptic communities through religious education for children in schools and in the churches. He lobbied for the introduction of Christian education in the khedivial schools and urged churches to instruct their young people. "Wherever he preached he ended his sermon with an urgent call to provide religious education for the children and youth in that place."[37] Furthermore, he worked to improve the religious education in the Coptic schools that were under supervision of the Community Council. In his eyes, Christian education in these schools had long been substandard: too few hours were dedicated to this topic, and trained teachers and proper material were both lacking.[38]

In spite of resistance from clergy and parents, the movement he initiated grew steadily; the number of schools increased rapidly from around only a half-dozen in 1892 to forty-six by 1907.[39] Among the main facilitators of this effort were the charitable societies that provided platforms for Girgis and other charismatic leaders to spread their ideas and to raise funds. Girgis himself was well respected. Unmarried, serving as one of Pope Cyril V's special deacons, and later ordained to the rank of archdeacon, his lifestyle was seen as matching that of a monk. Girgis advised the pope on his trips abroad and was even invited to attend the meetings of the Holy Synod.[40]

During this period of struggle between the Community Council and the pope, the Holy Synod twice confirmed the importance of educating Coptic youth and children. In 1898, more or less pressed by the Community Council, its members acknowledged the church's duty to provide Christian education. Only five years later, in 1903, the Holy Synod elaborated on this decision by requiring that Christianity and Coptic history be taught in all Coptic schools and that teachers and students attend weekly church services. Furthermore, it called on parents of children attending the khedivial schools to safeguard their children's upbringing in Orthodox Christianity by taking them to church.[41]

In 1918 Girgis formed a central committee to oversee the Sunday-school education for students in Coptic schools on Sundays and for those in the khedivial schools on Fridays. Originally Copts objected to the name, since the term *madaris al-ahad* (Sunday schools) was reminiscent of Protestant initiatives. However, for lack of a better alternative, the name remained.[42] The committee was based in the seminary, where Girgis started to recruit teachers and develop curricula and textbooks, for which he consulted materials used in churches outside Egypt. All involved were volunteers, while the projects were financed via donations and the support of the aforementioned charitable societies that played such an integral role in the reform of the Coptic Church and community. The Sunday-school teachers launched branches in towns and villages all over Egypt, where they grew into centers of spiritual activity with prayer groups, classes, and meetings for every grade.

Political Developments

The 'Urabi Revolt

The internal struggles of the church matched those within Egyptian society. On June 19, 1879, France and Great Britain forced Khedive Isma'il to abdicate. His grandiose projects had brought Egypt to a state of bankruptcy. His goal had been to create architectural projects and an infrastructure that would put Egypt on a par with western Europe. Instead, his ambitions led to European powers taking control. The high taxes and tyrannical rule needed to enforce his visions had evoked deep hatred among his people, while the emerging press questioned his financial policies vis-à-vis the western powers. Isma'il's successor, his son Khedive Muhammed Tawfiq (1879–92), was powerless.

As for Pope Cyril V, his period of papal rule bridged two centuries, and in each century he witnessed a major national revolution: the 'Urabi revolt of 1881, which brought Egypt under British control until the First World War, and the second uprising of 1919 that eventually resulted in an Egyptian declaration of independence three years later in 1922. Both times, Cyril found himself in the midst of the ensuing social turmoil, and took sides to support the nationalist causes that he found most beneficial for his community.

During the time of Khedives Isma'il and Tawfiq, deep discontent had taken hold of several influential sectors of the population. In his analysis of the 'Urabi revolt, Juan Cole mentions a complex set of socioeconomic developments that compounded the disgruntlement: high taxes, population growth, and competition for land and jobs between peasants and landowners, and between Egyptians and expatriates. The intelligentsia, guilds, and peasants all rebelled against Ottoman-Egyptian landowners and/or against the Europeans, forming new platforms for political resistance.[43] Religious activists such as the Iranian-born cleric Jamal al-Din al-Afghani (1838–97) empowered the Muslims with speeches against government corruption and foreign interference.

In this atmosphere, Colonel Ahmad 'Urabi (1841–1911) triggered a popular revolt when in January 1881 he presented demands to the khedive for better treatment and more influence for Egyptian members of the army. Pressure from the British to quell the unrest led to severe riots in Alexandria on June 11, 1882. The khedive appealed to Britain and France; partially at his urging, the British bombarded the city on July 11 and landed troops. The khedive placed himself under their protection, and a few months later he was reinstated. Colonel 'Urabi was sent into exile to Ceylon, whence his bold actions left an enduring impression on Egypt.

'Urabi's insurrection is often seen as Egypt's first national movement. Pope Cyril V fully agreed with the popular feelings against foreign intrusion. When the khedive tried to remove 'Urabi from his position as minister of war, on July 29 the latter called for a national congress of religious, military, and business leaders to declare Tawfiq's orders nonbinding and to depose him.[44] Of the 393 delegates, eighty-six belonged to the Muslim and Christian clergy, with the Muslim reformer Muhammad 'Abduh and Pope Cyril V as prominent representatives. Nationalist Egyptian sentiments were expressed in the demand that the meeting's language be Arabic, not Turkish. The Copts agreed with the choice of language, but insisted that the war against the British would be a patriotic one, not a religious one with potentially anti-Christian undertones.[45]

Although it would cost him the goodwill of the khedive, Cyril V was among those proudly affixing their seals to the document.[46] Perhaps in certain aspects the Coptic community benefited from the foreign presence, but the pope shared the prevalent sentiment that his primary allegiance was to his country.

Nationalism and Pan-Islamism

The British occupation did not merely fuel the anti-foreign sentiments and embryonic nationalism of the 'Urabi Revolt in Egypt, it also sparked a wider movement that strove to revive the pan-Islamic civilization from the early days of Islam. Jamal al-Din al-Afghani traveled the Middle East calling for unification of all Muslims into one nation to be ruled by a caliph. One of his most famous followers in Egypt was Muhammad 'Abduh (1849–1905), who tried to reform the leading Islamic university of al-Azhar and to reconcile the teachings and practices of Islam with the demands of modern life.

Resisting British colonialism, many of the leaders of the early nationalist movement followed this pan-Islamic agenda, which implied support for the Ottoman Empire. However, Mustafa Kamil (1874–1908), the founder of

Egypt's Hizb al-Watani (National Party), also stressed interdependence between religion and national identity, promoting equality between Muslims and Copts. He believed that these two principles were fully compatible and, referring to their shared heritage, considered Muslims and Copts as one family.[47] As for the Copts, they were wary of Islamic unity schemes and could not envision for themselves a meaningful place in an Islamic theocracy. As a result, few Copts joined this nationalist movement.

After Kamil's death in 1908, the party's agenda became more pan-Islamic and the relationship between the Copts and Muslims reached a nadir, the worst it had been for many centuries.[48] The *al-Liwa'* paper, founded by Kamil, ran an article titled "Islam is a Stranger in Its Own Land," an incendiary piece that set the Coptic community ablaze.[49] The fact that its editor was Tunisian only exacerbated matters. At the same time, Coptic complaints about inadequate representation in the bureaucracy and a lack of employment opportunities sparked acrimonious press debates. Finally, in 1910, Butrus Ghali, the first Coptic prime minister, appointed only two years earlier, was murdered, and Coptic emotions threatened to boil over. These interreligious tensions, along with the perception that the Coptic community was not unified in the face of these problems, led to the organization of the so-called Coptic Congress held in Asyut, March 6–8, 1911.

The Coptic Congress

From the start, Pope Cyril was against the congress because he thought it would reflect negatively on the Coptic community. Egypt's government administration equally feared that the meeting would create unrest and asked the pope to prevent the meeting. Cyril did not think his advice would be heard, and answered, "The people neither obey me, nor take my advice. But out of respect for the request of Your Highness I will try to prevent this Congress."[50] On March 2 the octogenarian pope issued the following statement urging the Copts to keep a low profile:

> We have learned that our beloved sons are in the process of arranging a large assembly of the people of our denomination to be convened in Asyut in Upper Egypt for the purpose of deliberating their national affairs. Whilst it gives us pleasure to see that a number of Copts have agreed to work together for the welfare of the community at large, we would ask our beloved children to refrain from building up a huge gathering in Asyut, which could result in agitation and render them liable to criticism. We would therefore urge everybody to exercise extreme prudence, wisdom and circumspection.[51]

The gathering made the pope uneasy because he feared that people in Asyut would "have no knowledge of councils among their customs, and thus it may be that an occasion be found for men without foresight to act unwittingly." He was concerned by the presence of a great number of Copts in the town, fearing that the motives of those gathering might be misunderstood.[52] Not only did Cyril fear that the congress would draw undue attention to the Coptic community, he also suspected that the British could exploit it to create discord among Egyptians.

The metropolitan of Asyut, Bishop Macarius, sided with the organizers of the meeting and in a telegram to the pope assured him that there was no cause for concern: "No personal or public damage is likely to result, the main objective of the Congress being the forging of stronger ties among all Egyptians through the safeguarding of the legitimate rights of Copts. I do not feel the slightest apprehension of its being held in Asyut."[53]

The Congress was cast as a nationalist exercise and discussions mostly revolved around points related to equal opportunity. The delegates pushed for the establishment of Sunday as a holiday, affirmed that ability should be the only criterion in hiring people for government service, advocated for proportionate representation in parliament, urged that village schools be open to all Egyptians—Muslims, Copts, and Jews—and that government taxes also be used to open Coptic schools, and, finally, insisted on equal financial policies regarding Coptic and Muslim institutions and regarding personal-status courts for the Copts.

The British consul general, Sir Eldon Gorst, commented that the congress had been the work of a clique of wealthy landowners and Copts who had benefited disproportionately from reforms introduced by the British. During a counter-congress called "The Egyptian Congress of Heliopolis," most of the Coptic demands were dismissed and Copts were accused of trying to break up the nation.[54]

The Wafd and Inter-communal Harmony

The dissonant atmosphere changed after the First World War, when the British placed Egypt under a military protectorate and an inclusive form of Egyptian nationalism emerged whose leaders were interested not in fostering a pan-Islamic movement, but in promoting Egypt's interests above all else. This movement coalesced into the Wafd party. In 1919, the Egyptian nationalist Sa'd Zaghlul led an Egyptian delegation, a *wafd,* to demand independence at the Paris peace conference. This delegation sparked the 1919 anti-British revolt that forced Britain to recognize Egypt as a sovereign state, albeit with the restriction that Britain retain its hold over military and diplomatic affairs. Copts were actively involved in the revolution, joining "demonstrations, strikes, propaganda, terrorism, organization, and policy-making."[55] The Wafd became a well-organized political party with a wide popular base that provided a neutral platform for the Copts to join the national struggle. Its central committee had several wealthy Coptic members, mostly landowners. In 1924, when Zaghlul formed the first Wafd cabinet, two of the ten ministers were Copts. Until 1950, whenever the Wafd won the elections, Christians held adequate representation in Egypt's governing bodies.[56] One of its most prominent leaders was an Egyptian Protestant, Makram 'Ebeid.

The 1919 revolution ushered in a virtual spring tide in Muslim–Coptic relations; peaceful coexistence was stressed and new bonds forged. Demonstrators carried banners depicting both a crescent and a cross; Coptic clergy and Muslim *'ulama* shared pulpits in mosques and churches. The activist priest Murqus Sergius, who later became the pope's deputy, led a demonstration to al-Azhar, where he was the first Coptic priest ever to give a public speech in its mosque. This period of time gave birth to the much-repeated credo that Copts and Muslims have lived in harmony since the Arab conquest and are one and not two peoples.[57]

The mufti of Egypt called on the pope, who returned the visit. Religious holidays became intercommunal affairs, with Copts joining the celebrations for the Eid al-Fitr, the feast at the end of Ramadan, and Muslims taking part in Easter festivities. In spite of his advanced age, Cyril seems to have been actively involved in the revolution, supporting it wholeheartedly. He received Copts and Muslims in the Church of St. Mark and was among the dignitaries who welcomed back Sa'd Zaghlul after the British exiled him between 1921 and 1923.[58]

Copts were committed to national unity and its corollary of full citizenship. The issue of citizenship rose to the fore in 1922, when Britain granted Egypt independence but reserved as one of three prerogatives the right to intervene in Egyptian affairs to protect minorities and citizens of foreign countries. The Copts protested vehemently. Fearing the destruction of national unity and British interference, they insisted they were not a minority, and that there was no division between Muslims and Copts.[59]

This period of peaceful coexistence was not to last. The Muslim Brotherhood soon began advocating for an Islamic order in which Copts would return to the status of *dhimmi*s, and by the late 1930s this viewpoint had become more influential in Egyptian society. By the 1940s, when the Palestinian question became a subject for international debate, relations between Christians and Muslims had deteriorated even more.

Negotiating Foreign Forces

For the Copts the British occupation was a mixed blessing. On the economic level it improved Coptic chances to compete for jobs. Although initially Copts were fired from certain government positions to make room for British subjects, by 1900 they were overrepresented in the state educational system and occupied around 45 percent of the government posts held by Egyptians.[60] On the social and religious level, the British presence placed the Copts in a double bind, in that it both restrained and encouraged Muslim animosity toward them. Pope Cyril V was engaged in a delicate balancing act. Even as he tried to accommodate the interests of his own community, the Muslims, and the British, he adamantly resisted the authority of foreign powers, whether a country or a church.

The presence of numerous rival Christian denominations in the country had challenged Coptic Church life and culture since the time of Pope Demetrius. Protestant and Catholic missions from Europe and North America increased after the British occupation. The American Protestant presence was at its peak during Cyril's reign, creating immense challenges and opportunities for the Coptic Church. Since converting the Muslims was forbidden, Protestant missionaries turned their attention to the Orthodox Copts, especially by opening schools.

The Copts also found themselves in conflict with other eastern Christian communities in Egypt. Since the days of Muhammad 'Ali, government rulers had preferred the services of Syrian, Greek, and Armenian Christians over the Copts. This preferential treatment aroused a certain level of animosity toward those groups. During the 1830s, British scholar Edward Lane remarked, "the hatred with which even the modern Copts regard the Greeks and all other Christians who are not of their own sect is much greater than that which they bear toward the Muslims."[61] And yet, in spite of feeling threatened by more cosmopolitan eastern Christian groups, at the end of the nineteenth century the Coptic community still occupied important sectors of society. The census of 1897 counted 608,000 Copts (around 7 percent of the population), who owned one-fifth of the land and buildings (around 1.5 million feddans and three hundred thousand houses). According to contemporary estimates, they ranked fourth in possessions after the tax apparatus, the khedive's family, and the highest civil servants.[62] Thus Copts represented 30 percent of the educated Egyptian population and held 19 percent of all the land. One of the reasons for this accumulation of land holdings was that Copts, in their capacity as tax collectors and moneylenders, could claim the properties of peasants who had borrowed money with their land as security. When crops failed, the moneylender took possession. By 1914 it was estimated that 50 percent of Egypt's wealth was in Coptic hands.[63]

At the time of the British occupation the Copts controlled a large part of Egypt's financial sector. According to Lord Cromer, the British consul general between 1883 and 1907, most of the accountants in government service were Copts, but "their system of accounts was archaic."[64] As a result, in the early days of the occupation, Syrian accountants replaced the Copts. However, during the 1920s when Banque Misr, the Bank of Egypt, was created, Coptic landowners became prominent shareholders in the new financial enterprise. Cromer's overall attitude toward the Copts was negative, to put it mildly. He tried to sympathize with these fellow Christians but had trouble understanding their particular practice of the faith and why they could not accept the fact that the British could not favor them over the Muslims. In his memoirs Cromer accuses the Copts of being double-faced: "Anglophobe and Anglophile according to the requirements of his audience." In short, in Cromer's eyes the Copts were "opportunists."[65] Copts resented the British for their inadequate support, but at the same time they realized that the foreign presence also meant a form of protection.

Due to his deep distrust of the British, Pope Cyril did not support the occupation until after 1900, when pan-Islamists leveled severe attacks against the Copts.[66] A well-known story about his interactions with Lord Cromer and Lord Kitchener (consul general 1910–16), which survives in various versions, was often recounted in order to illustrate how Cyril did not bow down to the colonial power. In the version told by Amir Nasr, when Cromer offered the pope protection from the Anglican Church, the pope answered,

> Oh my son, Copts and Muslims have lived side by side for centuries, sharing a house together. In matters of unity they share desks; they eat in one room from the same good earth; they drink from the same Nile; for better or for worse they are one in all matters of life. They cannot do without the other so we the Copts will not require protection except from God and from the throne of Egypt.[67]

With Lord Kitchener, the pope offered no dialogue at all. When Kitchener appeared at the papal residence unannounced, he was sent away with the message, "The Pope does not receive [guests] without an appointment."[68]

Monastic Ideals

Simple Lifestyles

Before moving into the beginning of the twentieth century, let us pause and consider the lifestyle of Pope Cyril. On this subject, we have some eyewitness reports from British visitors such as Leeder.[69] Cyril's piety not only embodied a spiritual heritage of hundreds of years; his persona also stood in stark contrast to the greed and negligence of which many of the clergy were accused. He was frugal and ran his administration effectively; by 1913 he allegedly had increased the papal revenue from LE5,000 to LE43,000 annually.[70] He had considerable real estate at his disposal that he used for religious purposes. In fact, he had sole power over the revenue of all churches. Lane observed during the 1830s that when a Coptic house was for sale in Cairo, the pope had the prerogative of bidding for it first and choosing a price to his liking.[71] He applied much energy to the building of new churches such as St. Mark's in Giza (1877) and the church of the Angel Gabriel in al-Saqaqqin (1881), and strongly supported the repair and restoration of existing churches and monasteries.[72]

According to Leeder, Pope Cyril V spent no more than sixty pounds a year for his own household and donated most of his income to build schools and churches and to provide for the poor. This observation was severely contested, however, by Coptic lay leaders who investigated the pope's personal expenditures. In 1907 they counted the amount of LE614 spent on the pope's food, which was staggering when compared to the LE235 used annually for an orphanage under Cyril's jurisdiction.[73]

Somewhere in the archives we might find the answer to what happened to that large sum of money, as it seems unlikely the pope spent it on himself. When Leeder visited him, he met a man dressed in a faded, threadbare black garment. Although well into his eighties, Cyril remained standing the entire visit. Leeder described the pope as a man of purity, simplicity, and self-denial.[74] He also mused about the attachment of the Copts to their pope, and how deeply moved they could be just by hearing him pray.[75] While many reform-minded Copts detested Cyril for his reactionary stances, others saw his struggle to preserve the *waqf* properties as an attempt to protect the monasteries.[76]

Anba Abraam

During Cyril's time other Coptic leaders equally evoked respect among both Copts and Muslims through their ascetic and humble lifestyles. The most famous example is the bishop of Fayoum, Anba Abraam (1829–1914), who was added to the official list of saints in 1964 and whose grave in Dayr al-'Azab in Fayoum has become a place of pilgrimage. Leeder paid him a personal visit because wherever he went in Egypt he heard incredible stories about this "most venerated man in all the valley of the Nile" who was revered for his "self-denial, his fastings, his mystical wisdom, his power of divination, his faculty to exorcise evil spirits and the cure of all manner of sickness and of the comfort his words gave to the afflicted both in soul and in body; of his unstilted kindness to the poor."[77] When the bishop prayed for the guests, Leeder felt that this man was "speaking in the clear presence of God Himself," and that by joining the heavenly powers, it was as if earth had fallen away.

Anba Abraam's way of living was countercultural in the pervading atmosphere of ignorance and greed. In fact, certain incidents in his biography confirm the complaints lay Copts had about the clergy. He became a monk with the name of Paul at the age of eighteen. His star rose quickly and he was elected abbot of his monastery, Dayr al-Muharraq. Practicing his concern for the poor, Abbot Paul opened the monastery's door to feed them, giving away large parts of its substantial annual income. As a result, infuriated monks accused him of wasting the monastic monies and forced him out. He found refuge in the Baramus Monastery where he befriended its abbot, who, after becoming Pope Cyril V, ordained him bishop of Fayoum.

Although educated in a simple village *kuttab*, he took learning seriously and was famous for his deep knowledge of the Bible, which he often used to defend his radical philosophy of charity. Not even the pope was exempt from his criticism. In a famous incident he chastised Cyril for wanting to defrock a priest who had fed and hosted a disgraced bishop.[78]

Cultural Awakenings

Pharaonic Roots

Coptic observers agreed that the century had been a good one for their community. Benefiting from Egypt's improved infrastructures, school systems, and international relations, and enjoying stronger legal positions, Copts had gained in wealth and stature, and participated in Egypt's written and cultural production and government. Khedive Isma'il's Majlis al-Nuwwab (Chamber of Deputies) had three Coptic members in 1866, two in 1870, and three in 1876. During that period five Copts held high positions in the state apparatus.[79] They had caught up with the other Oriental Christians such as Syrians and Armenians, who through their mobility as merchants often functioned as brokers between Europe and the Middle East. Following the winds of change in society, by the end of the nineteenth century Copts were deeply involved in education, print, and journalism, and had adopted the idea of benevolent societies. Within the boundaries of their country, many well-educated Copts embraced cosmopolitan lifestyles and nationalist causes, while still finding a place for traditional religious beliefs and practices.

A new-found awareness of Coptic and pharaonic heritage was one important aspect of this redefinition of Egyptian Christian religious identity during this period. Coptic schools provided serious study of the Coptic language beyond the rote learning of the traditional *kuttab*. They used works such as H. Tattam's Coptic–Arabic New Testament and Barsum al-Rahib's first-ever Coptic grammar in Arabic. At the turn of the century, Coptic historian Mikhail Sharubim (1853–1920) published a history of ancient and modern Egypt that included Coptic history from a national, not sectarian, point of view.[80] Following this national trend, Copts also became interested in their pharaonic roots, and Coptic scholars such as Claudius Labib (1868–1918) combined the study of Egyptology with Coptology.

European research into the pharaonic heritage had awoken in Egyptians the desire to rediscover their ancient roots themselves. As early as 1835, Muhammad 'Ali made a failed attempt to create an antiquities service and museum.[81] Khedive Isma'il increased general appreciation for the Egyptian heritage by opening important cultural institutions such as the Khedivial Library, the opera house, a state theater, and schools at various levels, including the influential Dar al-'Ulum teachers' college. Language became the vehicle of national identity. In 1867, Arabic replaced Turkish as the official language of the administration, and in 1868 the history of ancient Egypt was published in Arabic. Copts identified with this aspect of the national heritage and the Coptic press became an important vehicle for transmitting information about new discoveries. A defining moment in the Coptic imagination occurred in 1908, during a speech at the Ramses Club, when the French director general of antiquities, Gaston Maspero, explicitly identified the Copts as the purest descendants of ancient Egyptians. Interest in the pharaonic past skyrocketed in 1922, the year that Egypt unilaterally declared its independence from Great Britain, when Tutankhamun's tomb was discovered. At that point, Maspero reaffirmed that all Egyptians were descended from the impressive ancient civilization.[82] Inspired by discoveries of the ancient past, Copts became motivated to research their own Christian heritage.

Coptic studies had developed in Europe, where it grew out of biblical, patristic, and oriental studies, providing a gateway to Egyptology. More or less starting with the German Jesuit Athanasius Kircher's (1602–80) foundational work in hieroglyphics and Coptic, it gathered steam at the turn of the century with studies on language, literature, art, and architecture.[83] It took some time, however, before Coptic culture gained a place of its own among both foreign and Egyptian scholars. Ancient Coptic edifices erected in front of or inside pharaonic sites aggravated Egyptologists to no end. Invaluable remains of antique Coptic churches in front of the temple of Ramesses II at Madinat Habu were carted away.[84] Alfred Butler complained about the many Christian antiquities that were perishing; westerners were not aware of their existence and few Copts realized that "worn-out cult objects" were not merely valuable for their weight in silver but could be "priceless antiquities."[85] While some Copts were aware of the irreplaceable value of ancient churches, manuscripts, and art, well-meaning Coptic notables continued to replace ancient churches with structures covered with Italian marble and built in Greek style.[86]

With the founding of the Coptic Museum in 1908, Marcus Simaika (1864–1944) took it upon himself to raise awareness among the Copts about their Christian past rooted in Egypt. Unlike the Egyptian Museum (pharaonic), the Greco-Roman Museum, and the Museum of Arab (now Islamic) Art, this museum was the brainchild of an Egyptian who came out of Pope Cyril IV's Patriarchal School. In his capacity as the vice-president of the Majlis al-Milli, Simaika was also an avid advocate of communal and church reform.

Using Simaika's unpublished memoirs, Donald Malcolm Reid has provided a fascinating account of what it took to convince Pope Cyril of the need to preserve church treasures and artifacts in a museum. In fact, the idea for the museum was born when one day in the winter of 1908, Simaika witnessed the pope supervising a silversmith weighing out old silver gospel covers and church vessels with fourteenth- and fifteenth-century inscriptions in Coptic and Arabic to be melted down for reworking.[87] The pope's consent was indispensable, since the museum's premises and collection were church property and were situated in the midst of prominent historic churches in Old Cairo.[88] Initially Simaika tried to use the clout of the Khedivial Committee for Conservation of Monuments of Arab Art to propose preservation of historic Coptic churches and monasteries. The pope accepted its services reluctantly after the committee offered to pay part of the restoration costs. Simaika realized that this enterprise needed full Coptic involvement and decided to tone down his pro-reform agenda to focus on one of the ultimate symbols of reformation and communal identity—preservation of the Coptic heritage.

Much patience was needed. "The patriarch had tolerated rampant clerical corruption . . . tried alchemy to obtain gold to build new churches, and forced Simaika to dig for buried treasures under the altar of an Old Cairo church."[89] Yet Simaika worked hard to identify with the pope's point of view. Realizing that the pope had the backing of the clergy and the people, he even allowed himself to put some of the blame for the 1892–93 clashes between the Community Council and the pope on the lay Copts.[90] The change in tone paid off: Pope Cyril V allowed him not only to launch the museum, but also to comb through churches and monasteries to find Coptic objects to fill the museum with artifacts.

The museum provided an alternative, church-centered vision of Coptic identity and history. Within its walls, Coptic and pharaonic past complemented each other. It also served as a convenient ceremonial site for Muslim Egyptian officials to reconfirm their commitment to a shared national identity.

A Lay Church?

Pope Cyril V passed away on August 7, 1927, leaving behind a thriving church that had boldly entered the twentieth century. Copts had made gains in wealth, in access to education, and in political participation, and the devotional and academic lives of the church were reviving. Alumni of the seminary continued to launch Sunday-school meetings all over Egypt; the charitable organizations sponsored education and publications and cared for the poor and the sick.

Much of the work was done by lay Copts, although several bishops and priests also supported the new activities. One of the reform-minded bishops was Anba Macarius, who since 1897 had been the Metropolitan of Asyut and in 1944 became the 114th pope. He is remembered not only for supporting the Coptic Conference in 1911, but also for launching a series of initiatives that would stem the tide of the Protestant missions in his diocese.

As far as the pope's position was concerned, since the second half of the nineteenth century a shift had occurred in the relationship between the pope and the government. Popes Peter and Demetrius had commanded respect from the ruling khedives and seem to have been on good terms with the political powers. Although at times relationships were strained, the laity and clergy held great respect for Cyril throughout; his real struggle was against western trends in education that he opposed, but that were supported by the khedive, who backed the Coptic laity in their reform efforts.

While the laity gained in strength and influence during the reign of Cyril V, the ties between pope and government weakened, and continued to do so during the period described in the next chapter, which covers Cyril's successors, the 113th, 114th, and 115th in line after St. Mark: John XIX (1928–42), Macarius III (1944–45), and Yusab II (1946–56, followed by an interregnum from 1956 to 1959). As lay Copts joined national politics through the Wafd party, the government no longer needed to rely on the popes to represent the Orthodox community.[91]

6

Leading in the Midst of Political Change

(Pope John XIX,1928–42; Pope Macarius III, 1944–45; Pope Yusab II, 1946–56)

The three popes who reigned between 1928 and 1956 saw the proverbial best and worst of times in the history of Egypt and of the Coptic Church. Periods of revolutionary zeal during which Copts and Muslims joined in national unity alternated with times of inter-religious strife. Social and economic conditions deteriorated with the onset of the Second World War. The gap between rich and poor grew ever wider; farmers who had to increase their production for the rapidly growing population lost their lands to wealthy landowners; and social unrest grew. Neither the king nor the politicians vying for power had a vision or program to relieve the suffering of the population, and the people lost trust in their system of government. The Muslim Brotherhood was one of the few communal organizations with a comprehensive program to alleviate the socioeconomic suffering, and it grew rapidly in membership. The deteriorating conditions paved the way for the 1952 military coup that dethroned King Farouk: the leaders of this coup had as their goals the strengthening of the Egyptian army and the end of corruption, feudalism, and British interference.

Between 1923 and 1952, when Egyptians developed a western-style constitution with parliamentary government and political parties, several Copts became influential politicians. Concurrently, disagreements between the Coptic laity and the popes continued, ending in Pope Yusab II's removal from the papal throne by force in 1955, an unprecedented occurrence in Coptic history. The three popes who occupied the seat of St. Mark after Pope Cyril V were all controversial, and the struggle surrounding their election was symptomatic of the ongoing struggle between the laity and the pope. For each of these popes the beginning of their reign was mired in a contentious issue that split the community in two—the fact that each of them had been a diocesan bishop before being elected pope. John XIX had been the bishop of al-Beheira and Munufiya; Macarius III, the bishop of Asyut; and Yusab II, the bishop of Girga.

The Conservative Pope: John XIX (1928–42)

A Conservative Choice

Pope John, the 113th pope of the See of St. Mark, had served as personal assistant and close confidant to Pope Cyril V, whom he had joined in exile in 1892. Born in the province of Asyut in 1855,[1] and educated in the village *kuttab,* he entered the Monastery of Baramus at the age of seventeen. His many years of experience in papal affairs made him a natural choice to serve as deputy until a new pope was elected on December 7, 1928. Nobody, however, expected John to aspire to the papal throne himself. Having been the bishop of al-Beheira and Munufiya for over forty years, he was ineligible for the papal office, since the Coptic Orthodox Church strictly adhered to the rule that a bishop was wedded to his diocese and could not be removed from his seat. Becoming the pope would leave his congregation leaderless.[2]

In 1873, when Bishop Mark had been the locum tenens in the interregnum between Demetrius II and Cyril V, the electoral body, at that time the Holy Synod, had reconfirmed this rule and decreed that any bishop who sought to promote himself to the papal chair should be excommunicated.[3] Following tradition, candidates for the high spiritual office had to be chosen from monks of great sanctity and learning. Bishops, of course, had started their careers in the monastery, and some factions argued that bishops had the required experience to administer and govern a large and complex community. When the Holy Synod met in 1928, it decided to lift the ancient rule and promote Bishop John to Pope John. The community received this decision with anger and anxiety: letters of protest were written and demonstrations were held. Exasperated, Iris Habib al-Masri wrote in her history of the Coptic Church, "This was a clerical decision; what was the Majlis al-Milli doing?"[4]

In retrospect, the election of a bishop has been interpreted as a sign of the church's weakness—unified rules concerning the election of the pope were lacking or broken. But the main grudge the reform-minded lay Copts held against John was his arch-conservatism and persistent rumors that he had bribed his way into the papal position. Seldom had a pope received so little support from the people: "Many Copts detested John and the Coptic press was full of articles attacking him."[5] In December 1927, an assembly of 260 people—representatives of lay councils and Coptic notables—had tried to promote a more progressive candidate by electing a pope of their own choice. Since this election violated canon law, the government did not dare to accept the new 'pope,' and proceeded to organize proper elections during which a large majority voted for John.[6] His election did not bode well for the Coptic reform movement, which had gained in strength during Cyril's tenure.

Concerns about Money and Marriage

By 1926, the members of the Majlis al-Milli, realizing they needed to curtail wasteful expenditures and gain control of *waqf* revenues, submitted a proposal to the senate to expand the council to twenty-four lay members and grant it jurisdiction over the church's income. The Holy Synod protested vehemently, and in the end Macarius, the metropolitan of Asyut, was one of only three bishops to support this new reform effort. On behalf of an ill and frail Pope Cyril V, Bishop John submitted a petition to annul the proposal. However, just before the pope passed away, the Egyptian parliament passed the bill over the protests, and as a result the council's powers were expanded considerably.[7] John, upon becoming the pope himself, immediately tried to annul the new bill, and a few months into his reign he changed the locks of the papal residence to prevent council meetings from being held. The doors were not reopened to reform-minded Copts until Metropolitan Macarius, who had backed their efforts in 1926, became John's successor.

Apart from juggling perennial problems related to financial administration, the council during these years became heavily involved in revising the personal-status law. Reasoning that community-based codes prevented national unity, the emerging national government attempted to create one legal code that would apply to all citizens regardless of their religion. In order to reach this goal, Christians and Jews both had to renounce their autonomous personal-status law system. The new policies also meant that the state would train and control the body of judges.[8] Fearing the possibility that Islamic law would be imposed, Jewish and Christian communities protested vehemently.

When this effort at legal unification failed, the state required that each community publish its own code, which the Coptic Community Council did in 1938. (Later, in 1955, when President Nasser abolished the religious communal courts, he would still allow national family courts to apply the personal-status laws of the respective religious communities.) However, the rules submitted by the Coptic Community Council in 1938 had the effect of infuriating the pope and clerical members of the Holy Synod. One hotly contested issue was the matter of divorce. The new code contained nine grounds for the dissolution of marriage. Although the Community Council based these grounds on medieval documents, subsequent papal administrations have made efforts to reverse these laws, arguing that the Bible only allows two reasons for divorce—adultery and apostasy.[9] That the council at the time of Pope John could follow the medieval rules and ignore the Holy Synod shows its strength and influence at that time in history.

Educational Developments

As the right hand of Pope Cyril V, John had acquired a keen awareness of the necessity to strengthen the church's leadership by addressing problems related to the ignorance of clergy and cases of corruption. In 1928, he immediately launched a number of initiatives to further the educational and spiritual goals of his predecessor. Focusing on the education of the monks, he dedicated a large garden in Helwan, just south of Cairo, to the establishment of a theological college. The quiet location became a popular place for those used to living in the remote monasteries. Thirty students filled the first class, and a few years later the future Pope Cyril VI would become one of their number. The students followed a curriculum similar to that of the Cairo Seminary and received frequent visits from the pope, who dropped in to encourage them.[10] That same year, to enforce monastic rules and propriety, the Holy Synod required that monks who did not have a specific task within the larger community should return to and remain in their monasteries.[11] A decade later, in a second decree, the synod required that all those seeking the priesthood should be educated in one of the theological schools.[12]

While the pope was launching official projects, the lay movement was flourishing. During the period between 1935 and 1942 the Sunday School Movement gained traction and grew rapidly. In Cairo, four centers for Sunday-school education came into existence that would greatly impact Coptic Christian education and church growth throughout the land. In some cases, Sunday schools were started even before a church had its own priest.[13] Sunday-school teachers educated a new generation of Copts about the principles of their faith. Many of the teachers and students, although from modest backgrounds, eventually surpassed the new-style notables and moved into the church hierarchy, becoming monks, priests, bishops, and even popes.[14] They taught their students that what mattered most were not political and social squabbles but one's inner growth and individual spirituality. The idea took hold that a new generation with a strong inner spiritual life could bring about a revival of the church.[15]

Famous preachers such as Habib Girgis and Iskander Hanna fired up crowds of young adults to join this movement. Under the guidance of Metropolitan Macarius, they had started to copy Protestant revival meetings in Asyut, inspiring young Copts not only to join but to give part of their lives to the church by becoming *khuddam al-kanisa* (servants of the church). One of these servants, Azer Yusuf 'Atta, followed Iskander Hanna's intensive Bible studies and, to his family's great dismay, decided to become a monk. Later on, 'Atta became the charismatic Pope Cyril VI.[16] But it would take another quarter century for his generation to assume leadership of the church.

Growth and Challenges

Among Pope John's other noteworthy activities was a pastoral trip to Ethiopia, where he ordained several priests and bishops. Furthermore, he renovated the papal residence, had a memorable meeting during which he predicted that the monk called Mina al-Muttawahid one day would hold the papal staff, and twice presided over the special and rare ceremony of the preparation of the holy *mayrun*, the sacred oil used in liturgical ceremonies of consecration. The last time this holy oil had been consecrated was 110 years earlier, during the papacy of Pope Peter VII (1809–52).[17] The production of this oil is thought to go back to the time of the apostles and follows a strict procedure supervised by the pope. The ceremony is not only a joyous spiritual occasion but also a sign of the church's growth and vigor. One year after preparing the *mayrun* for the Egyptian church in 1930, John held the ceremony to replenish the oil for the Church in Ethiopia.[18]

In spite of his significant efforts to invigorate the pastoral and spiritual life of the church, Pope John's reign was overshadowed by two political events—one local and one international—that dealt serious blows to Coptic pride.

The first event took place in 1931, when the Egyptian government passed a law that the Coptic Museum should be supervised by the state and thus nationalized, just like the other main museums. On a local level, the nationalization of the museum was an especially thorny issue. Not only did the museum belong to the church's properties and endowments, it also housed liturgical artifacts that could be used in the celebration of the Mass, and adjoining its campus was the Mu'allaqa Church where regular worship took place. This nationalization effort did provide for a rare moment of unity between the pope and the Majlis al-Milli, however. When John called for a special meeting of the Community Council, all agreed that they should raise an objection. Unfortunately, their letters and statements of protest proved to be of no avail.[19]

The second event was the Italian invasion of Ethiopia in 1935. Over a period of time, this change in the political landscape would lead to a break in the Coptic Church's historical relationship with the Ethiopian Church.

The Church in Ethiopia

Since the fourth century, the Ethiopian Orthodox Church had been dependent on the Coptic Church for its ecclesiastical life. In every generation until the year 1881, one bishop called the *abun*—Egyptian by birth, chosen and consecrated by the pope of Egypt—had been in charge of the affairs of Ethiopian Christians, who by the nineteenth century far outnumbered the Copts. For several hundred years, requests had been sent by Ethiopian emperors to increase the number of prelates; however, fearing a gain in Ethiopian power, Egypt's rulers had never given their approval. This situation changed in 1881 when, after an Egyptian–Ethiopian armed conflict, the Ethiopian emperor negotiated for four bishops to be sent from Alexandria instead of just one *abun*. That year the Holy Synod decreed that an archbishop and three Egyptian bishops would be appointed to the church in Ethiopia. One of the reasons Copts in Egypt were reluctant to relinquish their privileged position was that Ethiopian dependency made the Coptic Church an important diplomatic conduit between the two countries. Consequently, Egyptian politicians closely monitored negotiations between the two churches.

By 1924, internal Ethiopian developments pushed for greater independence from the Egyptian church. Growing nationalist pride was compounded by feelings of growing discontent: Ethiopians increasingly viewed their relationship with the Coptic Church as a form of 'religious imperialism.' Crown Prince Ras Tafari (who would later become Emperor Haile Selassi) envisioned a future in which the imperial throne would represent a unified Ethiopian identity based on Amharic Christian culture. He needed Ethiopian bishops to hold the provinces together and to face down internal ethnic and regional challenges. Improving the general level of education of his country was one of his important goals as ruler. Connecting education with cultural pride, he ordered the Bible and liturgy, which were traditionally recited in the dead language of Ge'ez, to be translated into the Amharic tongue. This project was completed by 1934.

During his visit to Cairo in 1924, Ras Tafari tried to advance his national cause by demanding that Matewos, the Egyptian archbishop to Ethiopia, be succeeded by an Ethiopian vested with the power to appoint bishops.[20] He further demanded that the keys of the Dayr al-Sultan Monastery adjacent to the Church of the Holy Sepulcher in Jerusalem be returned to the Ethiopians. The monastery had been occupied by Ethiopian and Egyptian monks since the fifth century; the Copts had appropriated the keys in 1834 when Jerusalem was briefly under Egyptian control and when the Ethiopian monks residing there had fallen victim to the plague.

Ras Tafari's wishes were denied, but after Matewos passed away in 1926, Ras Tafari spent three years negotiating for Ethiopian monks to be consecrated as bishops. In 1929, Pope John appointed the new Egyptian archbishop, Cyril VI, together with three Ethiopian bishops; a fourth Ethiopian bishop would be added later that year during John's planned pastoral visit to Ethiopia.[21] Consistent with his educational vision, Ras Tafari stipulated that the new archbishop should be a man not only of great piety, but also of learning: he should be fluent in both English and French, and versed in contemporary sciences.[22] In June 1929, Cyril and the three Ethiopian bishops followed in the footsteps of the prelates who had been appointed from Egypt before them. Traveling to Addis Ababa via Djibouti and Harare, Cyril reported exuberant crowds along the road: "In most of the stations we passed through we were hailed by large delegations headed by men of the cloth carrying crosses and censers and chanting verses from the psalms of David."[23]

On December 23, 1929, Pope John followed the same route when he undertook a historic trip to Ethiopia to strengthen diplomatic and religious ties and to finish the work envisioned by Pope Cyril V forty years earlier. He was the first Egyptian pope to make the trip to Ethiopia, and was so exhausted that after arriving in Addis Ababa on January 3, 1930, he could not celebrate Mass the next day.[24] The pope established two schools and laid the first stone for a church. In the imperial palace he presided over the Christmas celebrations of 1930, and that same day visited the Egyptian Consulate, where he drank tea.[25] Later that week, the frail and elderly Empress Zewditu Menelik made the exceptional move of coming down to the train station in person to bid the pope farewell.[26] Before John embarked on the boat that would take him back to Suez, he received a message from the king of Egypt wishing him a safe trip home.[27]

In November of that same year the empress died, and Archbishop Cyril crowned Ras Tafari as Emperor Haile Selassi I. The bishop chosen to represent the Coptic papal delegation at the ceremony was the future Pope Yusab II, who supported independence for the Ethiopian Church. After he became pope in 1946, the Holy Synod would take the historic decision that an Ethiopian should replace Archbishop Cyril upon his death, and in January of 1951 Yusab would consecrate the first Ethiopian *abun*, Basilios.[28]

In 1930, however, the goodwill between the Coptic and Ethiopian Churches evaporated when the Ethiopians learned that Pope John had ordained eighteen priests for the church in Eritrea. Under siege by Italian missionaries, the Eritrean Church had been without a leader since the First World War. By bypassing the Ethiopian Church for the ordination of these priests, John de facto accepted Eritrea's political independence from Ethiopia. It was an action that the emperor in his turn interpreted as papal political interference.[29] Thus, in November 1935, when Mussolini invaded Ethiopia, "the only independent country in Africa," and started to press the Ethiopians to declare independence from the Church of Alexandria, relations between the two churches were put on hold.

With the onset of the Italian occupation (1935–41), Emperor Haile Selassi had fled to England, whence he let it be known that he was against splitting with the Coptic Church. The Italians continued to press Metropolitan Cyril, to the point that he traveled to Rome to discuss his cause directly with the invading authorities. They could not reach an agreement and Cyril returned to Egypt. While he was preparing to return to his diocese, the Italians installed their own metropolitan in Addis Ababa.[30]

Egyptian reactions to these developments were vehement. Copts and Muslims joined in rallies to protest the severance of a relationship that had lasted more than sixteen centuries, and to support the pope's stance against intervening in Ethiopia's political affairs. *Al-Ahram* reported that among the demonstrators were many Muslim youths carrying placards bearing patriotic slogans and other moving messages such as "All Egyptians are brothers" and "Muslims and Copts are sons of the same nation and condemn the separation of the Abyssinian Church from its mother Coptic Church."[31]

Ethiopians in the meantime were observing with concern the rise of the Muslim Brotherhood and Islamic–Arab sentiments in Egypt. By the 1940s it no longer made sense to them that a Coptic minority that was losing political influence in its own country should hold the final religious authority over a country with a much larger Christian population and whose religious identity defined their model of state.[32] With an Ethiopian *abun* in place, the emperor gained complete control over the nationalized church, which supported his cause for Ethiopian centralization and national unity. Nonetheless, for the time being, the Coptic pope continued to appoint and consecrate Ethiopian bishops.[33]

Communal Solidarity and Communal Discord

The looming severance of relations with the Ethiopian Church was an issue of Egyptian national interest that allowed Pope John to maintain a prominent public role. It also served as a cause around which Copts and Muslims could unite. During the 1920s, when Egypt's independence and the emergence of the Wafd party had created a strong bond of national unity based on a secular political model, relatively few cases of communal violence had occurred. However, the secularist model had been challenged shortly afterward.

Despite their title of 'king,' the rulers of Egypt maintained the ideal of heading an Islamic state, and the Muslim Brotherhood (established by Hassan al-Banna in 1928, the year of Pope John's election) advocated for a reform via the Islamization of the national laws in order to realize such a state. By the end of John's reign, the Brotherhood's social and economic development programs had gained it a popular base of an estimated two million members, and its sectarian ideologies and calls for a return to an Islamic state in tandem led to increased intercommunal tensions.[34]

In this atmosphere, election campaigns became occasions for heightened anti-Coptic rhetoric and accusations that Copts had gained too much influence, power, and wealth in Egyptian society. The fact that from 1937 to 1942 Makram 'Ebeid, the prominent Protestant politician, was the number-two leader of the Wafd party served as proof among such circles that Coptic influence in politics had become too great and needed to be limited. At the same time, due in part to internal power struggles, the Wafd party lost much of its influence during this period, and its liberal, secular agenda was increasingly drowned out by proponents of a pro-Islamic state.

For his part, Pope John did his best not to involve himself in this political acrimony, repeatedly reaffirming the Coptic community's support of the Egyptian state. At the time of King Farouk's coronation (1936), when sentiments flared up over the question of whether or not the ceremony should be an Islamic one, the pope simply sent a note to the palace confirming Coptic loyalties to the throne.[35] When Muslim–Coptic strife drew the attention of the British, the pope and several notables visited Egypt's prime minister, which provided the government with an opportunity to showcase public support for the Copts.[36]

Pope John's response to public debates over religious instruction in state schools is another case in point. During his tenure as pope, several educational bills were put forward to expand general education and make school compulsory for boys and girls between the ages of seven and twelve. The 1933 law instructed that schools should offer Islamic education and devote one-third of the curriculum to memorizing the Qur'an. Despite the constitutional principle of equality between Egypt's citizens, no alternatives were offered for non-Muslims. At first, the Community Council and the pope refrained from commenting at all on this delicate issue. When he finally did respond, the pope simply chose to support the government's position, with the result that this issue regarding the education of Coptic children was never resolved systematically. In the end, local schools and ministerial authorities could excuse Christian children from Qur'an lessons; however, such dispensations depended on the whim of local administrations, and might or might not be granted. Across the board in his policy, Pope John followed the time-tested pattern of refraining from making direct pleas to the government or the palace. For their part, his critics claimed that the pope was too afraid of offending the king.[37]

While Pope John was a conservative, rather timid leader who tried to stave off conflict with the ruling authorities, it should be noted that his deputy, Murqus Sergius, by contrast, was one of the most activist and radical priests in the church. During the 1919 revolution he had been the first priest ever to speak from the pulpit in al-Azhar, and he had devoted most of his career to defending Coptic rights. In previous generations, saintly monks who could criticize those in power had served as natural alter egos for Coptic administrations; by contrast, during the time of Pope John and his successors, this role came to be filled by a reform-minded priest who carried the agenda of the highly educated laity into the papal residence.

John died in 1942 and again there was great discord about who should be the next pope. And once again the ancient church rule that a bishop could not hold the highest office was broken.

The Reforming Pope: Macarius III (1944–45)

Macarius III, the 114th pope, only held office for eighteen months. For forty-seven years prior to his election on February 13, 1944, he had served as the metropolitan of Asyut. Born in 1872 in the town of Mahalla al-Kubra, he had entered the monastery at the age of sixteen and was ordained a priest at seventeen. Before his consecration as metropolitan, he had been the private secretary of Pope Cyril V for two years.

The Reform-minded Metropolitan

Macarius was one of only a few reform-minded bishops. He had hosted the Coptic Conference of 1911 and throughout his diocese he launched activities to counter American and English missionary activities. His goal was to revitalize the community by building new churches, renovating old ones, and opening schools. To reach this goal, in 1900 he opened the first Coptic school for boys in Asyut, and in 1909 one for girls. He also initiated several charitable societies, and built thirty more schools and fourteen new churches throughout his diocese. Apart from providing education for Coptic children, Macarius encouraged Coptic preachers and church volunteers to copy the Protestant strategies of revival meetings, intense Bible study, and social services. In 1932 he ordained Iskander Hanna, the master preacher, to the rank of archdeacon and allowed him to preach every day during Lent.

It was in Asyut that the concept and role of *khadim al-kanisa* (servant of the church) emerged; it came to designate a special category of lay volunteers who dedicated much of their time and income to the church.[38] Young 'servants' started to deliver moving sermons, slowly pushing an older generation of priests to the sidelines. During the 1930s, when a number of these servants moved to Cairo to pursue university studies, they took their ideas with them from Asyut and started to apply them in the four Sunday-school centers in the city.[39]

Electoral Discord

After Pope John XIX passed away, Anba Yusab, the metropolitan of Girga, became acting pope for the interim prior to the election of an official successor. Before new elections took place, however, the Holy Synod and the Community Council changed the regulations, establishing a larger electorate consisting of clergy and community members. In accordance with tradition, all preferred a monk as candidate. Two monks were put forward on the docket; one of them had entered the monastery only recently and both received minimal votes.[40] As a result, three bishops were nominated as final-round candidates: Yusab, Macarius, and Theofilos, the metropolitan of Jerusalem. This decision again split the community in two. Macarius' candidacy reveals the division of the Coptic community into several competing and powerful factions. In order to gain the majority of the votes, he not only had to lobby these different groups, but also earn the trust of the press. In her multi-volume *Qissat al-kanisa* (The Story of the Church), the Coptic historian Iris Habib al-Masri decries this divergence from tradition as "shameful" and "wrong,"[41] and goes on to describe at great length how her father, Habib al-Masri, the vice-president of the Majlis al-Milli, fulminated against this situation.[42]

Habib al-Masri understood why many were in favor of Macarius' eventual election. He knew the metropolitan from childhood, had grown up under his guidance, and visited him regularly. A photo of the metropolitan graces one of the first pages of the sixth volume of his daughter's history of the Coptic Church. She describes him as a person with eyes that shone with "a spiritual light," a face "beautiful with kindness," and a beard reminding her of "Aaron's beard in Psalm 133 with the precious oil running down the collar of his robes."[43] Yet this did not stop Habib al-Masri from challenging Macarius, asking him how he could agree to be a candidate for the papal throne when it was against all the church laws. The metropolitan's answer that "the people want me" did not satisfy him.[44]

A Pope for Eighteen Months

In Asyut, Macarius had focused on spiritual revival and left the local Community Council in charge of the practical and financial issues related to running the church. Delegating the material church affairs won him great sympathy with the people, as did the elaborate reform plan he proposed in 1920. The plan proposed a division of tasks that left the pope in charge of ecclesiastical and spiritual matters, while a council would supervise Coptic properties and *waqf*s, and an educational committee would monitor instruction in religion and the Coptic language. The plan drawn up after his election proposed the pope as chair of the council and transferred the administration of all monastic trusts to the papal offices in Cairo. It also called for the church to show special concern for poor families. The ultimate goal of spending the *waqf* monies on communal needs was to bring about a spiritual and educational revival.[45]

However, when Macarius proposed this governance structure to the Holy Synod, it caused a storm of protest. The clergy accused him of breaking church law and filed a complaint with the government, which nonetheless accepted the reform measure and granted control of church property (including the monastic endowments) to the Community Council. After a few months the pendulum swung the other way: the council, as it turned out, had equally mismanaged the funds and its members had been so demanding of the pope that this time he appealed to the government to annul the new measures. In protest of the council's attitude, he withdrew to the Monastery of St. Anthony for several months.[46] Shortly after his return to Cairo he passed away. Although he had failed to solve the issue of the supervision of church property, he had continued to renovate churches and monasteries and purchased new land for schools.[47] The spiritual revival that he had started in Asyut continued to grow and sow seeds for the future leadership of the church.

Sharing his authority over church property with the Community Council had been a revolutionary move. Unfortunately, this model did not work, and the popes elected after Macarius never tried it again. On the contrary, they all chose to wrestle with the council to regain their papal powers. Part of the rationale for electing Macarius, who was already over seventy when he became pope, had been his advanced age. It was hoped that his period of rule would give all parties time to sort out the issues of papal elections and community governance. However, when he died in 1945 after a mere eighteen months in office, there were no new monastic candidates yet on the horizon. Into this leadership void stepped Metropolitan Yusab, who had already been acting pope and a papal candidate prior to Macarius' election. He was brought forward as a candidate again, and this time he was elected.

The Ill-fated Pope: Yusab II (1946–56)

The story of Pope Yusab II is such a painful episode in Coptic history that Iris Habib al-Masri, his one-time personal secretary for foreign correspondence, omits an outline of his reign in her extensive history of the Coptic Church. Of the three popes discussed in this chapter, Yusab's image is by far the most memorable. In the gallery of popes in the Mu'allaqa Church he is the only one wearing sunglasses. His decline started when a group of eighty-seven young Coptic militants, calling themselves al-Umma al-Qibtiya (The Coptic Nation, short for Jama'at al-Umma al-Qibtiya), forced their way into the papal residence and kidnapped him late at night on July 26, 1954. At gunpoint they demanded that he resign and sign a document of abdication. He initially refused, but over a year later, on September 20, 1955, Yusab finally acquiesced. He resigned and was banished to the Monastery of Muharraq, where he passed away on November 13, 1956.

Developments in Church and State

The tumultuous end of Yusab's reign makes it easy to forget that during his ten years in office several formative events took place that would profoundly influence both Egypt and the Coptic Church. His weak and malleable personality brought out the worst in the Coptic community, exacerbating already existing conflicts. Factions fought each other, bishops conspired with laypeople, and the prevailing impression was that the church was without a head, drifting through Egyptian society like a ship without a rudder.

Ironically, Yusab's election was less divisive than that of the two preceding popes. After months of arguing, the clause that a monk should be elected pope was struck from the regulations and Yusab became eligible. A public strike kept a large part of the electorate home while army trucks shuttled his supporters to the polls.[48] He was considered eminently prepared for the job. Born in 1880 in the province of Girga, he had entered the Monastery of St. Anthony at the age of seventeen. After his ordination as priest in 1901, he studied at the Theological College in Athens, where he became fluent in Greek and French. He had been the abbot of the Coptic monastery in Jaffa and the metropolitan of Girga since 1920. He accompanied Pope John XIX during his trip to Ethiopia in 1930 and returned there a year later as the pope's official representative on the occasion of the coronation of Emperor Haile Selassie.[49] And he was neither too young nor too old to hold the office.

Yusab's reign coincided with one of the most turbulent political episodes in Egypt's history. In July 1952, Nasser and the Revolutionary Command

Council overthrew the monarchy, and in September of that year the government issued a land reform law that nationalized private estates, including those of many influential Coptic families. The following year, all political parties, including the Wafd, were eliminated, and Copts lost much of their political influence. We have little information on how Yusab guided his already distraught community through this time of profound change.

Yusab also had to deal with ongoing developments concerning the personal-status jurisdiction. Based on the Ottoman millet system, the community councils of the respective Christian communities handled personal-status issues such as marriage and divorce via their respective religious courts. After the millet courts were abolished, the government made several failed attempts between 1918 and 1956 to reform the system. Frequent drafts submitted to parliament had been blocked due to protests from Christian and Jewish communities.[50] The system was finally abolished just after Yusab's banishment in 1955 and personal-status issues were transferred to the civil courts.

The Sunday School Movement

For all this turmoil, there were positive developments under Yusab. On the ecumenical front, in 1954 the Coptic Church joined the network of global Christianity for the first time, when Yusab sent a Coptic delegation to the World Council of Churches (WCC) meeting held in Evanston, Illinois. On the domestic front, Yusab's decision to integrate the work of Sunday schools into the official clerical system proved to be vital to the movement's growth.

On March 18, 1948, the pope asked Habib Girgis to create a *lajna 'ulya* (Higher Committee) that granted the movement official status within the church. In his letter to Girgis, the pope described the Sunday schools as "our only hope on which we can build a new generation that will adhere to the Orthodox faith and guard its principles."[51] Yusab furthermore instructed all the priests in Cairo whose churches did not yet host a Sunday school to open one.[52]

Despite the fact that it had often worked on the fringes of churches, being tolerated but not encouraged by the clergy, by the 1940s the Sunday-school movement had instituted a strict organizational model and series of annual conferences.[53] Its journal, edited by Nazir Gayed (later Pope Shenouda III), criticized the church hierarchy regularly and exerted significant influence over church debates and developments.[54] With corruption rampant in the church, Sunday-school leaders started to question the pope's right to force a community to accept unpopular bishops and protested openly when they knew a position had been bought.[55]

Among the Sunday-school leaders a new model of church service developed—*takris,* the dedication of one's life to serving the community.

By the 1940s, several of those practicing *takris* became priests and monks, thus joining the official church hierarchy. One of them, Yusuf Iskander, became Matta al-Miskin, the influential abbot of the Monastery of St. Macarius. In seclusion, he started to publish the works of the early monks and church fathers. These publications allowed Sunday-school and seminary students to become familiar with their own theological tradition.

Intra-communal Strife and Corruption

In the meantime the clashes between the pope and the Community Council continued. Before his election, Pope Yusab had promised to transfer the administration of the *waqfs* to the council. However, once in office, he ordained the abbots of monasteries to the rank of bishops and charged them with the administration of the *waqfs*. Then, in 1947, when the pope wanted to elect an entirely new body of members to the council, the council members ceased their work in protest, and a backlog of tasks, including many unresolved personal-status cases, began to accumulate. Yusab left Cairo in frustration. Further twists and turns followed. The next year the government reinstalled the pope as head of the Community Council (in response to a request originally filed by Pope Macarius III),[56] but the elections that followed in 1950 resulted in a majority win for the reformers.

Yusab's lack of leadership qualities was exacerbated by the actions of his personal servant Milik, who had been with him since his time as metropolitan of Girga. Milik manipulated his employer's high position for personal benefit. Illiterate but shrewd, he influenced all of the pope's political and administrative decisions.[57] When he sold as many as sixteen of the nineteen available bishoprics, accusations of corruption and incompetence mounted. After a public outcry in the press, Milik and five of his associates were removed from their positions in September 1952. When Milik returned a few months later, al-Umma al-Qibtiya saw no other solution to end the intolerable situation than to attack the papal residence.[58]

The Holy Synod and the Community Council acted in rare unison when they banished Pope Yusab on September 20, 1955. It took something of a legal battle: as head of the Synod, the pope did not consent to his own banishment. However, the government backed the decision, stating that it "agreed to relieve the Patriarch of his powers in response to the wishes of the Coptic people and the leaders of the church after all agreed that His Eminence is not fit to carry out his duties."[59] A committee of three bishops was elected to run the church until Yusab's death on November 14, 1956. At that time Anba Athanasius, the bishop of Beni Soueif, was appointed acting pope.

The pendulum had completely swung to the side of the laity. Pope Yusab had been stripped of all authority and not even the government was willing to defend his position. Infighting and corruption had weakened the church during a time when it needed more strength than ever. Naturally, in this atmosphere, the Copts were eager to elect a new pope, and this time they insisted on someone who would fit the requirements of the traditional law, a monk of exceptional spirituality and wisdom. It was not until May 10, 1959, that Cyril VI, the 116th pope in the line of St. Mark, would be elected to the papal office.

7

Reviving Tradition, Reviving the Church

(Pope Cyril (Kyrillos) VI, 1959–71)

When Pope Cyril VI ascended the papal throne as the 116th pope on May 10, 1959, Copts were still reeling from the unprecedented events surrounding the forced abdication of Pope Yusab II. Yusab had died on November 13, 1956 at the height of the Suez War, and the election of a new pope had dragged on for several reasons. In an attempt to gain more control over the church, Nasser's government introduced new regulations for the election, which delayed the process for two and a half years.

The Copts themselves could not agree on the required qualifications of the candidates, and one could fairly characterize their process of selection as mayhem. The Community Council preferred a bishop, while the Holy Synod preferred a monk. The young leaders trained for and active in the Sunday School Movement lobbied for a reform-minded pope, while the bishops of the Holy Synod lobbied for a conservative candidate. To prevent the nomination of younger reformers, the Holy Synod barred their candidacy with a decree that the new pope should be over forty years old and have been a monk for at least fifteen years. The government agreed, adding that the monk should be "of good reputation and a holy man."[1]

Backed by the voice of the people, the names of twenty-one monks were presented as candidates. In spite of his varied career as a church leader, Pope Cyril had avoided becoming a bishop, and therefore was eligible. Although Cyril had been intensely involved with the young leaders, he was not identified as a representative of the Sunday School Movement. To underscore that this pope would be elected by divine providence, the electoral body also decided to return to the rarely used tradition of choosing by altar lot. Following the apostolic tradition of Acts 1:26, it was a child, five-year-old Rafik Bassili al-Toukhy, who selected the slip of paper with Cyril's name on it.[2]

Innovative Tradition

Defining Cyril VI

Copts consider Pope Cyril VI "the last of the traditional popes."[3] The word "traditional," in this context, needs clarification. During his reign as pope (mostly in the 1960s), air travel had not yet developed sufficiently for Cyril to travel the world; consequently, he went no further than taking two trips to Ethiopia. His lifestyle was traditional; he not only maintained the ascetic regimen of a monk, but added additional fasting and praying to the already grueling spiritual schedule that a Coptic pope is expected to follow. Following in the footsteps of his predecessors, he made himself accessible to the community and allowed people to see him without prior appointment. When seen from a present-day perspective, this custom belonged to another time when almost no one kept an agenda and phones were few and far between.

And yet, even though his reign as pope may be viewed as "traditional" in this sense, Pope Cyril's mindset, ideas, and actions were innovative and oriented toward change. He ruled the Coptic Church during a time of great hope and upheaval, when a new government in Egypt sought to transform society and position itself as a uniting force of Arab Muslims. After 1930, an urban, literate population emerged—a population who were not as oriented toward the west as were the much smaller educated elite before them. Their nationalist sympathies differed from those of the earlier generation, in part because they had to find new ways to identify with Egypt's emerging Arab and Muslim character. In spite of the new pressures felt by their community, Copts were united with Muslims in their strong feelings of nationalism and anti-colonialism, a political orientation that distinctively marked this era and that characterized the outlook of both the government and the pope.

Although the national arena was new to Cyril, he was adept at negotiating church politics. As a monk, he had found ingenious ways to challenge and critique the clerical hierarchy; he had been part of it while distancing himself from its internal squabbles. He also stood at the forefront of the lay reform movement that developed alternatives to traditional models of teaching, learning, and pastoral care. After his ascendancy to the papacy, this affiliation put Cyril in a position to reorganize some of the church's fundamental structures. Concerning the role of women in the church, the new pope was simultaneously non-traditional and profoundly traditional. In line with the Orthodox tradition, he never wished to include them in the official hierarchical structures, yet he was the first pope to create leadership spaces for women, encouraging them to become nuns, deaconesses, and Sunday-school teachers. In the relatively short time span of twelve years, he laid the foundations for a spiritual, pastoral, cultural, and intellectual revival that carried the Coptic

Church into the twenty-first century and still provides direction to its communities around the globe. His disciple and successor, Pope Shenouda III, who himself was part of this formative period, has continued to build upon these foundations, sponsoring a host of new Coptic institutional structures. Because of their close relationship, we cannot divorce Cyril's time from that of Shenouda, and at times the discussion of their reigns will overlap.

Nowadays, Cyril's image remains omnipresent in Coptic life on posters, stickers, key chains, clocks, and other trinkets. It has become part of the Coptic subconscious. At the Monastery of St. Menas in Mareotis near Alexandria, crowds of believers continue to visit his tomb asking for his intercession. Although the number of photos taken during his life is fairly limited—most in black and white—they have become an integral part of Coptic visual culture. They illustrate the covers of the many books published about his asceticism, his remarkable spiritual gifts, and the myriad of miracles credited to his prayers.

Not only do we see Anba Cyril's face more than that of any of the 115 popes before him, we also know more about his childhood and his career as a monk than about those of his predecessors. His time as pope was relatively short in comparison with the three decades he spent living the monastic life in a solitary and semi-solitary state. Indeed, his pre-papal biography is vital to understanding his influence on the history of the Coptic Church. This is because so many years were spent guiding the reform-minded activists to find their place and role in a church that could not yet envision the importance of their contributions. In the process, Cyril initiated a *nahda*, a revival or renaissance, that not only affected the church's spiritual and pastoral governance, but also its social life, education, and research institutions, as well as its position vis-à-vis the Egyptian state.

Cyril's rule started at a time when the church and Egyptian society were both in a state of chaos and facing profound transformations. Church prelates were at odds with the Community Council that had lost important parts of its jurisdiction in the wake of Nasser's reforms of the court system. The confiscation of farmlands had diminished the wealth of the monasteries and of the Coptic gentry. The Coptic laity was suffering. President Nasser's (1954–70) industrial and land reforms had taken away many of their possessions and destroyed the influence of the old feudal landowning class. Many moved from the countryside to the cities, where they turned to the church for solace and encouragement. Yet lay programs were flourishing: hundreds of foundations and churches, for example, still taught children and youth the essentials of the Coptic faith. Sunday-school students had gone on to become teachers, and while studying for prestigious careers in society, they also contemplated how they could dedicate their lives to the church. Anba Cyril was at the heart of this movement, inviting the brightest and most pious to join him in the small quarters around the St. Menas Church he had built in Cairo. There he invited them to consider a call to the monastic life.

Authors writing about this pope have struggled to describe him adequately in language that fits our time. He has been called "a man above words,"[4] "practical and mystical,"[5] "patriarch and solitary,"[6] "al-Mutawahhid, the solitary," "symbol of the renewal of tradition,"[7] "a healer," and a "wonder worker." Capturing his personality and actions in a few words is a challenge; yet he was, in the words of Anglican priest John Watson, "an undivided man."[8] Before becoming a public figure he lived as a hermit, and during that time developed his singular focus on the spiritual life. This undivided vision, paired with keen psychological and political insights, allowed him to understand the needs of his time while standing at the crossroads of massive changes in the church and Egyptian society. He knew what the community needed and created new opportunities for the believers to discover and assert their faith and identity as Copts.

During his life many "felt like sons when they were in his presence,"[9] and Copts continued to feel as if they had a personal relationship with Anba Cyril after he passed away on March 9, 1971. Decades after his death, the number of books appearing about him has continued to grow. Abuna Rafa'il, who served as his personal deacon and now lives in the Monastery of St. Menas (Dayr Mari Mina), has dedicated his life to collecting all the stories printed about Cyril and annually publishes a book detailing the miracles that happened that year through the pope's intercession. More than one hundred volumes have appeared in this series so far, including those translated into other languages that are available in Coptic churches around the globe. The information in these publications is predominantly of a hagiographic character. For more historical information about his life, we have to consult the biographies written by Iris Habib al-Masri, Amir Nasr, Abuna Rafa'il Ava Mina, and his own brother, Hanna Yusuf 'Ata.[10]

The Monk Mina al-Mutawahhid

Inside the Monastery

Cyril was born 'Azer Yusuf 'Atta in 1902, the second of three sons. His family was well off and lived in the village of Toukh al-Nassara in the district of Munufiya. Later on, they moved to Damanhur and then to Alexandria where his father, a manager, served as deacon, cantor, and calligrapher in the local church. The parents were deeply devout and taught their children the stories from the Bible and about the saints. They regularly undertook a pilgrimage to the Church of St. Menas in Abyar near Tanta. One of their frequent house guests seems to have been the Bishop of Munufiya, later to become Pope John XIX.[11] As a young child 'Atta urged his family to share their food with neighbors who were less well off, and he preferred to spend his time in church or in his room, praying or reading the Bible. His family witnessed other indications of his future religious calling when an old monk from the Baramus Monastery visited the family and announced that their three-year-old boy was from their stock and would be one of them.[12]

At the age of twenty-five, 'Atta entered the Baramus Monastery, where he stood out for his diligence in prayer and dedication to chores, especially taking care of the monks who were old and sick. Tonsured a monk and ordained a priest in 1931, he took the name of Mina, after the well-known Egyptian military saint, Menas. A short time later, he entered the newly opened theological college in Helwan. During one of Pope John's frequent visits, the long sermons of Father Mina so impressed the pope that he was chosen to be bishop of Gharbiya and al-Beheira. Greatly disturbing his superiors but in line with a historic spiritual practice, Cyril fled to avoid this high office. The church called upon his family to locate him. When he was found, he revealed for the first time his wish to live as a hermit.

After his return from Helwan, his monastic superiors allowed Cyril to move into the desert, where he became inspired by the model of Father 'Abd al-Masih al-Habashi, the Ethiopian hermit, who lived in the desert for thirty-five years (1935–70).[13] Using the cave that had been the retreat of Anba Sarabamun, the monastery's former abbot, Cyril returned to the monastery every week to attend the celebration of the Mass. During this period, he devoted much of his time to studying the church's spiritual heritage and to the craft of restoring old manuscripts. He especially studied the writings of the early fathers, focusing on the teachings of the seventh-century Syrian Nestorian ascetic, Isaac of Nineveh. His solitary state was at times interrupted when pilgrims undertook the one-hour walk between the monastery and the desert. One of the most memorable visitors was Pope John, who came to be blessed by the cave and also to bless *al-mutawahhid* (the hermit) in return.

Outside the Monastery

In 1936, two events happened that were formative for Cyril's career as monk and future pope. Showing a keen understanding of the national and Coptic condition, that year Cyril, then still called Mina, sought Pope John's permission to move to the ruins of the ancient monastery of his namesake, St. Menas at Mareotis, in the desert west of Alexandria. Together with St. George, Menas was the most popular saint not only among the Copts but also among Muslims, and in the 1920s his name had entered nationalist, anti-colonial discourse. In a speech denouncing the British presence in Egypt, nationalist leader Ahmad Husayn had referred to the saint as a "national hero" who had resisted colonial oppression.[14]

According to one version of his life story, Menas was born in the year 285 in the province of Gharbiya in the Delta and was later appointed military governor of Pentapolis. After practicing his religion in secret for several years, he publicly confessed his faith and was martyred as a result. The resting place of this saint became a thriving center of pilgrimage and healing in late antiquity until it fell into disrepair around the tenth century. Nearly a quarter century before becoming the pope, Cyril realized the symbolic, religious, and national value of restoring the shrine of this Christian national hero. He envisioned it as a gesture that would fulfill the aspirations of both Copts and Muslims. While his request to inhabit the ruins at Mareotis was denied, this holy site would become indelibly associated with his legacy: as we shall see, he would later be buried there.

Another incident at Easter that same year caused Cyril to leave the desert and move to Old Cairo. Returning to the Baramus Monastery before Palm Sunday for the Easter celebrations, he ran into a group of officials (including the local governor and a police officer) who were recruited by the abbot to remove seven monks from the monastery for criticizing the way it was managed. The idea of expelling these monks during Holy Week offended Cyril. Finding the monks beyond reproach, Cyril defied the abbot's orders and took them to Cairo, where he rented a house for them. Although facing reprimands from his abbot and from Pope John XIX, Cyril stood his ground and the incident came to represent his fearlessness, his irreproachable courage in telling the truth, and his skill in negotiating church and political hierarchies. When meeting the pope, he reminded his superior that expelling monks without good reason contradicted the monastic rule. In similar fashion, he turned the tables on a metropolitan who abused the expelled monks verbally by rebuking him for his luxurious gown and lifestyle.[15]

Although Cyril revived Coptic monastic life and is considered its prime model, he actually spent thirty-nine of his forty-two years as a monk outside his monastery. After resolving the issue of the seven monks, he did not return to the Baramus Monastery but took the unusual step of renting a windmill on the Muqattam mountain, east of Old Cairo, that had been abandoned since the end of the French occupation in 1801. He converted part of the windmill into a chapel and started his famous daily celebration of the Mass. The late Bishop Mina, who became a monk in 1937 and joined Cyril in the remote mill, later related that they would pray and celebrate the Mass between 6 and 8 a.m., fast until 3 p.m., receive guests, and then spend the rest of the day reading and praying.[16] Cyril taught that celebrating the Mass (which according to a rough count he did at least 12,500 times) not only strengthened the participants' daily relationship with God but also guaranteed that the angel in charge of the altar would pray and intercede for them all day.[17]

Living in the windmill from 1936 to 1942 transformed Cyril from a solitary hermit to a public monastic figure—a holy man well known for the power of his prayers, which brought healing and consolation to those who visited him. Interacting with the public, his fame grew and his message began to reach a wider audience, transforming the daily spiritual practices of individual Copts.[18] In 1942, during the Second World War, when the British forced him out of the windmill, Cyril's reputation as a man of prayer and a spiritual director living a solitary life in the midst of bustling Cairo was well established.[19] The move back to the city allowed him to pursue his visions for monastic renewal in several ways. Calling on the network of believers and highly placed personalities that had formed around him, he built a church dedicated to St. Menas at the foot of Muqattam. His cell was on top of the church, and university students who had moved to Cairo from the provinces and who had shown special leadership skills and dedication used the adjoining student hostel. The complex was called the Monastery of St. Menas, and in 1948, not one, but an entire group of bishops gathered for its consecration.

In 1944, Cyril was appointed head of the dilapidated Monastery of St. Samuel, where he used his skills to rally people and raise funds to renovate its buildings in Maghagha and the Qalamun Mountain. Due to his presence and the improvement of the monastic facilities, the monastery started to attract new monks (one of them the theologian Matta al-Miskin). Visitors and a new influx of income followed, which allowed Cyril to pass on the daily managerial duties to a prior. He returned to Cairo, where he dedicated himself again to working with the university students living in the church hostel. Only those students meeting his strict requirements could join: a certificate from their priest back home had to testify to their impeccable record of church attendance and service and their devotion to the monastic rules.[20] All of them would go on to assume strategic positions of leadership within the church, the most famous of them being Cyril's eventual successor, Pope Shenouda III. When a papal order was issued that all monks should return to their monasteries, Cyril's position as head of the Monastery of St. Samuel allowed him to continue the work in Cairo.

Under Cyril's direction, this new generation of church leaders practiced the regimen they had learned and taught in the Sunday schools, combining a strong sense of *takris* (selfless service to the church) with strict discipline, assiduous prayer, and study of the Scriptures. While they pursued their university studies, Cyril trained them in the monastic life, and upon graduation many of them joined monasteries. During the 1950s, few abbots were prepared to accept such highly educated novices: the choice of placement was limited to the Monastery of the Syrians (Dayr al-Suryan) in Wadi al-Natrun. Its head, Anba Ta'ufilus, was one of the few bishops who understood the potential of this new generation and welcomed their presence. Activism, scholarship, and piety were conjoined in the lives of young monks such as Abuna Makari, Abuna Mattias, Abuna Antonius, and Abuna Macarius, who had been among the most important actors in the Sunday School Movement in Cairo.[21] After Cyril was elected pope, he created a new generation of bishops and leaders by selecting candidates from these reform-minded, scholarly monks.

The Church and the Egyptian State

The New Regime

The Free Officers' coup of 1952 that brought President Nasser to power aimed to eradicate the remnants of British colonial control and overthrow the monarchy, which was considered to be corrupt and removed from the concerns of the people. The new government's ideology was secular: as a result, citizenship was not to be determined by religion. In spite of this, the outlook of the new rulers was deeply religious. Hailing from the lower middle classes, they had neither studied at western institutions nor did they know the European languages the ruling elite spoke. Their orientation was Arab and Islamic. Religious expression was encouraged, although Nasser did not condone radicalism or violence and suppressed the Muslim Brotherhood. In his speeches, Nasser stressed the value of religious minorities for the nation, while, at the same time, the foundation was being laid for the cultural supremacy of Islam.

With the new regime, the Copts lost much of their political influence: there had been no Copts among the officers leading the coup and only one Copt was given a (relatively insignificant) post in the resulting cabinet. Only around ten of the 350 seats in parliament were reserved for Copts. Furthermore, the Islamic heritage that was foundational to Nasser's pan-Arab ideology (with its premise that Arab nations are unified by language and history) was disconcerting to the Copts. School curricula were 'Arabized' in order to rid them of western colonial influence. Concurrently, curricula became infused with study of the Qur'an and the life of the Prophet. The economy was nationalized, and the bureaucrats who ran the state ventures operated under the assumption that a Copt could never be the president of a company or business. The Coptic gentry, who had lost large parts of their landholdings and income when Nasser nationalized most of their property, started to consider leaving Egypt and, over time, more and more did. Despite these disadvantages, the new policies opened up additional opportunities for bright students from the lower and middle classes to enroll (for free) in universities and graduate in coveted subjects such as medicine and engineering.

After the revolution, many whose finances had dwindled felt that the pope should stand up against the regime and protect Coptic interests. Cyril's reputation as a holy man protected him from much of this unrest, which was transferred instead to the monks who served as his assistants.[22] Although at times they had their tugs-of-war, there was mutual respect between Cyril and Nasser and they backed each other's policies. Nasser allowed Cyril to put the Community Council on ice, while Cyril praised Nasser when he reduced *waqf* holdings to two hundred acres of fertile land and two hundred acres of barren land, reasoning that the government could use the appropriated lands for industrial and reconstruction projects.[23] Both were fervent nationalists who disdained any reminder of colonial or imperialist influence.

Immediately after he was consecrated pope, Cyril drew a line between church and governmental politics. He refused to be the first to pay the president a courtesy visit, explaining that "not Nasser but God elected me; the Church is not his but my problem."[24] The president must have appreciated this subtle show of strength, since a robust relationship developed between pope and president. The late Otto Meinardus, a long-time observer of the Copts, lived in Cairo during the papacy of Cyril and commented on how much the two leaders had in common. They both led frugal lifestyles. Both lived in humble dwellings and wore simple clothing. While Nasser often dressed in shirt and trousers, Cyril seldom changed his monastic tunic for the regal papal vestments.[25] In an unusual gesture of respect and admiration, the president invited the pope to his private residence. Cyril's independent stance toward the president reflected his view that the church should be a full partner and supporter of the regime.

A National Church

At the time of the British withdrawal after the Second World War, a strong anti-British and anti-western sentiment had fueled attacks on Coptic churches. But the nationalization of the Suez Canal and the ensuing international crisis of 1956 united the country in ways that were reminiscent of the euphoric declarations of unity that had resounded during the 1920s. In the fall of 1956, a few weeks before Israel, France, and England attacked Egypt, Muslim and Christian dignitaries gathered at the papal residence to declare their solidarity with Nasser, who had become the symbol of Arab and anti-colonial resistance.[26] Interreligious strife also diminished when, in 1954, Nasser banned the Muslim Brotherhood, whose members had stirred up much animosity against religious minorities. Feelings of harmony still prevailed at the time of Cyril's election, when large crowds gathered in the streets chanting slogans such as "Muhammad and Jesus are both God's prophets," and "Our Arabic nationalism belongs to the Gospel and the Qur'an."[27]

Pope Cyril translated these feelings of nationalist fervor into solidarity with churches in Africa and other communities suffering oppression. As a result, he became the first pope in Coptic history to actively engage in Egypt's foreign politics. His regular comments on international and national affairs created new opportunities for intercommunal bonding that went beyond the customary exchanges of good wishes during Muslim and Christian feasts. He sent congratulations to President Nasser, for example, when in 1967 the conflict with Yemen was resolved. When Egypt was involved in international summits he called upon all Coptic churches to pray for their success, and in 1966 he declared a week of prayer to end the Vietnam War.[28]

Pope Cyril especially agreed with Nasser's policies with respect to the newly founded state of Israel, which in his view was the product of western imperialism, dividing the world and displacing the region's original inhabitants.[29] When the Shah of Iran officially acknowledged Israel in 1960, Cyril ordered his action to be condemned in all Coptic dioceses, and he sent the future Bishop Samuel to the World Council of Churches with a proposition that the council denounce this act as well. Cyril also disapproved of the decision taken by the Catholic Church during the Second Vatican Council (1962–65) to exonerate the Jews from crucifying Christ, as he considered it to be an un-Biblical and imperialist view.[30]

While these opinions were in line with other Middle Eastern churches, they placed the Coptic Church in an ambiguous position in relation to western churches. As a member of the World Council of Churches, the Copts belonged to a body that supported the founding of Israel and therefore was among the beneficiaries of funds that could be regarded as 'imperialist' monies. However, the Six-Day War with Israel (June 5–11, 1967)—a debacle that continues to reverberate throughout Egyptian society today—solidified Cyril in his stances.[31] Pope Cyril joined the entire Middle East in protest against the occupation of Jerusalem: in August of that year, he cancelled the annual pilgrimage during the Feast of St. Mary, and in the following year Coptic Orthodox and Catholic churches in Egypt both refrained from public Christmas celebrations.[32]

The New Cathedral

The amicable relations between the pope and the president were advantageous to the church in many ways. With demographic changes caused by population growth and Copts moving from the countryside to the cities, the community was growing and needed new houses of worship. The rules concerning building permits were still governed by the the Hatt-i Humayun decree of 1856. Reconfirmed in 1934 by King Fouad, the law required special permission from the head of state to build new churches or renovate old ones. Requests from Christian communities required such a long and tedious bureaucratic process that Cyril decided to approach Nasser directly to expedite the process, and he received permission to build twenty-five new churches a year.[33] In addition to these churches, Nasser also facilitated the building of a new cathedral, a dream that had initially seemed unlikely to be realized, given that the Coptic gentry had lost most of its disposable income.

Nasser realized the benefits of such a new cathedral for the largest Christian community in the Middle East. It was not only a project of national pride, but its opening would be an international affair, highlighting Egypt's prestige as the symbolic leader of the Middle East. Thus, he was present at every milestone of its construction and contributed the considerable sum of LE500,000. On July 24, 1965, Nasser laid the cornerstone, and three years later, on June 25, 1968, he attended its dedication along with many other luminaries, including the Ethiopian emperor Haile Selassi.

The consecration of one of the largest cathedrals in Africa was a symbol of the church's strength and of its recognition as one of the original churches that had defined Christian dogma and teaching. A milestone for the Copts was the return of a portion of the relics of its founder, the Apostle Mark. These relics had been taken from Egypt by Venetian merchants in 828 and had been in Italy ever since. Benefiting from its newly developed ecumenical ties, the Coptic Church negotiated with the Catholic hierarchy for the saint's relics to be returned. In Rome, a small relic was handed over to a delegation consisting of seven Coptic bishops, three Ethiopian bishops, and three Coptic lay notables. The relic was met at Cairo Airport by the pope himself. The day after the cathedral's inauguration, a special liturgy was celebrated in commemoration of the 1,900th anniversary of the saint's martyrdom, during which the silver reliquary containing the relic was enshrined in the crypt beneath the high altar.[34]

The Church at Home and Abroad

After being enthroned as pope on Sunday, April 19, 1959, Cyril wasted no time in addressing the most pressing political issues that were undermining the church. These were the position of the Majlis al-Milli and the ongoing controversy surrounding the administration of the *waqfs*, and the Coptic Church's ecumenical relations with other communions, especially the Ethiopian Church.

Cyril and al-Majlis al-Milli

The first problem Cyril had to solve was the simmering conflict over the *waqfs* and the changing role of the Community Council. Due to changes in the legal and political system, the council's influence had greatly diminished under the new regime. With the abolition of the religious courts, it had lost its jurisdiction over personal-status cases (marriage, divorce, alimony), while supervision of Coptic schools was transferred to the Ministry of Education, and regulation of the benevolent societies to the Ministry of Social Affairs. Moreover, observers at the time noted that the council had not done enough to represent the interests of the Copts in the new political landscape.[35] In 1960, Cyril petitioned President Nasser for a decree that allowed him to create a new board consisting of six bishops and six community members to supervise the *waqfs*.[36] Five years later, in 1965, when a potential conflict arose between Cyril and the members of the council about money spent on the new Monastery of St. Menas in Mareotis and on the construction of the new cathedral in Abbasiya, the pope requested another decision from President Nasser to grant him greater financial autonomy.[37] In 1967, with the council facing serious financial problems, he then stripped that body of its remaining administrative responsibilities for the theological institutes and the pope's offices, appointing a new committee instead.[38] Cyril himself also assumed one of the council's main diplomatic tasks—that of maintaining relationships with the state. By relating directly to President Nasser, Pope Cyril became the community's political voice vis-à-vis the state.

The Ethiopian Church

At the time of Cyril's election, the Egyptian political climate had become of great concern to the Ethiopians. Nasser's regime had deprived the Coptic Church of a great deal of its institutional autonomy through the state's intervention in church affairs, and the president had prevented an Ethiopian representative from attending Cyril's consecration. Relationships were initially so strained that the new pope considered finding a solution to the ongoing conflict with the Ethiopian Church a top priority. On June 1, 1959, he sent a delegation of bishops to Addis Ababa to meet with Emperor Haile Selassi and the ruling *abun*, Bishop Basilios, to negotiate the autonomous status of the Ethiopian Church. The terms of the new status were as follows: The Egyptian pope would consecrate his Ethiopian counterpart and his name would continue to be mentioned in Ethiopian liturgical prayers. The leader of the Egyptian church would retain the title of patriarch or pope, while the Ethiopian prelate would be called "Catholicus," following the title of the Armenian patriarch.[39] On June 29, 1959, in the presence of the emperor, Pope Cyril elevated Basilios to the rank of catholicus.[40] In October of the next year, Cyril made a pastoral trip to Ethiopia that opened the door for new types of cooperation between the two churches, such as the exchange of students, professors, and monks. In 1969, the Ethiopians regained control over Dayr al-Sultan in Jerusalem, and in 1970 they abolished the prerequisite that the Coptic pope should consecrate their catholicus. Over a period of just over forty years leading up to his dethronement in the 1974 revolution, Emperor Haile Selassie had reached his goal of establishing an independent Ethiopian church, which served as the foundation for his autocratic rule.[41] However, in spite of Ethiopian ambivalence concerning Egypt's new orientation toward Arab–Islamic ideology, strong relations between the two churches remained a priority, and the emperor visited Egypt when the new Cathedral of St. Mark was dedicated.[42]

Ecumenical Relations

Pope Cyril's rule coincided with the emergence of ecumenical networks and large international Christian conferences throughout the world. By the 1960s, the pressure on the Coptic Church from foreign mission organizations in Egypt had lifted, since these groups no longer were trying to expand their churches by recruiting Orthodox Copts. Instead, in a new spirit of ecumenism, western missionaries sought to be of service to the Coptic Church. With a growing number of internationally oriented members, the Coptic Church was ready to join this global movement. In 1954, Pope Yusab II had sent an official delegation to the assembly of the World Council of Churches in Evanston, Illinois. Under Nasser, a Coptic delegation participated in the first meeting of the All Africa Council of Churches (1963).

Concurrent with Egypt's political transformation under Nasser, the Coptic Church began re-identifying its national and international partners. Initiating ecumenical relations with the Oriental, non-Chalcedonian churches—the Ethiopian, the Syrian, and the Armenian Orthodox—seemed a natural step in this process. For a long time, Syrians and Armenians had had their own churches in Egypt and, in 1961, through an official delegation sent to Egypt, the Syrian Orthodox Church in Damascus pressed the need for an official alliance.[43] Thus, when Emperor Haile Selassie invited Cyril in 1965 to chair the first conference of non-Chalcedonian churches in Addis Ababa, it was a historic event. Not only did Cyril become the first Coptic pope to visit Ethiopia twice,[44] he also fulfilled the dream of unity among the churches that his predecessor and namesake Pope Cyril IV had expressed over one hundred years earlier.[45] In his speech at the conference, the pope stressed the importance of this unity, comparing the rains that fall in Ethiopia and that flow from there to water different countries to the work of the Holy Spirit that streams through the different churches to reach the people.[46] During a follow-up meeting in Cairo the next year, specifics of cooperation between the churches were worked out, and it was decided that Bishop Samuel (whose special assignment was to maintain ecumenical relations) and Bishop Athanasius of Beni Soueif would be permanent representatives to the new conference in order to intensify connections and cooperation.[47]

Around the same time, discussions opened between the Copts and the Chalcedonian Orthodox churches, with which official relations had been broken off since the Council of Chalcedon in 451. During the 1960s, Coptic delegations led by Bishop Shenouda attended theological consultations to prepare the way for renewed ecumenical relationships. In 1985, these preliminary activities gained official status. Two Coptic observers attended the Roman Catholic Second Vatican Council (1962–65), also in the name of strengthening relations; this gesture was one factor that led to the return of St. Mark's relics.

Mission to Africa

During the nineteenth and twentieth centuries, Coptic church involvement in other African countries was not limited to Ethiopia. After Muhammed 'Ali invaded Sudan in 1823, Pope Peter VII consecrated the first Egyptian bishop to be delegated to that country. It was not until over a century later, in 1948, that a Sudanese bishop became the metropolitan of Khartoum and Omdurman. During the reign of Pope Yusab, this connection with Sudan led to a brief Coptic presence in South Africa spearheaded by Bishop Morqos, who in 1950 was ordained to found a Coptic church in South Africa. Due to logistical and material obstacles, the bishop only lasted a few months before returning to Cairo, but the Coptic prayer book was translated into the Zulu language and one of the two priests who had accompanied him stayed until 1969.[48]

Under Cyril, this nascent interest in Africa as a mission field was accelerated by President Nasser's promotion of his so-called "three circles of interest" related to Egyptian international policy—namely, the Arab, the Islamic, and the African circles.[49] This new political mindset, in combination with the postcolonial ideal that indigenous churches should be freed from foreign missionary influences, challenged the Coptic Church to reconsider its relations with African Christians. It was in the context of this concern for pan-African unity that Pope Cyril began highlighting sub-Saharan churches in his speeches. For example, in 1962, he mentioned that Christians in countries such as Uganda and Kenya would have preferred to belong to the Coptic Church, had it not been for the imperialistic missions that had alienated them from "the message of Jesus Christ, and the message about love and peace."[50] Encouraged by Nasser's regime, the Coptic Institute added Africa specialists to its staff and started to train future missionaries. These young Copts would carry the authentic Orthodox message to the people of Africa who were living under the shadow of colonialist Protestants and Catholics. The guiding vision for this new type of mission was to make the Coptic Church the predominant African communion. As a reflection of this goal, the pope's title now stipulated that he should oversee "all of Africa."[51]

Into the Nations

The new political realities under President Nasser and a stagnant economy led many Copts to seek new opportunities outside Egypt during the 1950s. This demographic trend of Copts leaving their homeland was unprecedented. The Nasser regime's nationalization policies led many upper-class families to leave Egypt. Those with financial resources and those who were educated in foreign languages—doctors, pharmacists, and engineers—began to emigrate in droves. Schoolteachers left to work in neighboring Arab states.

By the mid-1960s this trend was significant enough for Pope Cyril to respond. He charged Anba Samuel, the Bishop for Public, Ecumenical, and Social Services, with the task of planning the establishment of Coptic churches abroad and commissioning priests to serve these new communities. The first such Coptic churches were founded in North America. In 1965, a Coptic Orthodox church was registered for the first time in Toronto, Canada, while in the same year, communities were planted in the United States—one in New Jersey and one in Los Angeles, California.[52] To cater to Copts working in the Gulf countries, Pope Cyril also established a church in Kuwait.[53]

These expatriate communities have since proved vital for the church in Egypt and have left a deep imprint on its international work and self-image. Emigrants, often successful in their adopted countries, began sending donations to the mother church, and their numbers increased in the early

1970s, when the easing of immigration restrictions in the United States and other countries made leaving Egypt easier for the middle class. The church's ranks were swelled further by non-Egyptians joining the Orthodox communion in Africa. In order to support this international expansion, the church in Egypt began translating its literature into other languages.[54]

The Church and Its History

Reviving Traditions

On the occasion of his enthronement, interviewers had asked Cyril about his vision for the church in the face of the ongoing disagreements among the clergy and the Majlis al-Milli. The new pope answered, "Pray to God that he would return to the Church her original glory with the cooperation of her sincere sons." His first papal letter was an appeal to "all sons, brethren, deacons, church members, priests, bishops, metropolitans, members of El-Majlis al-Milli, organizations and community groups" to "work in unison and self-denial."[55]

These statements sound idealistic, but in retrospect reveal a realistic and comprehensive plan—a plan that included the renewal of Coptic physical spaces and visual culture, literature and education, service and prayer, as well as the formation of clergy and laity. Part of Cyril's strategy involved revitalizing collective Coptic memories of the early Christian centuries. His goal was to use interpretations of the church's past to infuse its present sense of identity—to foster a historical sensibility that would empower Copts to claim their place within Egyptian society.

The Monastic Tradition

Cyril's first step toward recapturing the church's glory was to fulfill his dream of 1936. On November 27, 1959, the pope traveled in a convoy of cars to the tomb of St. Menas in Mareotis, where he celebrated the Divine Liturgy on an improvised altar and laid the foundation stone for a new monastery. This act baffled many, who wondered why the new pope did not give priority to more pressing church problems.[56] For Cyril, however, the act of laying this stone was a public performance that symbolized the revival and reformation of Coptic monastic life.

Through the cultivation and renewal of monasteries, Cyril sought to transmit the ideals of virtuous living he derived from his studies of the church fathers. According to his memoirs, the monastic rule contained all the values associated with "deprivation, love, modesty, prayer, reading, fasting, social interaction, work, guidance, self-examination and confession, the Divine Liturgy, seclusion, trial, the train of victory, admonishments, and spiritual sayings."[57] Patterned on the examples of the early desert fathers and mothers, the monks were to follow a regime of spiritual discipline, voluntary poverty, humility, and charity. In Cyril's time, these traits seemed refreshingly countercultural to a church community that had been riddled by financial scandal in previous generations. In the desert, monks were understood to possess the power to reverse the secular order and to counterbalance corruption in the church and in Egyptian society.[58]

The new monastery dedicated to St. Menas was located strategically between the two large cities of Cairo and Alexandria. This was especially meaningful to Copts who had moved to these cities from the countryside and who, as a result, could no longer easily attend the popular *mawlid*s (annual religious festivals) or perform pilgrimages to the graves of their favorite saints in their home territories. During their visits to such sites, pilgrims—from the illiterate to the highly educated—prayed for intercession with the firm expectation that miracles would take place. Since this first stone was laid at the Monastery of St. Menas in 1959, following Cyril's initiative, dozens of dilapidated monastic sites have been rediscovered and restored. As a result, today, trips to monasteries and holy sites have become more popular than ever, serving as crucial centers for educational and spiritual formation in the Coptic faith.

Under Cyril, new media technologies made these initiatives accessible to a much larger audience than ever before. For the first time in history, Egyptians could follow the liturgies of the Christmas and Easter celebrations on the radio. Not only did they read about the new Monastery of St. Menas and other papal news in the papers, they heard about it on the radio and could even witness some events via live broadcasts. One famous video clip shows Cyril walking purposefully in the empty desert toward the ruins of the St. Menas complex. We hear the wind blowing and see his robe billowing. Later videos after his death show Cyril's grave, with the nearby monastery and its churches thriving on once-arid lands.[59]

Rewriting the Past: Hagiographies and Holy Fathers

During the few years he spent in the Baramus Monastery, Cyril had started to produce a monthly newsletter called *Mina' al-khalas* (The Harbor of Salvation). This counterpart to the Sunday-school bulletin was revolutionary, as it seems to have been the first publication to address the monastic community.[60] During his time as a hermit, Cyril had studied the teachings of the seventh-century Syrian Nestorian ascetic Isaac of Nineveh. According to Isaac's biography, after only five months as bishop of Mosul (Nineveh) he realized that the administrative duties did not suit him, and he abdicated to retire in extreme solitude. He withdrew to the southwestern desert of Iran, where he practiced a rigorous spiritual and religious regime. There, as a result of an intensive reading regimen, he is said to have lost his eyesight. By the ninth century, Isaac's homilies on asceticism and the inner spiritual life had been translated into Arabic, Coptic, and Greek, and were included in a work on the spiritual life called the *Philokalia*.

Thus, while he was still a monk, Cyril had begun writing letters encouraging his fellow monks to develop a reading regime like that of Isaac: "I hope that you have developed your own library, and have some good books to read, for this is a useful and spiritual exercise. I hope that you continue reading in the Coptic language."[61] He stressed the importance of reading and advised his spiritual sons to read only spiritual books, such as the writings of the church fathers and the lives of saints, since these transmitted the rules of the monastic life. He wrote to one of them, "Persist in and honor reading, if possible more than prayer. Reading is the spring of intelligent prayer."[62]

By the 1960s, thanks to the government's education policies, the literacy rate had risen considerably and was continuing to climb. In the Coptic Church, the 250 charitable organizations and more than 2,500 Sunday-school centers had reached an estimated forty-three thousand children and adolescents.[63] To cater to the increased needs for educational materials, churches in Cairo and Alexandria started to publish the stories of the lives of saints; during the 1960s their production grew by 200 percent.[64] Up to the 1940s, spiritual literature had mostly been authored by monks and priests. By the 1960s, lay Copts had started to write hagiographical and other religious materials. Two churches in Alexandria were especially productive: between 1959 and 1971 the Church of St. George in the Sporting Club area and the Church of the Holy Virgin in Muharram Bey published 40.3 percent of the total number of Christian hagiographical literature in the country.[65] The most productive churches in Alexandria and Cairo also ran vibrant youth centers; the one at the church in the Sporting Club area was led by the famous Father Bishoi Kamil (1931–79), who was one of the engines behind this publication effort. Organizations such as the St. Menas Association, the Bayt al-Takris, and the Mahabba Bookstore also contributed to the rapid increase of publications.

As Copts began to study their own heritage, newly discovered manuscripts yielded the names of scores of largely forgotten or hitherto unknown saints, including popes, bishops, and theologians. By 1951, sixty names of saints were added to the Synaxarium: twenty-five popes, nine saints, twenty martyrs from the early Christian period, and six 'neo-martyrs' from the period after the Arab invasion. Among them were Anba Abraam, the bishop of Fayoum, and Pope John XIX, as well as Coptic notables such as Ibrahim al-Gawhari.[66] Churches bearing the names of more obscure saints felt compelled to discover and publicize their stories. The young martyr, St. Aba Nub, whose relics lie in the Church of the Holy Virgin in Sammanud, is an example of a saint from the early Christian era whose story was unearthed during this period. Snippets of information about the lives of the newly discovered saints were gleaned from manuscripts. Some claimed that saints appeared to believers in order to convey or correct their story, and creative writers invented vivid dialogues to spice up the accounts for an eager audience. These exercises were vivid illustrations of Saphinaz-Amal Naguib's observation that "texts are performative mediators of knowledge; they are neither direct expressions of reality nor are they completely estranged from it."[67]

With pressure from society on the Coptic community mounting, the stories of the saints and martyrs regenerated communal identity and faith by keeping the past alive, as heroic tales took on new forms that served the needs of the present. Stories of miracles and apparitions circulated widely. Children in the Sunday schools memorized the lives of the saints whose features, dress, and environment were being visually reimagined by artists on icons and posters. Pictures of saints and martyrs were no longer restricted to churches but entered everyday spaces—homes, shops, and cars—where they inspired the believers daily.

In monasteries and convents, monks and nuns started to compose the life stories of their patron saints from church history, as well as the stories of the saintly monks and nuns who lived among them. The need arose for more works on monastic discipline and the examples of the early desert fathers and mothers as they were preserved in their sayings. These sayings were systematized and published under the name of *Bustan al-ruhban* (The Garden of the Monks).[68]

During this period, the writing career of one of the most prolific Coptic theologians, Father Matta al-Miskin (1919–2006), began with intense study of the early monastic and church fathers, such as Athanasius and Cyril of Alexandria, and the aforementioned St. Isaac of Nineveh. One of al-Miskin's earliest works, *Hayat al-salat al-urthuduksiya* (Orthodox Prayer Life), published in 1952 while he was living in the Monastery of the Syrians, is now considered a classic. Using the sayings of the fathers from any sources he could find, al-Miskin's goal was to provide a comprehensive course of Coptic Orthodox prayers for contemporary times. Presenting the different levels of prayer and analyzing how the believer can make progress in spiritual life, the work reaffirms the vision of Orthodox Christianity as found in the Holy Scriptures and the writings of the fathers.[69] During the 1960s, this book reached the

Sunday schools via the deacons at the Bayt al-Takris, and it has since been reprinted many times and translated into several languages. Among monastic communities east and west, al-Miskin came to be considered one of the most inspiring voices of the twentieth century, and his book *The Communion of Love,* published by St. Vladimir's Press (New York) in 2004, made him well known far beyond Coptic circles.[70]

New Forms of Leadership

By selecting the best and the brightest of the Sunday-school leaders, Cyril, in part, took up the mantle of the charismatic and visionary Habib Girgis, who had passed away in 1951. By that time, expressions of enthusiasm and renewal took several forms. Following the spirit of *takris,* individuals launched or joined monastic and semi-monastic groups. Many Sunday-school leaders eventually became monks or hermits, while others dedicated themselves to a life of service and *kiraza* (celibacy) in church settings.

Reforming Churches

A few churches need to be mentioned in this context for the pivotal role they played in these developments. Between 1940 and 1944, a group of young Sunday-school teachers active in St. Mark's Church in Giza decided to "dedicate their spirits to the Lord."[71] Sa'ad Aziz, Yusuf Iskander, Zarif Abdallah, and Wahib Zaki—now known respectively as Bishop Samuel, Father Matta al-Miskin, Father Boulos Boulos, and Father Salib Suryal—spent many nights together in prayer and experienced a common spirit of dedication and calling toward service. By 1948, three of them made history as the first Sunday-school leaders to enter the church's monastic or clerical leadership: Sa'ad entered the Monastery of the Syrians, Yusuf that of St. Samuel, and Wahib was ordained a priest.[72]

The focus at St. Mark's Church was service to the poor, especially those in the countryside. The Sunday-school program initiated by the future Bishop Athanasius at the Church of the Holy Virgin in Faggala had a similar focus. This commitment to rural development led to the establishment of a center for social and religious services in Damanhur by Father Boulos Boulos in 1957. By 1959, this initiative had developed into the Rural Diaconate Project, which aimed at strengthening the Christian identity of Copts living in villages without a church and educational or other facilities. The approach was comprehensive, with volunteers offering spiritual, religious, educational, social, medical, and agricultural services. Priests with portable altars would travel the countryside to celebrate the Eucharist. The male and female volunteers, including many deacons and deaconesses who were graduates of the Coptic Orthodox Theological Seminary, improved their understanding and skills via weekly and annual meetings.[73] The project started in the province of al-Beheira with twenty villages and then snowballed after the church officially sanctioned and adopted it. By 1966, twelve dioceses had rural diaconate services and the number of families being served had risen from 3,275 in 1961 to 71,914.[74] Together the architects of these programs laid the foundation of the comprehensive social-service system for the church that is nowadays known as BLESS.

At the Sunday-school center of St. Antonius Church in Shubra, Yusuf Iskander (the future Father Matta al-Miskin) and Nazir Gayed (the future Pope Shenouda III) focused on studying the heritage of the early church as it was transmitted in the sayings and teachings of the first centuries. Gayed was among the most active Sunday-school instructors, focusing on educating the teachers. As the editor-in-chief of the *Sunday School Magazine*, he verbalized the criticism of his generation against the uneducated and conservative ruling clergy. In 1954, Gayed became a monk at the Monastery of the Syrians (Dayr al-Suryan), taking the name Father Antonius. He, too, followed the call of the desert and lived as a hermit for several years before being called to Cairo to become a bishop.

These various church and monastic initiatives generated another form of dedicated living for those who neither were ready to join a monastery nor wanted to enter the priesthood. They were called the *mukarrasin* and *mukarrasat*—the men and women dedicated to *takris*. In order to involve women in social-service activities, in 1959 Father Suryal asked Pope Cyril's blessing to launch a house of *takris* for women. This later developed into the current system of deaconesses in the Coptic Church. A few years later, in 1965, Bishop Athanasius of Beni Soueif (1923–2000) took the same step and received permission to accept three women into the Community of the Daughters of St. Mary, which later became a convent for nuns.

While these initiatives for women grew rapidly, a similar center for celibate men in Helwan, the Bayt al-Takris l-il-Khidma al-Murqusiya, opened in 1959 and met with somewhat less success. Most of its members eventually moved on to become monks and priests elsewhere. However, those who remained have been prolific in research and publishing related to the writings of the early church fathers. In 1982, they launched the Patristic Studies Center.[75]

Reforming Bishops

In May 1959, immediately after his enthronement, Pope Cyril gave Coptic scholar Wahib Atallah (the future Bishop Gregorius) the task of redesigning the church's governance structure. One of the main suggestions was to appoint general bishops who could assist the pope in the areas of religious/theological education and social services, and in matters concerning Copts abroad. [76] As a result, Pope Cyril took the historic step to ordain three general bishops who had no diocesan connection but who were charged instead with special assignments. On September 30, 1962, two of Cyril's close protégés, Anba Samuel and Anba Shenouda, were consecrated as Bishop for Public, Ecumenical, and Social Services, and Bishop of Christian Education, respectively. Each of these bishops was put in charge of areas in which they already had considerable experience.

Anba Samuel (1920–81) had been among the delegates to the Conference of the World Council of Churches (WCC) in 1954 and had graduated from Princeton Theological Seminary in 1955. In addition to his strong relations with the churches who were members of the WCC, he was also involved in all the other ecumenical contacts the Coptic Church developed during this time. His large network of contacts benefited the church when raising funds for Coptic development projects. Through his work at the church in Giza, Samuel envisioned and planned comprehensive forms of mission and service to Egyptian villages. Put in charge of the Department for Social Studies at the Coptic Theological Seminary, he taught an integrative approach for the development of rural areas.[77] Furthermore, he also gave high priority to the Copts who had emigrated to the west and, in 1963, he started to visit them on an annual basis.

In addition to being named Bishop of Christian Education, Shenouda (1923–) was also appointed dean of the theological seminary. Critical of the ignorance that hindered effective communication between many members of the clergy and the increasing number of educated Copts, his priority was to strengthen the training of monks and priests. Women were encouraged to take courses in the Coptic seminary as well, to support them in their role as mothers and Sunday-school teachers. These new ideas were met with great enthusiasm, and within ten years of Shenouda's appointment, registration rose from 130 day and evening students to a total of 570.[78]

Considering individual spiritual growth foundational to a vibrant church, Shenouda also introduced the practice of giving a public lecture every Friday. These lectures became an important platform for the transmission of church teachings. Their topics included not only spiritual themes, but also Coptic theology, apologetics, and canon law. Those in attendance were allowed to ask questions about theological, practical, or personal matters of faith—a novelty for Egypt. The meetings were so popular that, after becoming pope in 1971, Shenouda continued to hold them on Wednesday evenings. Copts attended by the thousands, feeling the message was addressed to them personally and enjoying the opportunity to interact publicly with the church hierarchy.[79]

In 1967, when Atalla was consecrated Bishop Gregorius (1919–2001) and made responsible for higher theological education, Coptic culture, and academic research, a third general bishopric was added. In 1955, he had been the first Sunday-school leader to earn a PhD from a British university. After graduation, he had spent time mentoring the *mukarrasin*, but after many of his disciples became monks and priests, he himself entered the Muharraq Monastery in 1962. His work paralleled that of Anba Shenouda, albeit with a stronger focus on research. He was put in charge of the Institute for Higher Coptic Studies, which had been launched in 1954 by several lay Copts, including Professor Aziz Suryal Atiya. The institute offered courses in a variety of Coptic studies, ranging from Coptic music, art, and canon law to social studies and African studies. Under the guidance of Bishop Gregorius, the institute expanded and gained in academic importance. Several of its professors gained international fame for their work in preserving and reviving Coptic culture: Ragheb Moftah (1898–2001) recorded the Coptic Orthodox Liturgy of St. Basil,[80] while Isaac Fanous (1919–2007) created a new genre of Coptic iconography. The liturgy and icons produced in the institute can now be heard and seen in churches both within and outside of Egypt.

On the same day that Anba Samuel and Anba Shenouda were consecrated, Anba Athanasius (1923–2000) became the first Sunday-school leader to be consecrated a diocesan bishop. Fluent in English, he was internationally involved in ecumenical relations. At home, his focus was on social development. As the bishop of Beni Soueif and Bahnasa, in his diocese he applied the vision that he and Anba Samuel had developed while working in the Sunday schools and on the Rural Diaconate Project. Via his weekly public Bible-study meetings he transmitted the basic ideas of Christian living and responsibility for the poor. Following in the footsteps of his spiritual father Pope Cyril, he committed himself to visiting the poor, and allowed them to call upon him whenever they were in need.

Reforming Monks and Nuns

The official church hierarchy could not flourish without changes in the leadership models of the monasteries where the formation of future leaders was taking place. At the same time, Cyril's insistence on a life of prayer also made ascetic practices part of everyday life for the laity. Of the many who could be mentioned here, the names of one man and one woman stand out for their innovative style and ideas: Abuna Matta al-Miskin and Ummina Irini.

A vision prompted al-Miskin to launch an alternative monastic experiment. In imitation of the fourth- and fifth-century Christian hermits, a group of monks would live in complete isolation from the world. The inspiration for this experiment came to al-Miskin in 1958 when he was wandering through the desert as a monk at the Monastery of St. Samuel. In his meanderings, he hit upon Wadi al-Rayyan (an oasis 192 kilometers southwest of Cairo), where he spent one week sleeping under a palm tree. One night he had a vision of an old man telling him, "I have waited here for thee for many years and I shall give unto thee this mountain."[81] On August 11, 1960, he moved into the wadi with several of his disciples. Following the model of St. Macarius of Scetis, living in cells 150 feet apart, they filled their days with prayer, reading, and copying spiritual writings. al-Miskin was spiritual guide of the group, which eventually comprised twelve monks. Bedouins guided them to an ancient Coptic cave church where they gathered once a week to celebrate the Eucharist. In al-Miskin's own words, the nine years spent this way were "perfect but hard, the most difficult time in my life."[82] The oasis was uninhabited; its date palms few and far between; its well yielded only brackish water that eventually made him sick.[83] The monks survived on their own vegetable gardens and on supplies of basics such as flour brought to them every two months by camel caravan from Cairo.

Nowadays, this monastic experiment has taken on mythical proportions, but it was not well received by Pope Cyril at the time. Cyril had wanted al-Miskin to use his considerable talents to restore the Monastery of the Syrians in Wadi al-Natrun (where he was spiritual father to, among others, Father Antonius, the future Pope Shenouda III). However, al-Miskin had insisted on following his vision. On the night before his planned withdrawal into the desert, a delegation arrived at his doorstep with a note from Pope Cyril ordering him not to leave Cairo. As al-Miskin remembered the incident, one of the delegation, Bishop Benjamin of al-Munufiya, countermanded the papal order and sent them off with the words, "I am an archbishop of the church and know its laws. You are all free to go with blessing. Build altars, pray, and celebrate the Eucharist, and the responsibility toward God and the church will rest upon me."[84] Al-Miskin's decision to ignore Cyril's appeal was not without consequence, however. In October of that same year, the bishop of the Monastery of the Syrians publically announced that all those staying in Wadi al-Rayyan had been stripped of their priesthood and could no longer be considered monks. They had not only left behind the world; in his eyes, they had also left behind the church and were now excommunicated.

By 1969, Cyril decided that he wanted this group to return to the fold. Allowing them to stay together, he called upon them to relocate and take up residence in the Monastery of St. Macarius in Wadi al-Natrun. Based on a settlement inhabited by the early Christian hermit St. Macarius the Great (300–90), it had been one of the church's strongest spiritual and scholarly centers, supplying thirty of its popes. In the 1960s, it had become a shadow of its former glory: having been ransacked and rebuilt several times, it now housed only four ailing monks. The monastery provided al-Miskin with a new center in which to apply his ideas for spiritual growth and renewal. He accepted the pope's offer, and that spring (on May 9) the monks' excommunication was lifted.

Al-Miskin and his group of disciples transformed the Monastery of St. Macarius into a testing ground for monastic labor, research, and living the solitary life in community. With prayer at the center of their vocation, they added the ancient monastic practice of performing physical labor as a means of spiritual growth. The new generation of monks who joined them were increasingly educated: many of them had previously worked as medical doctors, engineers, and architects. Their project of reclaiming the desert through the application of advanced agricultural methods gained national and international attention. By growing new varieties of crops, such as a new type of beet fodder, and by adding new types of livestock and poultry, the monks reclaimed traditional practice while helping to address contemporary social problems related to farming and land use. In addition, the monastery purchased a printing press to publish al-Miskin's writings and journals. Their practice of receiving visitors for retreat and spiritual direction helped strengthen ties not only with Coptic churches in Egypt, but also with monasteries in Belgium, France, England, and Lebanon, and in the process the monastery's international reputation grew.[85]

Such agricultural experiments, which traced their roots to a garden planted by the famous Anba Abraam in 1925, were later replicated by other monastic leaders. Ummina Irini (1936–2006), the abbess of the Abu al-Sayfayn (St. Mercurius) Convent in Old Cairo, was one who took up this initiative. She purchased a plot of land overlooking the Mediterranean at Sidi Krir, where her nuns transformed the barren ground into a blooming fruit orchard and vegetable garden, as well as another plot in al-Qanatir al-Khayriya, an area known for its especially fertile land. These plots not only provided income, but also expanded the living space for the nuns and offered the Coptic faithful new opportunities for retreat and renewal.[86]

When Irini became a nun in 1954, entering a convent had been viewed as less acceptable than entering a monastery was for men. Nuns typically lived under one roof but, apart from meeting once a day for communal prayer, they had no rule or regime guiding their monastic lives. One of Ummina Irini's goals was to revive women's convents by applying a new monastic discipline. A manuscript found in the convent's library led her to rediscover the system of communal or coenobitic living that St. Pachomius (290–346) had established for both his monastery and the convent of his sister Mary. Unlike solitary living, this system involved eating once a day at the communal table and praying together three times a day, especially at the midnight hour. In Irini's hands, the Pachomian system was reapplied to women's life in the convent in a particular 'gendered' way that was quite different from the more mixed organizational systems found in Egyptian men's monasteries.[87]

Shortly after becoming a nun, Irini had met the future Pope Cyril, who had foretold that under her guidance the convent would bloom, its buildings expand, and its ranks of nuns grow.[88] This encounter was the beginning of a lifelong relationship. According to popular stories, Irini had prayed that Cyril's name would be drawn at the time of his election, and on October 15, 1962, Cyril chose her as the convent's abbess, despite the fact that she was the youngest of all the nuns.

Cyril and Irini shared a common devotion to military saints. Just as Cyril had done in the case of the Monastery of St. Menas, Irini renovated and rebuilt her convent as a way of honoring its patron saint, Mercurius.[89] Cyril fully supported Irini's quest to renew the convent's physical surroundings and religious life. They also both conversed with the Virgin Mary regularly. One time the Holy Mother appeared to each of them conveying the same message: she wanted a church dedicated to her to be built in the convent's garden.[90]

The Church in Heaven

In death, Cyril and Irini remain united not only through the many expressions of visual culture transmitting their images, but also through their burial in custom-built shrines within the houses of their guardian saints. On March 9, 1971, Cyril "traveled to heaven," and one and a half years later his body was transported to the Monastery of St. Menas, where he is buried under the altar of the cathedral. Irini died in 2006 and was laid to rest in a shrine beside the convent's altar dedicated to St. Abu al-Sayfayn. Both graves have become centers of pilgrimage, and believers come from near and far to ask for their intercession.

Now, forty years after Cyril's death, books about his interventions and prayers on behalf of the Copts continue to appear annually. While during the first years of his papacy critical voices were heard from those displeased with his policies, as time passed those voices fell silent.[91]

Toward the end of his reign, starting on April 2, 1968, the Virgin Mary appeared on top of the Church of the Holy Virgin in Zaytun, a site associated with the Holy Family's journey during their flight into Egypt. These sightings of the Virgin as a white figure surrounded in lights continued until 1971. Healings and miracles were reported by many witnesses, including crowds of Orthodox Copts, Catholics, Protestants, Muslims, and Jews. Accounts of the apparitions emphasize how people of different faiths were united across denominational and religious lines. Lacking alternative interpretations, even the Egyptian government acknowledged the phenomenon. To verify the apparitions, Cyril appointed a special committee consisting of three bishops and a team of medical specialists who investigated the phenomenon and made a full report. The pope declared the apparitions to be genuine, and Egyptians—Christians and Muslims alike—were convinced that the Holy Mother had appeared not only to console the nation (which had been battered by economic woes and by the Six Day War), but also to honor the unusually gifted Coptic pope.

Befitting his image as a holy man, Cyril knew when the end was near and bade farewell to those around him. As in life, he paid attention to details, leaving behind envelopes with money and checks to finish construction projects such as the renovation of the old St. Mark's Cathedral. He is now part of the glorious tradition himself, and Copts young and old still watch clips of his funeral; some even have them on their cell phones.[92] "Take care of the church. May God be with you and attend to its needs" were among his last words.[93]

By utilizing all of the church's human resources, by allowing its members to apply their passions toward church service, and by paying attention to dissenting voices and opinions, Cyril had transformed the structure of the Coptic community. He had not just reclaimed the papal authority, but had also changed the structures that governed the church. Once a body torn apart by a civil war between the clergy and the rich, highly educated laity, the church had become a place of refuge for all Copts where they could turn for guidance and empowerment. Its priests now received obligatory education before being ordained. Monks, nuns, and bishops were now recruited from among the Coptic community's best and brightest. The ceremony to make a new supply of holy *mayrun* oil during Holy Week of 1967—only the 26th time in Coptic history—testified to a vital and growing church.[94]

Cyril had created a tight-knit community in which people were bound together not by their status, educational level, social stratum, or accident of birth, but by their Christian belief and active service to the church. Considering Egypt's tenuous political and religious climate, it was miraculous that this pope had managed to remain aloof from what could have been disastrous political intricacies. At the same time, he had molded the church into a platform from which the Coptic community still could act as "a unified political actor."[95]

8

Negotiating Political Landscapes

(Pope Shenouda III, 1971–)

Introduction

Before he was elected the 117th pope of Egypt, Shenouda III had already played a prominent role in the church revival that had begun to flourish during the reign of his predecessor and mentor Pope Cyril VI. Having been at the forefront of the lay church reform movement, he had gained a reputation as one of the most outspoken critics of the dismal state of the Coptic clergy. He was among the first of his generation to enter a monastery, and in 1962, when Pope Cyril ordained him as bishop, he became part of the official church hierarchy. In his position as general bishop of Christian education, he had greatly improved the educational and spiritual level of the community. Shenouda's election followed the procedure established in 1957. Nominated as one of three candidates (the others were Abuna Timoteus al-Maqari and Bishop Samuel, who garnered the most votes in the preliminary round), Shenouda's name was drawn from an altar ballot by a blindfolded child, whose agency represented the providential activity of the Holy Spirit in the process.

Since 1971, Shenouda III has guided the Coptic community into an era far more complex than the church had ever previously faced. The administrative, educational, social, and clerical reforms he introduced have been the most expansive in Coptic history. Throughout his career, he has remained grounded in monastic prayer and contemplation. But he has also had to act as a skilled politician in order to respond to local political vicissitudes. Accelerated population growth, urbanization, and unemployment in Egypt have required new church programs and reforms. With the Coptic community outside Egypt growing fast, he has also taken on the added role of international diplomat. Intricate ecumenical negotiations with Catholics, Byzantine Orthodox, and Protestant churches have required strong theological skills.

In addition, the church has faced external and internal pressures from other Christian groups such as Pentecostals and other evangelical forms of Christianity that have called Coptic beliefs and practices into question.

The incorporation of lay servants into the church hierarchy also has escalated during the time of Shenouda. He has continued the 'clericalization' of the laity started by Cyril: volunteers and clergy alike have to meet educational requirements and high moral standards, and their areas of work are more precisely defined. This corps of church workers has become increasingly well educated, Internet-savvy, cosmopolitan, energetic, critical of the church hierarchy, more individualistic, and less patient than the generations before them.

Shenouda has managed to gain control over almost all areas of the Coptic Church, thus creating a church-based civil society.[1] Following in the wake of Pope Cyril, he has taken on a full-blooded political role vis-à-vis the Egyptian government. This role was not immediately embraced by President Sadat, who succeeded Nasser and served as president of Egypt from 1970 to 1981, and whose style of leadership did not appreciate an assertive Coptic pope.

Shenouda is certainly the most visible pope in the history of the Coptic Church. Through his travels, ecumenical relations, and excellent command of English, he has greatly contributed to the Coptic Church's visibility in the world. During his first thirty-five years in office, he made eighty-nine pastoral journeys and visited thirty-eight countries. Since he took office, the Coptic Church has become a full member of the World Council of Churches, the All African Council of Churches, and the Middle East Council of Churches. And as Coptic churches have been founded on other continents, it has also joined local church councils in places such as Australia, North America, and Europe.

His high profile has gained him widespread international recognition, numerous academic awards, and eight honorary doctorates from foreign universities. He is well respected in other countries of the Middle East as well. In 2003, for example, Libya's President Muammar Qadhafi awarded him the "Qadhafi Prize for Human Rights" followed by a celebration in the president's desert pavilion.[2]

Well before his election as pope, Shenouda began producing a voluminous body of writings. Over the course of his career, he has authored numerous books and has published countless articles in the *Sunday School Magazine* and in *al-Kiraza,* the biweekly church newsletter that he launched in 1965.

The available material about this pope is enormous, in steady production, and translated into several languages. For example, a series of massive volumes in Arabic entitled *Historical Records for His Holiness Shenouda III* was at its eleventh volume in 2006.[3] It summarizes and expands on the pope's duties, travels, and activities as reported in *al-Kiraza*, documenting the churches and monasteries he has visited, people and places he has consecrated, festivities and celebrations he has attended, guests he has received, and speeches he (or his guests) have given.

The list goes on and on. Two books compiled on the occasion of his eightieth and eighty-fifth birthdays provide overlapping overviews of his accomplishments and main activities up to the year 2008.[4] Among others things, they catalogue his foreign travels, the major conferences he organized, the 110 bishops he ordained (seven were for the church in Eritrea), the titles of eighty-one books written about him in Arabic, and titles of the 141 books Shenouda has himself written. The available body of works in English consists mostly of translated materials: exceptions are S.S. Hasan's book *Christians versus Muslims in Modern Egypt* and shorter article-length studies by John Watson.

These days, the pope's visibility is no longer limited to printed media. His speeches are now available on audiocassettes, CDs, and DVDs. Since 2005, Copts have been able to tune in daily to see him on one of the two Coptic TV channels, Agape TV and CTV, and his website provides streaming videos of every word he utters.[5] In sifting through this abundance of available material, I will necessarily have to be selective in highlighting the particular economic, political, and religious challenges that Shenouda has faced during his tenure as pope.

A daunting task faced Pope Shenouda from the day of his enthronement. Yet he was eminently prepared to take on the challenges of public ministry. Born to a middle-class family as Nazir Gayed Rufa'il on August 3, 1923 in Asyut, the youngest child in a family of three boys and five girls, he was orphaned at a young age. His mother passed away shortly after his birth and his father died a few years later. He spent his childhood with his older brother, whose job forced the family to move to a different town every few years. As early as 1939, he started teaching Sunday school at a church in Cairo, and from there he moved to St. Anthony's Church in Shubra. Between 1946 and 1954, when he entered Dayr al-Suryan (the Monastery of the Syrians), he concurrently earned degrees at Cairo University and the Coptic Theological Seminary, while also fulfilling the requirements for military officer's training and serving in the first Arab–Israeli war of 1948. He taught, wrote columns in the *Sunday School Magazine*, became its main editor, and also published several volumes of poetry he had been composing since the age of fourteen.

After entering the Monastery of the Syrians on July 18, 1954, he took the name of Antonius al-Suryani, and he began applying his scholarly talent as head of the monastery's library. When Pope Cyril asked him to serve as his secretary in 1959, he demurred, withdrawing to the desert to practice the eremitic life in a cave several miles from the monastery. This period he has often referred to as "the happiest days of my life." However, on September 30, 1962, life in the desert ended abruptly when Cyril took the historic step of consecrating two extra-diocesan bishops and Father Anthony became Bishop Shenouda. He was appointed president of the Coptic Orthodox Theological Seminary, and later took over the direction of the Coptic Institute that had been opened in 1954. Eventually he controlled all Coptic education, from kindergarten Sunday-school classes to graduate-level seminary education. He also introduced his open lectures—first held on Fridays, then later on Wednesdays—that drew thousands of believers and that have remained his personal trademark throughout his papacy.

While Bishop Shenouda expanded and strengthened Coptic religious education, Anba Samuel was appointed bishop for public, ecumenical, and social services. In that capacity, Samuel widened his sphere of influence from rural ministries to include urban social development projects. In Cairo, for example, he started projects that would lift the *zabbalin* (garbage collectors) out of deep poverty and brought language classes and other types of education to Shubra and other districts with large Christian populations. Under his guidance, homes for drug addicts, delinquents, the mentally handicapped, and unwed pregnant girls started to spring up all over Egypt. These initiatives triggered new demands and expectations concerning the training of church workers, the services they rendered, and the role of the church within the Coptic community at large. Opportunities opened up for women as the need for their services in the new projects increased. When Shenouda became pope on November 14, 1971, he thus faced a community whose educational level had risen and whose expectations had changed. Copts no longer expected just religious guidance and liturgical celebrations from their church, but also educational and social services, job training, and assistance finding work.

The community was not all that was in transition—the character and role of the papacy had also changed. Now that the Coptic gentry and the once-powerful Community Council had lost much of their influence, the church's political and social roles were expanding and Pope Shenouda was firmly ensconced as the church's foremost political representative.

One Pope, Two Presidents

Shenouda's reign has coincided with the presidencies of Anwar al-Sadat (1970–81) and Hosni Mubarak (1981–2011). The policies and personalities of both of these presidents have profoundly impacted Shenouda's time in office. When assessing the pope's political role and relations with the government, the forty years of his papacy may be divided into four distinctive periods. The first two were during the Sadat era, beginning amicably and in a spirit of mutual trust and cooperation, but ending with a breakdown in relations between pope and president, culminating in Shenouda's exile (1981–85). Indeed, during the first decade of his reign his approach toward defending the community's rights and voicing its demands became increasingly assertive and even, at times, confrontational.[6] The third period corresponds with Mubarak's tenure until around 2005 when the pope supported the president unconditionally. Beginning in that year, various new forces within the government (and within the church) began to challenge some of the pope's decisions, and since then he has become noticeably more critical of government policies once more.

In dealing with the Egyptian state, Shenouda has been forced to walk a fine line. Following an unwritten agreement, he always needed to stay within the limits that Egypt's government and the Islamic environment placed on his community. Since the Copts are woven into the fabric of the nation, the state and the Coptic community remain engaged in a symphony that goes off key when certain issues arise, such as those related to freedom of religion, citizenship rights, conversion, the building of churches, and the Coptic community in diaspora.

While Egypt has ratified core human rights conventions, including those concerning freedom of religion, the church faces ongoing challenges from mixed marriages, conversions, and Islamist pressure on poor and vulnerable communities. Although reliable figures are hard to come by, Copts do convert to Islam, and one of the church's main problems is that those who regret their choice and would like to return to its fold are forbidden to do so.[7] At the same time, high-profile incidents, such as the case of Wafaa Constantine (2004), a priest's wife who tried to escape an abusive marriage by converting to Islam, caused deep furor within the community and revealed the difficulties of applying fundamental religious freedoms in Egypt.[8] Because of her position as the wife of a priest, Constantine was handed over to the church and more or less confined to a convent.

In spite of attempts to introduce more transparent rules, the building of new churches and the repair of old ones has remained an issue of contention. To counterbalance the laxity of the security apparatus during times of sectarian violence, the government has regularly held out olive branches to the Copts. A watershed moment was in 1998 when about 70 percent of the *waqf*-endowed lands that had been confiscated under the Nasser regime were returned to the church. That same year the cumbersome process of applying for permits to build and repair churches was simplified by referring the decisions to local governors and Mubarak signed thirty-nine permits at once: two for new churches and the rest to allow repairs. Decentralization meant that the burden of negotiation no longer rested on the pope alone; the national network of bishops could work the red tape locally.

The fact that Pope Shenouda viewed the political landscape from the vantage point of a Christian community subject to Muslim control provoked the wrath of Copts both inside and outside of Egypt, who interpret issues like conversion and church building with reference to basic human or civil rights. Over time they were not alone in fostering such ideas, however. During Mubarak's rule, Muslim intellectuals reflecting on the status of the Copts and the Coptic Church also began voicing criticism of the state's ways of dealing with their Christian compatriots.[9]

The Sadat Era (1970–81)

Although at the time of Shenouda's election Sadat had been pleased with the choice of the young pope, within a few years their relations became strained. The president of Egypt had expected a malleable figurehead, not an assertive leader whose every move was watched across the world. Nasser, whose regime had greatly damaged Coptic wealth and employment opportunities, had been keen on avoiding sectarian strife by maintaining good relationships with Pope Cyril. He had also curtailed the activities of the Muslim Brotherhood. In 1954, when its agenda became politicized and its members tried to assassinate him, Nasser had put many of their leaders into prison, where they stayed during the rest of his time in office. Yet throughout his tenure, the message and activities of the Brotherhood had worked their way through society and had awakened a renewed sense of religiosity among Egyptian Muslims. In spite of Nasser's repressive measures, religio-political tensions continued to grow throughout the 1960s, especially after Egypt's defeat in the 1967 War, which the Brothers blamed on a general lack of religious dedication among Muslims.

Although the Sadat era started and ended with strife, violence, and confrontation, the years between 1972 and 1977 were relatively quiet. As most popes had done before him, Shenouda tried to maintain a good working relationship with the government. Being a nationalist at heart, he squarely backed the October War with Israel in 1973 and unflaggingly supported the Palestinian cause. Convinced that "anger does not solve a thing," in 1977 he asked the president why he avoided Copts but made it a point to converse with all other groups in society, from artists to students. Sadat promised to come visit every year on the feast at the end of Ramadan. However, the promise was not kept: when the feast came around in the following year, Sadat happened to be in Jerusalem.[10]

As Nasser's successor, Sadat knew that initial expectations about his presidency were quite low. To strengthen his position, he reorganized Egypt's economic and political systems via the so-called *infitah,* a set of liberalization policies that would open up Egypt's economy to the world. This entailed seeking closer relationships with oil-rich Middle Eastern and western states and cutting ties with the Soviet Union, which had become one of Egypt's prime economic partners during Nasser's socialist regime. The new economic model made Egypt attractive to foreign investors and resulted in a rapid growth of multinational companies, which made a few Egyptians very rich and led to a sharp increase in the cost of living for the rest of the population. Copts, who were bypassed for many state offices and public service positions, relied increasingly on the private sector for income. Thus, Coptic businessmen and shopkeepers were not altogether averse to the new policies, since for many it meant economic growth and the creation of new commercial jobs. But most Egyptians suffered from the high rate of inflation, especially those in the lower and lower-middle classes who had strongly supported Nasser and who consequently felt betrayed when Sadat curtailed their security net of subsidies for food, electricity, and rent control.

In the face of growing unrest, Sadat turned to Islam as a force to help consolidate his constituencies. He released political prisoners, including the leaders of the Muslim Brotherhood, and allowed them to reorganize and publish their journals *al-Da'wa* and *al-I'tisam.* In an attempt to silence the opposition, Islam became Sadat's tool for political mobilization. Casting himself as Egypt's devout Muslim leader, he unleashed forces that ultimately caused his demise and alienated the Coptic community. He clashed frequently with the Coptic leader, Pope Shenouda, who was bold, critical, and outspoken. Shenouda had no intention of suffering in silence.

By stressing Egypt's character as an Islamic country, Sadat hoped to undermine Nasser's supporters and the socialist cause. In 1971, Sadat promulgated the so-called permanent constitution that included a clause declaring the shari'a law to be "one of the sources of legislation." Furthermore, he supported the Islamic societies (or *jama'at*) that, over time, became more militant than the Brotherhood. With great efficiency they took hold of student unions, and by the mid-1970s were harassing Copts and moderate Muslim students on university campuses and forcing their militant preachers upon the general mosques.[11] Mass media and pulpits became filled by Islamist voices espousing conspiracy theories about the Coptic Church. Between 1977 and 1980, certain of these societies started anti-Christian campaigns in Upper Egypt that caused recurring sectarian clashes. Copts were accused of hoarding weapons in their churches, creating a Coptic state, and impeding Islamic law.[12] With this radical fervor taking hold of society, mosques mushroomed. Meanwhile, for the Copts, the difficulty of obtaining building permits for churches remained a pressing problem. Very few permits were granted at a time when many Egyptians were moving from the countryside into the city and urban communities badly needed more houses of worship. Coptic communities often ended up building illegal structures out of necessity.

This tense climate galvanized the Islamists, whose actions were often tacitly condoned by the government. The first major sectarian clash took place on November 6, 1972 in a village close to Cairo called Khanqa, where fights broke out when Muslims protested a chapel that had been built without the proper permissions. The violence escalated and the chapel was burned to the ground. The pope reacted by sending a group of bishops and priests to the site of the chapel, ordering them to celebrate a Mass on the ruins. This act of defiance provoked riots, and Christian homes and shops in Khanqa were torched.[13] Sadat was furious at the pope.[14]

While clashes between Muslims and Christians flared up throughout the 1970s, Sadat's own honeymoon with the Islamist militants did not last long. By 1974, they attacked what they considered to be the regime's 'symbols of authority.' For example, in 1977 a violent group called al-Takfir wa-l-Hijra kidnapped and murdered the minister of religious endowments.[15] Sadat's attempts to appease the radical Muslim groups elicited Coptic responses that placed his policies in a negative light. In 1977, when the government submitted a draft law proposing the Islamic penal code for apostasy, Copts both within and outside Egypt revolted, since the law could mean a death sentence for Copts who had converted to Islam and wanted to recant. The pope organized a conference in Alexandria to voice the Coptic community's concerns and declared a five-day fast. Coptic communities abroad, especially in the United States, were fuming and pressured the regime to withdraw the proposal.

On the eve of Coptic Christmas, January 6, 1980, bombs exploded in several churches in Alexandria. When the government did not move to punish the perpetrators, Pope Shenouda decided to take a public stance, canceling that year's Easter celebrations and withdrawing to a monastery with his bishops. Government and Muslim dignitaries could not convey their customary greetings. Sadat, who since the 1978 Camp David agreement with Israel had cherished his international image as a peacemaker, was utterly embarrassed, since he missed his annual opportunity to showcase national harmony. Shenouda angered the president even more when, on March 26, he alleged in a public speech that Islam was being used as a new form of Egyptian nationalism.[16] In Sadat's eyes, the pope was a master politician whose influence reached as far as the United States, where he had orchestrated the Coptic protests awaiting the president during his visit there. On top of that, Sadat was infuriated because Shenouda refused to lift the ban on Coptic pilgrimage to Jerusalem. To reciprocate the steady flow of Israeli tourists visiting Egypt, the president needed Copts to visit the holy shrines and increase the number of Egyptian tourists. But the pope refused to betray the Palestinian Arabs and would not budge.[17] The escalating situation put Shenouda in a difficult spot. Moderate bishops and lay leaders wanted him to retract his position, but many within the Coptic community supported his firm stance. When he held his first public Bible study after the Easter events, on April 25, massive crowds filled the cathedral chanting, "Shenouda is our president," and "We will sacrifice ourselves for you."[18]

In May 1980, relations between Sadat and Shenouda came to a breaking point. In a final attempt to appease the militant groups, the government proposed a constitutional amendment which made the principles of shari'a the basic source of legislation rather than simply one of several sources of law. For the Copts, acceptance of this proposal meant a de facto return to the status of *dhimmi*. In his address to parliament that month, Sadat accused the pope of acting as a politician and of plotting to set up a Christian state within the state.[19] He won thunderous applause with the words, "But the pope must understand that I am the Muslim president of a Muslim country." The speech was as historic as it was unusual since, even in the worst of times, the Egyptian state had refrained from openly attacking the Copts. "No Egyptian ruler, since the early 19th century, had attacked publicly a Coptic Patriarch."[20]

Egged on by this public rebuke of the pope, leaders of militant societies devoted their sermons to vilifying the Copts. Religious tensions came to a head in June 1981 in a district of Cairo called al-Zawya al-Hamra'.[21] An angry Copt opened fire on Muslims who tried to build a mosque on land that by court order had been designated for a new church. Several days of extreme communal violence erupted. The police stood by while eighteen people were killed, 112 injured, and 171 shops destroyed. Following a familiar strategy, Sadat (and much of the Egyptian press) blamed the pope. At the same time, the president faced several antagonistic and aggrieved forces in society. Some were angry at him for making peace with Israel and others for letting the economy spiral out of control. Islamists declared Egypt an un-Islamic country. On September 3, Sadat used the strife as an excuse to silence his opponents and detained 1,536 opposition figures. Most were Muslim activists, but eight bishops, twenty-four priests, and numerous other Copts were among those imprisoned. Two days later, Pope Shenouda became one of the most prominent detainees: Sadat ordered that he be confined to the monastery of St. Bishoi, where he was to remain for 1,213 days.

The Papal Committee (1981–85)

The period of Shenouda's exile put great strain on the Coptic community. Sadat decided to revoke his presidential decree concerning Shenouda's appointment and referred to him as the "ex-pope."[22] He not only banned *al-Kiraza,* the pope's newsletter, but also the only other Coptic newspaper, the weekly *Watani*. With the Copts deprived of their own press, Sadat started a media campaign against Shenouda, accusing him in various registers of waging war on the government.[23]

During a televised speech on September 5, Sadat announced that the pope's responsibilities had been transferred to a specially appointed committee of five who would take over the church's affairs while the pope was in exile. Bishop Samuel was appointed the committee's chair. Its other members were Bishops Gregorius, Athanasius of Beni Soueif, Maximos of Benha, and Yuhanna of Tanta (who was the secretary of the Holy Synod). Each of these bishops had disagreed with Shenouda's confrontational approach, preferring that the church concentrate on strengthening the community economically and educationally, or that it limit its role to the spiritual realm.

Their willingness to serve on this committee was motivated by their fear that the latest confrontations between the president and Shenouda would increase the church's tensions with the government and might generate an Islamic backlash. But even though Sadat considered Shenouda to be the "ex-pope," the committee made it clear that he had been chosen for life according to canon law and would remain the spiritual head of the church. The majority of the Coptic community did not dwell on this sophisticated legal point; they simply maintained their deep love for their pope, since he had been the only one brave enough to stand up for them. As he left Cairo for what turned out to be forty months, they lined the streets, crying out, "Bi-l-ruh, bi-l-damm nafdik!" ("With our souls and our blood we will vindicate you.")[24]

The formation of this interim committee nearly ripped the church in two; it exposed divergent lines of thinking about the church's public role that had developed since the 1950s. When the conflict spilled over onto the international stage because of the activism of the expatriate communities cultivated by the pope, it also revealed how profoundly the Coptic Church had changed over the course of Cyril's reign. Thanks to its new international ties, the Coptic Church had become a known entity in the ecumenical networks, and modern communication tools and media—much less available during Cyril's time—were quick to broadcast and publicize the opinions of opposing factions.

The crisis also caused irreparable rifts between former friends and colleagues. Pope Shenouda and the other formidable church leader, Father Matta al-Miskin, found themselves at odds. Matta's relations with Sadat remained cordial, and shortly before Shenouda's exile Sadat had summoned him to discuss the situation. According to al-Miskin's memoirs, the day he heard the news of the pope's exile was the "second black day" of his lifetime (the first was when Pope Yusab was ousted).[25] In the span of one generation the impossible had happened twice: a pope had been forced out of office. It was during the meeting with Sadat that Matta al-Miskin proposed the formation of a committee as one of several solutions to defuse the crisis between the pope and the president. In the end, it was the only idea Sadat would accept.[26]

On September 28 of that same year, still less than a month after Shenouda's exile, Matta al-Miskin greatly upset the pope. In an interview with *Time* magazine, he blamed Shenouda for the religious discord, referring to his appointment as "the beginning of trouble." In al-Miskin's view, the church had gone from bad to worse.[27] Under Shenouda, logic had replaced inspiration and planning had supplanted the life of prayer. He fully supported the government's policies by saying that "Sadat's actions protect the church and the Copts. They are from God."[28]

The pope's banishment infuriated many Copts outside Egypt. The communities in the United States protested heavily, but their ranks were equally divided and few of the clergy spoke out publicly. Two U.S.-based Coptic priests and one in Great Britain openly criticized the committee that was replacing the pope. One voice even found a platform in the U.S. court system. Father Markus al-Askity protested the pope's exile in a public demonstration outside the Egyptian consulate in Houston, Texas. Originally from Kenya, he had converted to Coptic Orthodox Christianity and been ordained by Pope Shenouda. Afterward, Shenouda sent him to a new congregation in Bellaire near Houston. This public act of defiance by the non-Egyptian Father Markus aggravated the members of the committee and on March 10, 1982, they defrocked and excommunicated him. Since he could not appeal to the pope, Father Markus filed an appeal with the U.S. court. In June of that year, a letter from Pope Shenouda refuting the committee's actions against the priest was accepted by the U.S. judge, who decided to uphold the canons of the Coptic Orthodox Church.[29] The Committee's act of excommunicating a serving priest gave previously neutral Copts pause and many found that their sympathies returned to the pope.

During the pope's exile, many of the western partner churches had no clue as to how to react. Most of them had maintained close relationships with the amicable and diplomatic Bishop Samuel who, among others, had been a permanent member of the Central Committee of the World Council of Churches (WCC) and vice-president of the All Africa Conference of Churches. Over the years, his contacts had helped swell the church's coffers with funds for social and educational activities. Supporting Bishop Samuel was almost a natural reaction for most of the churches in the west. This picture changed on October 6, 1981, when he was murdered along with Sadat while viewing a military parade. A year later, representatives from the Catholic Church and the WCC made carefully planned and guarded visits to the exiled pope. With these visits from foreign dignitaries, the position of the committee became more precarious.

While the committee continued its work in relative quiet, the ice between the pope and the government was breaking. In 1983, the pope exchanged New Year's wishes with the new Egyptian president Hosni Mubarak. Then, suddenly, in January 1985, Pope Shenouda was allowed to return to Cairo to celebrate the Christmas liturgy in St. Mark's Cathedral. This reentry began a new phase in the pope's reign. Now it was the members of the committee who were being banned. Bishop Gregorius withdrew into his academic work and the other bishops returned to their dioceses. They all became *personae non gratae*, including Matta al-Miskin, whose books were removed from the papal libraries and bookstores.

Bishop Athanasius had assumed the committee chair after the death of Bishop Samuel, and for the many Copts who highly respected him, it was painful to see how he endured years of subsequent public humiliation. Once I asked him about the Catch-22 of his having to pacify the president who appointed him to the committee while maintaining his desire to remain obedient to his superior, the pope. His answer was that they had all felt "squeezed." He went on to comment further:

> It was a terribly difficult time and we felt a strong sense of duty to maintain bridges between the state and the church, knowing that it would involve suffering, hatred, and repulsion. I felt like a soldier in an army that had withdrawn and left a few behind. But suppose

> history would say that there had been a crisis in the church which lasted for forty months and a man called Athanasius had acted as a traitor. Even then the main fact would remain that the church survived the crisis. Never mind the person.[30]

Bishop Athanasius expressed deep gratitude for living to old age to see his reputation and image restored. He kept trying to build bridges with Shenouda and, over time, the pope reconciled with him over their past "differences." The pope visited Athanasius as he lay in the hospital dying and presided over his funeral, which was attended by forty-four bishops. Eulogizing the bishop in front of a crowd of fifty thousand, Shenouda fondly recalled the times when they had been young Sunday-school teachers and had entered the same monastery.[31] Born around the same year as Samuel and Athanasius, Shenouda had survived all of the committee members. During interviews, Shenouda often referred to the period in exile as a time when he could pray, study, and write. Athanasius agreed and called him "a model of good faith and patience." The bishop used to say that one of the pope's greatest qualities was his "calm behavior in a time of extreme duress."[32]

The Mubarak Era (1981–2011)

Pope Shenouda's first message after his return from exile in 1985 stressed love, peace, and friendship between Egyptians. He supported the new president unequivocally. Since then, the Holy Synod, led by the pope, has issued decrees at regular intervals to back Mubarak's re-elections and to urge all Copts to vote for him. According to political scientist Mariz Tadros, the lines between religious and political allegiances became blurred, especially when church bells rang to celebrate the president's victories.[33]

However, this strong support was not enough to prevent continued sectarian violence, which intensified during the 1990s. Islamist groups did not stop promoting the application of the shari'a law, which asserted the *ahl al-dhimma* status and the *jizya* tax for the Coptic community as its corollaries. For several decades, activist proponents, such as the popular Sheikh Muhammad Mitwalli al-Sha'arawi, aired their views daily via radio and TV, shaping young, impressionable minds with Islamist propaganda. By the mid-1980s, militant groups had reorganized themselves and resumed their attacks on Christian homes, businesses, and churches. The list of incidents is long. To name just a few, Copts readily recognize the names of Sanabu (1992), Abu Qurqas (1995), al-Qusiya (1996), Kush (1998), al-Kusheh (2000), Alexandria (2005 and 2011), Dayrut

(2009), and Nag Hammadi (2010)—places associated with episodes of anti-Coptic violence.

With state protection still faltering, the pope continued to rely on diplomacy. He chose to serve as the church's chief government liaison himself rather than sending out protesting delegations of clerics. Wisely, he focused on efforts at reconciliation, such as hosting high-profile annual Ramadan *iftar* meals (held in the early evening at the time of the breaking of the fast) for Muslim leaders and government officials. These meals were replicated in dioceses all over Egypt, offering opportunities for Christians and Muslims to get to know each other better. He launched the Committee of National Unity to improve relationships with Muslims. Copts were encouraged to invite Muslims to discuss problems such as job discrimination and difficulties in obtaining licenses to build churches.[34] These activities promoting national unity and harmony did not generate much enthusiasm among government officials, nor, for that matter, among their Muslim Egyptian neighbors, but they did help promote knowledge about the Copts. Following familiar patterns in situations of majority-on-minority conflict, the dominant group knew all too little about the minority: the average Egyptian Muslim was woefully uninformed about the Coptic past, about who the Copts were and what they believed. The pope's activities represented modest steps to remedy this ignorance.[35]

In the 1990s, when the militants broadened their targets to include foreign tourists, security forces, and high-ranking officials, the church and the state suddenly had a common enemy. With militant Muslim attacks growing more indiscriminate, the government's rhetoric about and toward the Copts changed. The state started to disseminate information about the Copts via an array of initiatives. One of the projects for *al-wahda al-wataniya* (national unity), the "Reading for All" campaign, launched in 1992–93, aimed at writing Coptic participation into the nation's past. History books examined the national struggles that Muslims and Christians had overcome together. Other publications related how members of both groups were killed in the October War or painted idyllic village scenes with locals living in joyous harmony.[36] Coptic characters were scripted into popular television shows featured on the state-controlled channels, and speakers at public dialogue events stressed that "all Egyptians have lived through many periods of struggle, in wonderful national unity."[37]

Highlights in the drive toward national unity were the bimillennial year celebrations and President Mubarak's decree that made Coptic Christmas (January 7) a national holiday. Celebrating two thousand years of Egyptian history naturally underscored the historical place of Coptic Christianity.

Sites related to the Flight of the Holy Family suddenly became reclaimed as part of the national heritage. Ironically, the new millennium started with one of the worst sectarian conflicts in modern Egyptian history. The violence in the village of al-Kusheh in Upper Egypt that erupted on January 4, 2000, was so brutal that it made the international press several times. Twenty Christian villagers were killed and thirty-three were injured. At the same time, thirty-three Christian-owned and forty-five Muslim-owned shops were destroyed.

The government's response was familiar: the police were still slow to interfere and the judicial system remained lax in punishing perpetrators of sectarian violence. Pope Shenouda's stance was to stress national unity unequivocally and express his trust in the authorities to deal with the crisis. But he protested when necessary and did demand justice for the victims.[38] On December 1, 2000, when eighty-nine defendants charged with the violence in al-Kusheh were released without bail, he challenged the ruling. So that the nation would not forget, all the victims at al-Kusheh were mentioned by name in *al-Kiraza*.[39]

The complex conditions of balancing concerns for national unity with the existence of a growing Coptic community outside Egypt were highlighted in 1994 when the Ibn Khaldun Center for Developmental Studies organized a conference on Middle Eastern minorities, including the Copts. This event triggered "one of the most passionate debates in the Arab World in recent memory."[40] In spite of recurring calls for the application of shari'a, Copts and Muslims vehemently rejected the suggestion that Copts be defined as a minority because this idea entailed returning to the Ottoman system. In the twentieth century, the Copts had been an integral part of the historical, cultural, and legal fabric of Egyptian society. For the sake of national cohesion, it was now unacceptable to propose the idea of minority.[41] Casting Copts in the role of minority not only invoked images of the *dhimmi* status of the rejected colonial past, but also was considered a form of foreign intervention in Egypt's affairs by outspoken Coptic communities in the United States and other western groups. Coptic intellectuals, such as Samir Morcos and William Sulaiman Qilada, whose publications focused on questions of citizenship, refused to attend. In an attempt to explain the conference's rationale, the center's director, Saad Eddin Ibrahim, wrote to Pope Shenouda. The pope maintained that the Copts should neither be on the agenda, nor think of themselves as a minority, nor be considered to be one.[42]

The crowning moment of Pope Shenouda's reconciliatory work came in 2000 when he received the UNESCO–Madanjeet Singh Prize for the Promotion of Tolerance and Non-violence. "There is a way to win your enemy over to become a friend," he said in his acceptance speech. "We will not allow victory to hatred but overcome it with goodness."[43] It was around the same time, however, that some elements in the church began to think that goodness too often meant giving up their individual and communal rights as Copts.

During the 1990s, numerous organizations, activities, and forums had developed inside and outside Egypt—forums that sought to create strong forms of Christian civil society. Some of these groups outgrew the church's close guidance and became increasingly assertive and vocal.[44] In 2006 and 2007, Coptic writers, intellectuals, and activists from various backgrounds organized two lay conferences to discuss their priorities for church reform and Coptic engagement in civil affairs. One of their main points of disapproval was "the increasingly political role of the church and its impact on citizenship"; they opposed the notion that Copts should "engage with the State as followers of church directions or guidance rather than as independent citizens."[45]

Another sign of discontent with Shenouda's public policies became evident in the aftermath of the sectarian violence that took place on Coptic Christmas 2010 in the town of Nag Hammadi. There, what seemed to start as a blood feud transformed into premeditated killings of Copts and destruction of Coptic property. According to activist Copts and Muslims, Pope Shenouda's non-confrontational stance in response to the crisis failed to account for the fact that the perpetrators of such crimes had changed. During the 1970s, 1980s, and 1990s, militant Muslim groups instigated the violence, but in the new millennium, ordinary citizens had begun to run amok, triggered by rumors or inflammatory sermons. According to Mariz Tadros, the fact that "the intolerance is now internally bred, not externally induced" led to unprecedented mass protests and rallies in front of St. Mark's Cathedral after the incident at Nag Hammadi.[46] With Egypt's security forces painfully slow to react, Muslim activists started to join the Copts in protest, publicly critiquing the window dressing of orchestrated reconciliation committees that denied the facts and claimed that "everything is just fine and we have come to establish a cultural dialogue!"[47] Here, entering the second decade of the new millennium, it is easy to see how a Coptic citizenry with new priorities and new ways to show its discontent has emerged. These groups and individuals even include some Coptic clerics who are no longer willing to let the church speak on their behalf, but instead wish to exercise their political and civil rights unhindered.[48]

The tipping point came early on New Year's Day 2011, when a suicide bomber killed over twenty worshipers and wounded dozens in the al-Qiddisayn Church in Alexandria. Mubarak called the bombing an attack on the entire nation, and the government was quick to blame groups such as the Mossad (the Israeli secret service) and al-Qa'ida. This time the public fury came from Copts as well as from Muslims. Demonstrators carried the national symbol of unity, the Crescent and the Cross, and Facebook users replaced their own pictures with this symbol.[49]

Pope Shenouda himself has recently resorted to more outspoken tactics as well. As a form of protest, he has regularly withdrawn to the Monastery of St. Bishoi, written public letters of protest, and appealed to the authorities to take action against the many cases of injustice. In these ways, he has signaled that he no longer lends the regime his unconditional support.[50] On February 15, 2011, a few days after Mubarak was forced from office, Pope Shenouda issued a statement in which he congratulated the Egyptian youth, paid tribute to the army, and emphasized that Egypt should now be a democracy and a civil nation. In an interview shortly thereafter, he explained that in such a nation Copts would no longer be marginalized; the country would be non-religious and non-military, and would uphold the principles of social justice and national unity.[51]

9

Reforming the Church for the Twenty-first Century

(Pope Shenouda III, 1971–)

As of the time of this writing, on the eve of Pope Shenouda's fortieth anniversary as pope, his policies and reforms have come to touch all aspects of church life. The most profound changes, however, have come through his efforts to improve the quality of monastic life, to redraw diocesan boundaries and ordain new bishops, to incorporate laypeople into various levels of the clerical hierarchy (including al-Majlis al-Milli), to invite youth and women into the official structures of lay service, and to raise the educational and professional levels of all involved.[1]

One Church, Many Ministries

Monasteries at the Heart of Renewal

Following Cyril's example, Pope Shenouda has continued to restore and repopulate abandoned monastic establishments. By 2008, the number of monasteries for men had expanded from nine to twenty-five and those for women from five to seven. The number of monks increased from 206 in 1960 to over 1,200 in 2001. The population in the contemplative convents saw a comparatively rapid growth. For example, between July 1992 and 1993, the pope consecrated sixty-one new nuns.[2]

Most of those who become monks these days have university degrees and serve their monasteries as engineers, architects, medical doctors, or pharmacists. In the monastic churches, they conserve the icons and frescos. In the libraries, they restore and study ancient manuscripts and write books about the histories of their monastic settlements. They cultivate gardens that make the desert bloom. And in the workshops, they fashion souvenirs that visitors can take home as a reminder of the holy places and as a source of blessing in daily life.

Paved roads created a silent revolution by making the once-remote monasteries accessible to the public. Priests come to make their mandatory retreats, while groups of church workers hold workshops and perform spiritual exercises on the monastery grounds. Through web pages, e-mail, and cell phones, the monks remain connected with Coptic communities around the world. The monasteries and convents have become an integral part of Coptic ritual life. Some organize annual festivals to celebrate the saints' days (*mawlid*s), while others receive church groups performing shorter pilgrimage visits *(ziyarat)*. Copts from all over Egypt come to gain blessing from the holy places and wisdom from those inhabiting them. The pope himself retreats into the desert weekly to his residence in the Anba Bishoi Monastery, where he often receives guests and holds conferences.

The regimen of women who enter convents differs from that of the men in several respects. Contemplative nuns cannot work in the community in any capacity; their vocation is lived out within the walls of the convent, and according to tradition a nun can only leave when her body is taken to the graveyard. Yet they have played equally formative roles in the revival of the church. One way that nuns serve the needs of the larger community is by guarding the relics of popular saints and organizing annual *mawlid*s. The convents dedicated to Abu al-Sayfayn (St. Mercurius) and Mari Girgis (St. George) in crowded Cairo can only afford to host one-day festivities, but the large *mawlid* at St. Dimiana's in the countryside close to Damietta lasts for days. Mother Irini (1936–2006), the superior of Dayr Abu al-Sayfayn, continued her pioneering revival of female monastic life, both materially and spiritually, during the first three and a half decades of Shenouda's reign. She inspired a movement that rediscovered women's contributions to monastic life in Egypt, applying the fourth-century coenobitic (communal) rules of St. Pachomius to the life of the nuns under her care, and transformed her convent into a place of visitation for women seeking spiritual and pastoral care.[3]

Entrepreneurial Bishops and Priests

All bishops in the Coptic Church are now trained in the monastic discipline. By 2008, the pope had ordained 110 new bishops, of whom seven belonged to the Eritrean Church.[4] In order to facilitate church governance and strengthen pastoral and spiritual care, large dioceses were split up, which increased the need for episcopal oversight. After the death of Anba Athanasius, his diocese of Beni Soueif, for example, was restructured into five diocesan units. From 1971 to 2008, the number of dioceses in Egypt more than doubled, from twenty-three to fifty.[5] Outside Egypt, new dioceses were added even more rapidly; by 2001, there were nineteen bishops serving abroad, compared to only three at the beginning of Shenouda's reign.[6] This increase in the number of bishops reflects the pope's vision "to have as many bishops serving the Christians of Egypt as there were during the Middle Ages."[7]

The most successful bishops multitask, operating as much as social entrepreneurs and political negotiators as spiritual leaders. One of their goals is to bring economic and social development to their dioceses by launching social-service programs ranging from orphanages, nurseries, clinics, student hostels, and homes for abused women, to literacy classes and Bible-study classes for girls. The model bishop succeeds in institutionalizing his programs: rather than running them alone, he divides and delegates his tasks and responsibilities among the consecrated lay workers around him so that they have a stake in the church's well-being.[8]

Contemporary bishops also play an important role in recruiting and training effective priests. Under Shenouda, the number of medical doctors, engineers, and teachers who have entered the priesthood has risen dramatically.[9] In poor areas, the presence of priests with such professional backgrounds has proven vital for economic and social development, especially in curtailing certain practices the church does not condone, such as forced marriages and clitoridectomies. One of Pope Shenouda's important reforms was to provide fixed salaries for all priests and to standardize their theological education. Retaining his position as head of the seminary after becoming the pope, he continued to give weekly lectures to the seminarians, and founded multiple branches of the seminary in Egypt, as well as in North America, Europe, and Australia.

Lay Leadership

Pope Shenouda's ambition has been "to integrate the Copts—every single one of them—into the church."[10] Such integration has started at the local level through church councils, church workers, church volunteers, deacons, deaconesses, and Sunday-school teachers.

At the local level, the *majlis al-kanisa* (church council) was reintroduced to communicate the wishes of parishioners to church leaders, supervise the church's finances, and monitor the performance of the priests. Originally established by the Community Council at the beginning of the twentieth century to carry out reform, nowadays its members include youth, women, and civil-servant representatives. These members, both inside and outside Egypt, are appointed by papal decree and their names are published in *al-Kiraza*.[11]

On a national level, after a twelve-year suspension, elections were held in 1973 to reinstate the Community Council, al-Majlis al-Milli. The council members still had an important role to play in selecting the papal candidates and appointing a locum tenens when a pope dies. However, the profile of its members changed radically. The majority no longer came from the cosmopolitan elite and landed gentry, but rather from the middle class—people who had gone through the Sunday-school system and oftentimes had taken courses in theology and Bible. By profession, they were lawyers, medical doctors, university professors, or successful business owners. During the first meeting of the revived council, Pope Shenouda III ordained the members to the diaconate, thus placing the council membership within the lower ranks of the church hierarchy.[12]

Deacons, Deaconesses, and Consecrated Women

For women, voluntary church service opened up many new opportunities to be active in the church: women were needed to teach, especially other women and children. Becoming a Sunday-school teacher, a *mukarrasat* (consecrated virgin), or a deaconess in the Coptic Church carries with it prestige, as it implies that a woman has been well educated through an extensive course of instruction in church doctrine and theology, and that she has gained the respect of a priest or bishop who recommended her for the position. The positions of deaconess and *mukarrasat* are new developments, but they were cast as a recapturing of early Christian tradition, when consecrated women were an important part of the official church.

By the 1960s, small groups of women emerged whose involvement in diaconal projects had inspired them to remain unmarried and continue this service as a career. Working with two women in the church in Giza, Father Salib Suryal (d. 1994) had cooperated with the future Pope Shenouda to formulate guidelines for women who wished to be officially recognized as unmarried servants of the church. In May 1960, the first house opened for *mukarassat,* who were addressed as *tasun* (sister).[13] Over time, the movement in Giza lost steam. Later, however, a small group of women in Beni Soueif under Bishop Athanasius developed the idea of the Banat Maryam, a community for consecrated women that opened in 1965. They also called themselves *tasun* and considered their center to be a convent for active nuns. The sisters started with a kindergarten and rapidly branched out into activities that were innovative for Egypt, serving groups that traditionally had been ignored. They launched mobile clinics serving the villages, opened schools and homes for the elderly and the mentally impaired, and established places of refuge for unwed mothers.

Pope Cyril had blessed these initiatives. However, Pope Shenouda was not happy with the Beni Soueif model (he considered it a Catholic innovation), and as a result he began prompting the Holy Synod to revise the system of initiation rites for female deacons. In 1981, the first official group of twenty-eight deaconesses was consecrated and a building on the premises of the Convent of St. Dimiana, supervised by the pope's right-hand man, Bishop Bishoi, became their national center. The rank of *mukarrasa* was designated as the preparatory stage to becoming a subdeaconess, which then led to the full rank of deaconess *(shammasa)*. To reach this full rank, a woman has to serve for an uninterrupted period of at least fifteen years. Because of this, a deaconess must be over forty years of age. Between 1992 and 1998 the Holy Synod refined the rules governing this vocation further, stressing that deaconesses could never serve at the altar or be consecrated by the laying on of hands.[14]

The Banat Maryam today continues to grow. Nowadays there are hundreds of *mukarrasat* working in various capacities alongside bishops and priests inside and outside of Egypt.[15] *Al-Kiraza* regularly reports on their work, including conferences and meetings with the pope. For example, conferences organized by Sister Rauth (who developed the school for the mentally handicapped in Beni Soueif) are mentioned regularly. After moving to Cairo, she became the director of the church's programs for the mentally and physically handicapped and was appointed to several governmental and international committees studying their condition.[16]

Youth

In each generation, high-school and university students constitute the future of the Coptic Church's leadership. In recognition of this fact, in 1980 Pope Shenouda ordained and appointed a special bishop for youth, Anba Musa, who occupies the only such position in the world. Young adults had long gravitated toward Shenouda, whose initial weekly lectures were aimed at them. By establishing the Bishopric of Youth, the pope hoped to channel their critical energies and supervise more closely the Bible-study groups and similar initiatives that sometimes developed without the oversight of local priests or bishops.[17]

Another pressing reason for creating this bishopric was that by the 1970s Christian university students had started to feel Islamist pressure on campuses. When tensions grew because of radical Muslim students who forced everybody on campus, including non-Muslims, to join daily prayers, the Christian students turned to the church for support. The church obliged and set up an alternative infrastructure for them. It has since built dorms for Coptic university students and organized activities such as summer camps, conferences, and sports tournaments.

Upon becoming bishop, Anba Musa, a medical doctor who himself had worked as a *khadim* (church servant) alongside Bishops Samuel and Athanasius, developed a host of programs that appealed to the interests of youth in different stages of their lives. Over the years, the bishopric has become a successful venue for recruiting future church leaders. Since 1995, volunteers have received special training in the Youth Servants Training Center that was launched to equip them with resources for theological and biblical study, as well as with knowledge about key social issues. In all areas of work Bishop Musa encourages them to practice "the four P's: Prayer, Preparation, Participation and Personal Touch."[18] In an article written in 2010, on the occasion of the thirtieth anniversary of Musa's ordination, Father Matthew Attia reported that the bishop's work had inspired the vocations of one bishop, three celibate priests, and over twenty-five deaconesses.[19]

Using various media—written publications, art, and the Internet—Anba Musa has aimed at binding youth to their family, to the church, and to Egypt.[20] Through its magazines, *The Message of the Church Youth* and *The Branches*, the bishopric has provided youth under twenty years of age with religious and social education. Articles explain Coptic doctrines and discuss issues of faith, but also address topics such as youth criminality, depression, drugs, dating, and the ethics of cloning. Apart from the many books, sermons, speeches, and articles by Bishop Musa himself, priests and volunteers working in youth ministry are encouraged to write books as well. Material for the educators and group leaders is published in a bimonthly magazine called *The Word*, and books with titles such as *200 Topics for Youth Meetings* and *Keys to Successful Youth Ministry* are bestsellers within the world of Coptic youth ministry.

The bishopric has also stimulated discussions about the role of Copts in civic society. The Coptic Center for Social Studies in particular has done pioneering work on citizenship. Connected with such scholarly platforms are interfaith activities. The bishopric organizes discussions with Muslim scholars and youth about challenges all young Egyptians face, such as difficulties in securing housing and the postponement of marriage for financial reasons. Bishop Musa considers having vigorous discussions with and about Muslims one of the bishopric's priorities. "We cannot wait passively," he says, "but have to reach out to our Muslim neighbors with Christian love. If we close ourselves off and withdraw from society, all will be lost."[21]

The work of this bishropic has also extended to the west. Two examples here will suffice. In Great Britain, Bishop Angaelos was appointed in 1999 as general bishop to Stevenage, Hertfordshire, with a special concentration on youth ministry. Born in Egypt, he grew up in Australia, which makes him a forerunner of a new generation of bishops raised outside of Egypt. In the United Kingdom, Angaelos established a national youth association and launched graduate conventions. In the United States, Bishop Serapion has started a Graduates and Young Professionals Committee in Los Angeles, California, an area with a large Coptic population and many university students. This committee organizes educational seminars, community service projects, and fellowship-building activities for young adults between the ages of twenty and thirty-five.

The anchor of the church's work with youth, however, remains the papal headquarters in Cairo. Once a year, the unity of all Copts is underscored when youth from Egypt and from the Coptic diaspora compete at the same time in a spiritual competition called Mahragan al-Kiraza. Over one million persons participate in seven age groups. Beginning in their local churches, and then progressing to the regional and national diocesan levels, the youth are tested (in Arabic or in English) on their knowledge of the Bible and church dogmatics.

One Church, Many Countries

The planting of churches in other lands has made Pope Shenouda the most well-traveled pope in Coptic history. Usually making one or two international pastoral visits every year, the pope has ordained priests in countries as far away as Pakistan, Bangladesh, and Japan. His first trip was to Libya in 1972, followed by a series of visits to Orthodox churches in countries such as Russia, Rumania, Armenia, Turkey, Syria, and Lebanon. In 1973, he was the first Coptic pope to travel to Rome where, in the ecumenical spirit of Vatican II, he met with Pope Paul VI (1963–78). In 1977, he went to North America for the first time, and then in 1979 he made a visit to Great Britain. In 1978 and 1979, he also visited Sudan and the Coptic mission churches in Kenya and the Congo.

At the same time, new churches were being consecrated. As of 2008, there were 450 expatriate churches on the roster, some of them with memberships of over two thousand families.[22] Although the precise numbers cannot be confirmed, according to current estimates more than one million Copts live outside Egypt.[23] When Shenouda became pope, there were three Coptic dioceses outside Egypt: one in Jerusalem and two in Sudan (Omdurman and Khartoum). Now there are bishops on five continents: in Brazil and Bolivia in South America, in several countries in Europe, in North America, in Australia, and in Africa.[24] Catering to the need for more acculturated priests, branches of the seminary in Cairo have been opened in Australia, North America, the United Kingdom, and Germany, and there are functioning monasteries in the United States, Australia, Germany, France, and Italy.[25]

Scholars researching the process of emigration/immigration have called it a "theologizing experience." The trauma of leaving their homeland draws people closer to their church as a center of communal and religious life. Communities of new immigrants go through stages of assimilation, with some transiting smoothly into the mainstream and others struggling with a conflicted sense of ethnic and national ties.[26] For Copts who have resettled in other places, the rise of a second generation abroad raises complex questions about how and what to teach the children, which languages to use, whether to endorse marriage to non-Copts, and how to adapt (or not) to the surrounding culture. With regard to the involvement of women and youth, expatriate Coptic communities face similar challenges, including the need to come to terms with new and different views on gender roles, hierarchy and authority, dress, and ethical values. For example, while women's voices are never heard in Coptic churches in Egypt, in the west there are mixed choirs that perform outside the official eucharistic service. Women head the Sunday-school programs and dress differently than they do in Egypt. Meanwhile, the Bishopric of Youth works overtime composing and translating booklets on social and sexual issues such as dating, premarital sex, and homosexuality. Yet, even as expatriate communities have adjusted (sometimes hesitantly) to their host cultures, they have made efforts to maintain close ties with the church leadership and culture in Egypt.

Immigrant Churches in North America

The first priest for North America, Wagdi Elias, was ordained in Egypt on August 9, 1964. Given the title of "Priest for the Altar of God at the Coptic Church in North America," he flew around the country, stopping in different areas to celebrate the Eucharist for communities of Coptic immigrants. The first officially consecrated church was established a year later in Toronto. The bylaws formulated at that time emphasize that the ultimate ecclesiastical authority belonged to the church in Egypt.[27] Elias, who became Father Morcos Morcos, was chosen for his education, his fluency in both Arabic and English, and his work experience. He had earned an MA degree in psychology of religion in the United States as well as a degree from the Coptic seminary. The choice of Father Morcos to occupy this role served as the model for Pope Shenouda's strategy of sending only priests with the highest credentials to communities overseas.[28]

From early on, Los Angeles has been home to a large and thriving Coptic population. Dr. Elhamy Khalil, a medical specialist and long-time church *khadim* who moved to the United States in 1959, has written about the earliest Coptic communities established in and around Los Angeles. He describes how the first immigrants set up the Coptic American Association and initially attended Syrian Orthodox churches.[29] A periodical published by the association kept Copts informed about the church in Egypt and bound all the North American Copts together in a sort of virtual community.[30]

The first priests in Los Angeles were the charismatic Father Bishoi Kamel and the scholar-priest Tadros Malaty. They purchased church buildings and attracted talented young people to church service; one of them was the future Father Antonious Henein, who in 1973 became the first permanent priest for the area. A survey of the priests who have worked in the Diocese of Los Angeles shows that nearly all had obtained advanced university degrees and were successful professionals before being ordained.[31] In 1995, when there were fifteen churches and nineteen priests in southern California, the pope decided it was time to form a diocese. During the installation ceremony of Bishop Serapion, the first and still-current bishop of this diocese, the service was held in both Arabic and English. In his speech the new bishop emphasized that his priorities were providing services to youth, supporting the nuclear family, and maintaining strong bonds with the church in Egypt.[32]

Missionary Churches in Sub-Saharan Africa

During Pope Shenouda's reign, the presence of the Coptic Church in Africa expanded considerably, with particular growth witnessed in sub-Saharan Africa, where churches were planted as a result of Coptic missionary activities. The training of Coptic missionaries for sub-Saharan Africa actually started in Ethiopia. After the Ethiopian Orthodox Church had become self-governing or autocephalous, the educational and clerical contacts between the Ethiopian and Coptic Churches needed to be reinterpreted. The Coptic Church workers started to assist the Ethiopian Church with educational and medical services. The first person to do this work was a young medical doctor who had grown up in the Sunday School Movement and been involved in the rural diaconate projects. He arrived in Addis Ababa on May 26, 1966, and stayed until 1975 when he was forced out by the revolution. During these years, this doctor—the future Bishop Antonios Morqos—acquired skills in translation, experience in acculturation, and a feel for local and national politics. He also broadened his network on the continent using the many relationships that Anba Samuel had developed, traveling to churches in Kenya, Zambia, and other African countries.

Upon his return to Egypt the young doctor entered the Baramus Monastery, where he was ordained Father Antonios al-Baramousy, and in January 1976 he was sent to Kenya, where a small Orthodox Christian movement had started spontaneously during the 1930s. A Methodist pastor hosted him during the first weeks.[33] Traveling from country to country, Father Antonius encountered numerous challenges, including incessant requests for money, threats of blackmail, and claims by several independent churches to be 'Coptic' or 'Orthodox' or both. In his memoirs he details a visit to a church with a leader who gave himself the title of "Holy Father" and who directed an all-day, Catholic-style service that involved beating drums and cymbals and dancing.[34] After the service, the Holy Father announced to Father Antonios that he was the patriarch of the Coptic Church in Kenya and all Africa and that even though his knowledge of doctrine might be lacking, it was based on the Holy Spirit.

Father Antonios' several decades of work marked the official start of the Coptic mission to sub-Saharan Africa, a mission now overseen by two bishops—Bishop Antonios Morqos in South and West Africa, and Bishop Boulos in East and Central Africa. Today there are over sixty churches, three monasteries, hospitals, vocational training centers, and schools in fourteen countries, and Coptic liturgies and prayers have been translated into several African languages. According to a rough estimate, the Coptic Church in Africa has nearly half a million members.[35] Since the Coptic presence is spread out over many countries, this number means that most of the churches are small. The work has been grueling and not many Egyptian priests have had the stamina to stay for long periods of time. As in the countries populated by Coptic immigrants, the church has encountered difficulties in making Coptic priests available in all locales. However, this missionary effort has received a boost as a result of Pope Shenouda's commitment to building up ecumenical relations in Africa and elsewhere.

Ecumenical Relations

Since his ordination as bishop, Pope Shenouda has worked to strengthen relationships with other denominations. The Coptic Church has become a full participatory member of the World Council of Churches, the Middle East Council of Churches, and the All Africa Council of Churches, and in 1989, Shenouda was elected one of the five presidents of the World Council Central Committee.

The Coptic presence in Africa and in the west generated the need for these contacts. Copts who immigrated to areas that had no Coptic church often attended services in one of the pre-Chalcedonian churches (the Syriac, Armenian, or Ethiopian churches), since these bodies are in full communion with the Copts. A point of disagreement arose in March 1998, however, when Pope Shenouda proposed joint representation of these churches at ecumenical consultations. The other churches balked. Some preferred to maintain their independent voice at such gatherings. In the case of the Syrian leadership, they were concerned about a prior agreement they had made with the Catholic Church concerning interchurch marriages, which authorized each of the partners to stay within his or her own communion.[36]

Discussions about the nature of Christ have been equally important in developing ecumenical relations with the Catholic Church. Just one month before his election in 1971, Shenouda had attended the Pro Oriente consultation between the Catholic and the Oriental Orthodox churches in Vienna, and at that meeting he had proposed that the historical Christological disagreement between the churches (dating to the Council of Chalcedon in 451) could be overcome by reliance on the teachings of Cyril of Alexandria, most notably Cyril's statement, "We believe that He was perfect in his Divinity and perfect in His Humanity and that his Divinity never departed from his Humanity, not even for a single instant nor a twinkle of an eye. His Humanity is one with his Divinity without co-mixing, without confusion, without division, without separation." In 1988, these suggestions resulted in an agreement about the nature of Christ. However, these theological discussions have more or less stalled and there still remain many subjects to be sorted out in this dialogue, such as the churches' differing views on the seven sacraments, the position of St. Mary, and eschatology.[37]

Consultations between the Coptic Church and the Chalcedonian Orthodox churches had started unofficially in Aarhus (1964) but became official in 1989 during a meeting held in the papal residence in the Monastery of St. Bishoi. A breakthrough was reached on the subject of Christology: the representatives agreed that there was, in fact, no real disagreement concerning the basic question, the doctrine of Christ's person. The divergence, as acknowledged earlier in Aarhus, lies only on the level of phraseology. Even though each side had its own preferred formula when speaking of one or two "natures," the underlying understanding of the Incarnation was the same.

During two follow-up meetings in Chambésy, Switzerland (in 1990 and 1993), this new understanding was reconfirmed and all parties involved proposed to lift the centuries-old mutual anathemas. However, in Russia and Greece, churches still find resistance from their members, who consider the Copts heretical. While efforts at rapprochement between the two Orthodox families continue, full communion has yet to be restored. Intensive inter-Orthodox consultations are ongoing, and their importance to Pope Shenouda has been confirmed by his several trips to Russia and Greece.

Until 1985, ecumenical relations with the Protestant churches mostly took place on the level of social-development initiatives, and Pope Shenouda did not see the need for meetings on Christology with Protestant churches. However, after he changed his mind about the issue, theological consultations (including one held in 1994) led to joint statements with the World Alliance of Reformed Churches and the Anglican Church. Contacts with these churches have become more vital now that there are Coptic churches in the west, where they have joined national councils of churches in the United States, Canada, and Australia. Furthermore, individual bishops have been instrumental in developing relationships with Protestant churches. For example, in order to find funding for the manifold social projects in his diocese, Bishop Athanasius of Beni Soueif maintained close contacts with German and Dutch Protestant churches. In addition, the Taizé-inspired Anaphora retreat center north of Cairo, built by Bishop Thomas of al-Qusiya and Meir, receives a steady stream of visiting groups from Scandinavian and other European churches.

Transnational Legal Debates: Marriage and Divorce

The recurring legal debates on marriage and divorce within Egypt have had consequences for ecumenical relations. Divorce has been the most pressing issue. In Egypt, the national courts continue to apply the family-law codes of the different religious communities, but in cases of mixed marriage (that is, the spouses belong to different churches), national Islamic-inspired law is applied. For example, if a Coptic spouse joins the Syrian or Armenian Orthodox Church, the national court will consider her or his case based on the shari'a law and grant a divorce on a legal basis not acknowledged by the Coptic Church. Copts who have emigrated and are obliged to follow the divorce laws of their new countries of residence follow the canon laws voluntarily. Thus, marriage and divorce serve as highly symbolic indicators of the church's sometimes conflicted relationship with other ecclesiastical and national cultures.[38]

Within the church, the grounds for dissolution of marriage have been cause for heated debate ever since the Majlis al-Milli created the 1938 code that established nine legitimate reasons for filing for divorce. In May 1945, Pope Macarius had argued that the only reason found in the Gospels for the dissolution of a marriage was adultery, and the Holy Synod had readily accepted this restriction. In 1962, Pope Cyril VI had confirmed that a second reason was if one of the spouses converted to another religion, and had instructed a committee, headed by then-Bishop Shenouda, to draft a new code according to biblical teaching. Shortly after his own enthronement, Shenouda not only confirmed this stance but also issued a decree prohibiting remarriage of anyone who had been divorced because of adultery.[39]

While such church rulings were strict, until the year 2000 the Islamic personal-status law applied in Egypt made it equally difficult for Muslim women to obtain a divorce. In 2000, a revised family law code granted a Muslim woman the right to apply for divorce via the so-called *khul'* option by which she forgoes her financial rights (including the return of her dowry). This new law also opened up avenues for Egyptian Christian women to file for divorce. A Coptic woman, by changing her denomination—for example, through conversion to the Syrian Church—could get her case heard according to the national law of the land, and thus she could apply for a divorce based on the Islamic personal-status law.[40] Pope Shenouda tried in vain to draft a reinterpretation of the personal-status law to close off such access to divorce. The state ignored his initiative, while the heads of other Christian communities feared that allowing divorce only in the case of adultery would drive their members to Islam.[41]

If obtaining a divorce in the Coptic Church is not easy, remarrying is even more difficult. On May 30, 2010, a furor erupted when the Egyptian Supreme Court ruled in favor of a divorced Copt who had sued the church for denying him the right to a second marriage in the church. Pope Shenouda was furious since, in his view, this ruling went against biblical teaching on second marriages. Only widowers and those who had obtained a divorce sanctioned by the church could remarry—that is, those who had not committed the adulterous act and were therefore the 'innocent' party. "Whoever gets a civil divorce is free to remarry but not in the Coptic Church," the pope maintained.[42] This stance on divorce, of course, was meant to apply to Copts outside Egypt as well. Coptic bishops and priests overseeing communities in other countries immediately discussed the issue with their congregations, underscoring that when Copts divorce and remarry (even for reasons of insanity or long-term absence), this can only be done outside the church and consequently one ceases to be a Copt. In such cases, one's legal status and religious identity come into conflict.

Keeping and Contesting the Faith

Shenouda's teachings on divorce and remarriage touch on the intersection of biblical interpretation and its application to the everyday life of the church. The foundations of his own distinctive theological perspective were laid while he was still teaching Sunday school, well before his election as pope. Many view his series of articles entitled *Intilaq al-ruh* (Release of the Spirit)—initially printed in the Sunday-school bulletin and later published as his first book in 1957—as his most important theological work. The book has been reprinted nine times and translated into several languages.

It is written in the tradition of Pope Cyril VI's teaching that God cannot be known except through prayer and contemplation. According to Shenouda, the human mind is prone to wrong judgments and unable "to comprehend or approach God on its own."[43] In his view, "Human wisdom even . . . made some people accept only what conforms to their views regarding the Bible and the Church laws and refuse whatever their intellect does not approve of."[44] In his theology, modernity and biblical criticism are considered dangerous—slippery slopes that guide the unsuspecting right into heresy. Casting himself as the guardian of the true faith, Pope Shenouda has battled theological viewpoints that differ from his own, including within his own community. While both of them wrote similar foundational works as early as the 1940s, Pope Shenouda's disagreement with Father Matta al-Miskin (1919–2006) extended to matters of theology and played out in public for the entire community to witness.

As mentioned earlier, al-Miskin was an avid reader of early church fathers such as Athanasius and Cyril of Alexandria. In their writings, al-Miskin rediscovered the notion of "deification," the idea that through Christ's Incarnation, humanity comes to participate in divine attributes.[45] For al-Miskin, this participation was embodied in monastic practices and in the liturgy.[46] For his part, Shenouda categorically rejected the idea that human beings can be endowed with divine properties, and in a series of seven articles, published in *al-Kiraza* over the course of 2003 and 2004, he refuted al-Miskin's teachings on this subject. In addition, he personally instructed students at the Coptic seminaries in Cairo and Alexandria about this deviation of the faith and encouraged Copts to destroy al-Miskin's books. After al-Miskin passed away on June 8, 2006, *al-Kiraza* published another series of seven articles against his teachings.[47] Shenouda's motives in attacking al-Miskin can be ascribed, in part, to awareness of the church's precarious position in a Muslim society, where the concept of human deification would ring as blasphemy.[48] Another reason for their disagreement lies in their very different ways of interpreting the Bible: while Shenouda focuses on biblical texts that emphasize human misery, al-Miskin prefers more the mystical stories in Scripture, such as the Transfiguration scene in Matthew 17:1–13, where Christ's human body was glorified and "shone like the sun before Peter, John, and James on the mount."[49]

Pope Shenouda's doctrinal feud with al-Miskin was not an isolated case. In fact, it sparked another internal debate soon afterward, this time with a former seminary professor, George Habib Bibawi. After Bibawi accused Shenouda of being ignorant of early church teachings and accused him of heresy, Bibawi was excommunicated by the Holy Synod on Wednesday,

February 21, 2007. The charges included "theological, dogmatic and ritual deviations that he published and misled others' thoughts with" and "his continual insisting on his errors and his movement among different doctrines."[50]

Neither did Shenouda shy away from polemical battles with Protestants, Jehovah's Witnesses, and Seventh-Day Adventists, whose views were regularly distributed through books, DVDs, and other media. In 1998, the Holy Synod's Educational Committee warned Copts against errant theological ideas and advised monthly meetings for priests and the examination of all religious books and movies circulating among the Coptic faithful.[51] Pope Shenouda himself wrote several volumes entitled *Comparative Theology* in an effort to refute "heretical teachings and contemporary theological errors." In conferences, articles, and books he has expanded his attacks on the "western specialization" of Biblical criticism, which is seen as simply another species of heresy.[52]

The cases of al-Miskin and Bibawi, and the effort to suppress non-Orthodox teachings, underscore an important part of Pope Shenouda's views regarding authority in the church. Viewing Protestant models of lay leadership as unacceptable, he has insisted that clergy be the ones to transmit Orthodox teachings, while laypeople are discouraged from "doing" theology. This has led to an intensive process of clericalization during his papacy: the laypeople most involved in official church activities are typically promoted to the clerical hierarchy, where they answer to the pope and his bishops more directly.

However, in a modern world filled with individuals wishing to exercise their autonomy and agency, Pope Shenouda's authority to deliver the final word on every aspect of Coptic life continues to be challenged on different fronts. During the 1990s, a monk called Abuna Daniel emerged as a popular preacher, attracting Christian and non-Christian youth to his often emotional revivals. This led to accusations of his being too "Protestant" and not complying with church doctrine. The case was made all the more controversial by the fact that Daniel was drawing in Muslim youth to hear his charismatic words. When the church excommunicated him, Abuna Daniel married and became a Protestant minister.

Another case is that of a rebellious deacon named Max Michel from Tanta in the Eygptian Delta. Max Michel went to Nebraska in the United States, where he somehow was ordained under a title that only Pope Shenouda should have been able to confer—"Archbishop for the Holy Synod for the Orthodox Church in Egypt and the Middle East." Endowed with a new name, Archbishop Maximos, the former deacon returned to Egypt. There he founded the Athanasius Association as a nongovernmental organization and opened a church of the same name in the area of Muqattam in Cairo. The church gained the approval of the Ministry of Interior, and de facto, Maximos oversaw a shadow Egyptian Orthodox church whose members were disgruntled Copts, many of whom were attracted by his more lenient stance on divorce. In 2006, he established a Holy Synod and ordained two bishops, who donned attire identical to that of Coptic Orthodox bishops.[53] Pope Shenouda raised a protest and requested that the government revoke their approval for this group, claiming that the creation of this association caused confusion among unwitting Copts. The fact that the Egyptian government was initially unwilling to honor the pope's request until he threatened to stage a protest reveals something about the complex cultural negotiations that help create and condition the power and legitimacy of the modern Coptic papacy.[54]

Marie Assaad, one of the lay pioneers of Coptic development work, once remarked that Pope Shenouda built "an empire, not just in Egypt but in the world."[55] In a May 2004 interview, Pope Shenouda himself highlighted the inner workings of this empire: "In Cairo alone, there are over thirty thousand Sunday-school teachers and we have pastoral care in every village and town." Over the course of his forty years in office, Pope Shenouda has reconsolidated the power and authority that most of his early-twentieth-century predecessors were forced to share with the laity. His autocratic rule is softened by a modicum of democracy—necessary in a community whose members have become as cosmopolitan as he is and who wish to exercise their individual rights. Despite his firm hand, he knows how to maintain the fine balance between imposing his rule and allowing the church's members to share in decision-making. For example, he will never simply impose his choice of bishop on a community, but allows congregations to air their opinions.[56]

At the same time, the power pendulum has started to swing back in the other direction. Influence is shifting to the periphery, where the pope's charisma is being transferred to new generations of priests, bishops, and laypeople. In part thanks to Shenouda's own work, the Coptic laity in the new millennium is showing marked assertiveness in matters of church life: well-equipped with biblical knowledge, their depth of service involvement would be the envy of other churches. With Shenouda at an advanced age, he and his church stand at the verge of another transition in papal leadership. Who will the 118th pope of Egypt be, and how will he meet the challenge of guiding a complex, multinational Coptic Orthodox Church into the coming decades of the twenty-first century? The answer to these questions rests with a new cadre of clerical, monastic, and lay leaders, who will continue to carry the church as they have during the past two centuries.

Works Cited

Primary Sources and Collections

Documents

National Archives in Cairo, *Dar al-Watha'iq al-Qawmiya* (DWQ)

Alexandria Shari'a Court Registers: 13
al-Salih Court Registers: 346
Bab 'Ali Shari'a Court Registers: 60
Dasht Boxes: 142, 144, 145, 293
Misr al-Qadima Court Registers: 98, 100
al-Qisma al-'Arabiya Court Registers: 45, 122, 123, 147
al-Qisma al-'Askariya Court Registers: 147

Coptic Patriarchate Archives

A3079 (28 Jumada al-Ula 927/1521)
D8, al-Salih Court (Rabi' al-Awwal 1146/August 1733)
D41, al-Salih Court (1 Muharram 1131/November 24, 1718)
D103, Bab 'Ali Court (28 Jumada al-Akhar 1146/December 6, 1733)
D189, Bab 'Ali Court (29 Jumada al-Ula 1181/October 23, 1767)
D216, al-Salih Court (8 Sha'ban 1133/June 3, 1721)
D217, al-Salih Court (13 Jumada al-Ula 1133/ March 12, 1721) b
D225, al-Qisma al-'Arabiya Court (7 Rabi' al-Akhar 1163/March 16, 1750)
D260, al-Salih Court (10 Shawwal 1192/November 1, 1778)
D286, Tulun Court (4 Muharram 1121/March 3, 1709)
D340, Babi Sa'dah wa-l-Kharq Court (1086/1675)
D331, al-Zahed Court (1206/1791)
D348, Qanatir al-Siba' Court (1186/1762)
D364, Qusun Court (12 Shawwal 1182/ February 19, 1769)
D397, Bab 'Ali Court (10 Rajab 1113/December 11, 1701)
D416, al-Salih Court (6 al-Hijja 970/July 27, 1563)

D466, Bab al-Sa'dah wa-l-Kharq Court (2 Dhu al-Hijja 1181/May 10, 1768)
D474, al-Zahid Court (Sha'ban 1178/January 1765)
G11, Bab 'Ali Court (26 Dhu al-Qa'da 1160/November 1747)
G278, Bab 'Ali Court (1077/1666)
G286, Bab 'Ali Court (14 Rajab 1116/12 November 1704)
G416, Bab al-Sha'riya Court (16 Dhu al-Hijja 1168/September 23, 1755)
G424, al-Salih Court (9 Rajab 981/December 1573)
G440 (9 Rabi' al-Awwal 925/1519)
M4, al-Salih Court (13 Ramadan 1191/15 October 1777)
S16, al-Salihiya al-Najmiya Court (15 Sha'ban 1165/28 June 1752)
S21, Bab 'Ali Court (25 Rajab 1133/22 May 1721)
U7 (15 Shawwal 1193/26 October 1779)
U22 (end of Safar 1195/Feburary 15, 1781)
Z25, Qanatir al-Siba' Court (14 Rabi' al-Thani 1192/August 13, 1770)
Z108, al-Salih Court (15 Safar 1165/January 3, 1752)
Z361, al-Salih Court (3 Safar 1141/September 8, 1728)
Z518, Bab al-Sha'riya Court (1 Muharram 1097/November 28, 1685)

Manuscripts

Bibliothèque Nationale de Strasbourg

MS 4314

Coptic Museum Library

MS 128/839 Liturgy, "Tarikh 'amal al-mayrun"
MS 220/155 Liturgy
MS 221/155B Liturgy
MS 222/155C Liturgy
MS 231/137 Liturgy

Coptic Patriarchate Library

MS 259/447 Theology, "Sermons and Message of Pope Butrus al-Gawli"
MS 291/301 Theology, "Kitab yahtawi mukatabat yahtaju ilayhum al-aba' al-batariqa wa-l-matarina wa-l-asaqifa"
MS 414/350 Theology
MS 434/377 Theology
MS 436/61 Theology
MS 437/77 Theology
MS 493/161 Theology
MS 512/134 Theology
MS 972/345 Theology, "Adraj al-baba Mark al-thamin"

MS 390/886 Liturgy
MS 68/94 Biblical
MS 70/118 Biblical
MS 74/174 Biblical
MS 76/77 Biblical
MS 82/7 Biblical
MS 85/140 Biblical
MS 79/124 Sacred

Other Primary Sources

Abna' al-Baba Kirullus al-Sadis, ed. *al-Baba Kirullus al-sadis tarikh . . . wa Amjad*. Cairo, 2002.

——. *Christian Behaviour According to the Saint Pope Kyrollos the Sixth*. Cairo, 2000.

——. *The Fruits of Love: The Saint Pope Kyrollos the Sixth*. Cairo, 1999.

——. *Jam'iyat al-ruh al-muqaddas*. Cairo, 1991.

——. *Service and Humility in the Life of the Saint Pope Kyrollos the Sixth*. Cairo, 1999.

Book of the Sinaksar [a collection of information on prophets, apostles, martyrs, and saints]. Vol. 2. Cairo: Maktabat al-Mahabba, 1972.

Convent of the Great Martyr St. Philopater Mercurius "Abu Seifein" for Nuns, ed. *Tamav Erene: The Jewel of Heaven and the Beacon of Monasticism*. Cairo: Convent of Abu al-Sayfayn, 2007.

Ibn Abu Surur al-Bakri, Muhammad. *al-Rawda al-manusa fi Misr al-mahrusa*. Edited by 'Abd al-Raziq 'Isa. Cairo: Maktabat al-Thaqafa al-Diniya, n.d.

Ibn al-'Assal. *al-Majmu' al-safawi*. Edited by Girgis Filuthaus 'Awad. Vols. 1 and 2. Cairo, n.d.

Ibn Idris al-Shafi'i, Muhammad. *al-Umm*. Edited by Muhammad Zahri al-Najjar. 2nd ed. Part 4. Beirut: Dar al-Ma'rifa, 1973.

Ibn Iyas. *Badai' al-zuhur fi waqa'i' al-duhur*. Edited by M. Mustafa. Vol. 5. Wiesbaden: Franz Steiner, 1931.

Ibn Kathir. *Tafsir al-Qur'an al-'azim*. Part 4. Lebanon: Dar al-Jil, 1990.

Ibn al-Muqafa', Sawiris. *Tarikh batariqat al-kanisa al-misriya*. Edited by Yassa 'Abd al-Massih and Aziz Suryal. Vol. 2. Cairo: Publications de la Société d'Archéologie Copte, 1959.

Ibn Qayyim al-Jawziya. *Ahkam ahl al-dhimma*. Edited by Subhi al-Salih. 1st ed. Damascus, 1961.

Ibn Taghribirdi. *al-Nujum al-zahira fi muluk Misr wa-l-Qahira*. Part 2. Cairo: Dar al-Kutub, n.d.

al-Jabarti, 'Abd al-Rahman. *'Aja'ib al-athar fi-l-tarajim wa-l-akhbar*. Vols. 1, 2, 4. Cairo: al-Anwar al-Muhamadiya Press, 1297/1897. Beirut: Dar al-Jil, n.d.

——. *Journal d'un notable du Caire durant l'expédition française 1798–1801*. Translation of *'Aja'ib al-athar fi-l-tarajim wa-l-akhbar*, translated by Joseph Cuoq. Paris: Albin Michel, 1979.

Khater, Anton, and O.H.E. Khs-Burmester, eds. and trans. *History of the Patriarchs of the Coptic Church of Alexandria (History of the Holy Church)*. Vol. 3, Part 3. Cairo: Publications de la Société d'archéologie copte, 1970.

al-Kiraza. Official magazine of the Coptic Patriarchate.

al-Miskin, Matta. *The Communion of Love*. New York: St. Vladimir's Seminary Press, 2004.

Mutraniya Beni Soueif, ed. *Bustan al-ruhban*. Beni Soueif, 1968.

al-Qalqashandi. *Subh al-a'asha fi sina'at al-insha*. Vol. 1. Cairo: Dar al-Kutub, 1978.

Qanun-name-i Misr. Translated by Ahmad Fu'ad Mitwalli. N.p., n.d.

St. Paul Monastery Manuscripts.

Secretary of the Holy Synod. *al-Qararat al-mujamma'iyat fi 'ahd sahib al-ghibta wa-l-qadasa al-baba Shenuda al-thalith (117)*. Cairo: Coptic Orthodox Patriarchate, 2001.

al-Sharanbalali, Hassan al-Wafa'i al-Hanafi. *al-Tahqiqat al-qudsiya wa-l-nafahat al-rahmaniya fi-l-rasa'il al-hasaniya*. Manuscript at Dar al-Kutub al-Masriya, Fiqh Hanafi Tala'at no. 622/microfilm 9222, folio 450 verso, 451 recto.

Shenouda III, Pope. *The Release of the Spirit*. Rockville, Md.: St. Mark's Orthodox Fellowship, 1990.

al-Tabari, Abu Ja'far Muhammad ibn Jarir. *Jami' al-bayan fi tafsir al-Qur'an*. Egypt: al-Maymaniya Press, n.d.

Secondary Sources

'Abd al-Fattah, Nabil, ed. *Tajrir al-halat al-diniya fi Misr*. Cairo: Al-Ahram Center for Political and Strategic Studies, 1995.

'Abd al-Ghani, Ahmad Shalabi. *'Awdat al-isharat fi man tawalla Misr al-Qahira min al-wuzara' wa-l-bashawat*. Edited by 'Abd al-Rahim 'Abd al-Rahman 'Abd al-Rahim. Cairo: al-Khangi Library, 1978.

'Abd al-Raziq, Ahmad. *al-Mar'a fi Misr al-mamlukiya*. Cairo: al-Hay'a al-Misriya al-'Amma li-l-Kitab, 1992.

Abu 'Abayd. *Kitab ahl-amwal*. Edited by Muhammad Hamid al-Fiqa. Cairo: 1353/1934–35.

Afifi, Muhammad. *al-Aqbat fi Misr fi-l-'asr al-'uthmani*. Cairo: al-Hay'a al-Misriya al-'Amma li-l-Kitab, 1992.

"Agreement on Interchurch Marriages between the Catholic Church and the Malankara Syrian Orthodox Church." Syrian Orthodox Resources. http://sor.cua.edu/Ecumenism/19940125SOCRCMarriageAgmt.html.

Amin, Muhammad Muhammad. *al-Awqaf wa-l-hayat al-ijtima'iya fi Misr*. 1st ed. Cairo: Dar al-Nahda al-'Arabiya, 1980.

Anderson, Benedict. *Imagined Communities: Reflections on the Origin and Spread of Nationalism*. 2nd ed. London: Verso, 1992.

Ansari, Hamied. "Sectarian Conflict in Egypt and the Political Expediency of Religion." *Middle East Journal* 38, no. 3 (Summer 1984): 397–418.

al-Antuni, Zakhariyyas. *al-Baba Kyrillos al-rabi' (Abu al-islah)*. Cairo: Dar al-Taba'a al-Qawmiya bi-l-Fajjala, 1994.

Armanios, Febe. *Coptic Christianity in Ottoman Egypt*. New York: Oxford University Press, 2011.

'Ashur, Sa'id. *al-Mujtama' al-misri fi salatin al-mamalik*. Cairo: Dar al-Nahda al-'Arabiya, 1987.

Assad, Maurice. *al-Anba Samu'il fi dhikrihi al-'ishrin (6 October 1981–2001)*. Cairo: Asdiqa' al-Anba Samu'il, 2001.

——. "Prägung der koptischen Identität." In *Koptisches Christentum*, edited by P. Verghese, 87–116. Stuttgart: Evangelisches Verlagswerk, 1973.

'Ata, Hanna Yusuf. *The Life of the Saint Pope Kyrollos the Sixth*. 2nd ed. Shobra, Cairo: The Sons of Pope Kyrollos VI, 2002.

'Ata, Hanna Yusuf, Rafa'il Ava Mina, and Rufa'il Subhi. *Mudhakkirat 'an hayat al-baba Kirullus al-sadis*. Cairo: Abna' al-Baba Kirullus al-Sadis, 1985.

Atiya, Aziz Suryal. *A History of Eastern Christianity*. London: Methuen, 1968.

——. *A History of Eastern Christianity*. 1968. Reprint, Millwood, N.Y: Kraus, 1980.

——, ed. *The Coptic Encyclopedia*. 8 vols. New York and Toronto: Macmillan Publishing Company, 1991.

Attia, Father Matthew. "Thirty Glorious Years. Anba Moussa, Bishop of Youth . . . The Three S's, Four P's, and the H Club." *Watani International* (May 23, 2010). http://youthbishopricsite.blogspot.com/2010/05/glorious-years30/html.

Ayalon, Ami. "Egypt's Coptic Pandora Box." In *Minorities and the State in the Arab World*, edited by O. Bengio and Ben-Dor, 53–73. Boulder, Colo: Lynne Rienner, 1999.

Baer, Gabriel. *A History of Landownership in Modern Egypt, 1800–1950*. London: Oxford University Press, 1962.

Bahr, Samira. "Coptic Congress of Asyut." In *The Coptic Encyclopedia*, edited by Aziz Suryal Atiya, vol. 2, 602. New York and Toronto: Macmillan Publishing Company, 1991.

Behrens-Abouseif, Doris. *Die Kopten in der ägyptischen Gesellschaft: von der Mitte der 19. Jahrhundert bis 1923*. Freiburg im Breisgau: Klaus Schwarz Verlag, 1972.

——. "Nationalist Party (Hizb al-Watani)." In *The Coptic Encyclopedia*, edited by Aziz Suryal Atiya, vol. 6, 1987–88. New York and Toronto: Macmillan Publishing Company, 1991.

Beldiceanu, Nicoara. "L'organisation de l'Empire ottoman." In *Histoire de l'Empire ottoman*, edited by Robert Mantran, 117–38. Paris: Fayard, 2003.

Beni Soueif Bishopric, ed. *al-Anba Athanasiyus, ayqunat hubb wa 'ata'*. Beni Soueif: Beni Soueif Bishopric, 2000.

Berger, Maurits. "Apostasy and Public Policy in Contemporary Egypt: An Evaluation of Recent Cases from Egypt's Highest Courts." *Human Rights Quarterly* 25 (2003): 720–40.

Bishoy, Metropolitan. "Revival of the Egyptian Church since the Middle of the Nineteenth Century." In *Christianity: A History in the Middle*

East, edited by Habib Badr, Suad Abou el-Rousse Slim, and Joseph Abou Nohra, 775–96. Beirut: Middle East Council of Churches, 2005.

Bosworth, C.E. "Christian and Jewish Religious Dignitaries in Mamluk Egypt and Syria: Qalqashandi's Information on Their Hierarchy, Titulature, and Appointment (II)." *International Journal of Middle East Studies* 3 (April 1972), 199–216.

Botiveau, Bernard. "The Law of the Nation-State and the Status of Non-Muslims in Egypt and Syria." In *Christian Communities in the Arab Middle East: The Challenge of the Future*, edited by Andrea Pacini, 111–27. Oxford: Clarendon Press, 1998.

Botros, Ghada. "Competing for the Future: Adaptation and the Accommodation of Difference in Coptic Immigrant Churches." PhD diss., University of Toronto, 2005.

——. "Religious Identity as an Historical Narrative: Coptic Orthodox Immigrant Churches and the Representation of History." *Journal of Historical Sociology* 19, no. 2 (June 2006): 174–201.

Brown, Peter. "The Rise and Function of the Holy Man in Late Antiquity." *Journal of Roman Studies* 61 (1971): 80–101.

Buri, V. "L'unione della Chiesa copta con Roma sotto Clemente VIII." *Orientalia Christiana* 23 (1931): 101–264.

Butcher, Edith. *The Story of the Church of Egypt*. Vol. 2. London: Smith, Elder and Co., 1897.

Carter, B.L. *The Copts in Egyptian Politics, 1918–1952*. London, Sydney, and Dover, New Hampshire: Croom Helm, 1986.

Chaillot, Christine. *The Coptic Orthodox Church: A Brief Introduction to Its Life and Spirituality*. Paris: Inter-Orthodox Dialogue, 2005.

"Chroniques." *Proche-Orient chrétien* 48, nos. 1–2 (1998): 381.

"Chroniques." *Proche-Orient chrétien* 54, nos. 1–2 (2004): 131–32.

"Chroniques des Pays." *Proche-Orient chrétien* 49, nos. 1–2 (1999): 168–69.

CIA Factbook. https://www.cia.gov/library/publications/the-world-factbook/geos/eg.html

Cole, Juan R.I. *Colonialism and Revolution in the Middle East: Social and Cultural Origins of Egypt's 'Urabi Movement*. Princeton, N.J.: Princeton University Press, 1993.

Coptic Catholic Patriarchate, ed. *History of the Coptic Catholic Church*. Cairo: Matba'at Sayidat al-Karmil, 2001.

Coptic Orthodox Church Network. "Commemorations for Mesra 1: The Departure of St. Kyrillos V (Cyril), 112th Pope of Alexandria." http://www.copticchurch.net/classes/synex.php?day=1&month=12

"Coptic Pope Rejects Egyptian Court Ruling on Remarriage of Divorcees." Assyrian International News Agency. http://www.aina.org/news/20100608192647.htm

Davis, Stephen J. *Coptic Christology in Practice: Incarnation and Divine Participation in Late Antique and Medieval Egypt*. Oxford: Oxford University Press, 2008.

——. *Early Coptic Papacy: The Egyptian Church and Its Leadership in Late Antiquity*. Cairo and New York: The American University in Cairo Press, 2004.

Dayr al-Qadis Anba Maqar, ed. *Abuna al-qummus Matta al-Miskin*. Dayr al-Qadis, 2006.

"Death of Pope Kirullos VI." http://www.youtube.com/watch?v=zdOUnbXgPak&feature=PlayList&p=F058CF13B38CE97B&playnext=1&playnext_from=PL&index=55.

al-Dimirdash, Ahmad. *al-Durra al-musana fi akhbar al-kinana*. Edited by Daniel Crecelius and 'Abd al-Wahhab Bakr. Cairo: Dar al-Zahra, 1992.

Duff Gordon, Lady Lucie. *Letters from Egypt (1862–1869)*. New York: Praeger, 1969.

The Earl of Cromer. *Modern Egypt*. Vol. 2. London: Macmillan, 1908.

Ehrlich, Haggai. "Identity and Church: Ethiopian–Egyptian Dialogue, 1924–1959." *International Journal of Middle Eastern Studies* 32, no. 1 (February 2000): 23–46.

Elaasar, Aladdin. *The Last Pharaoh: Mubarak and the Uncertain Future of Egypt in the Obama Age*. Missoula, Montana: Beacon Press, 2009.

Fahmy, Khaled. "The Era of Muhammad 'Ali Pasha, 1805–1848." In *Modern Egypt, from 1517 to the End of the Twentieth Century*, edited by M.W. Daly. Vol. 2 of *The Cambridge History of Egypt*. Cambridge, U.K.: Cambridge University Press, 1998, 139–79.

Farah, Nadia Ramsis. *Religious Strife in Egypt: Crisis and Ideological Conflict in the Seventies*. Montreux and New York: Gordon and Breach Science Publishers, 1986.

Faruqi, Suraya. "Ottoman Guilds in the Late Eighteenth Century: The Bursa Case." In *Making a Living in the Ottoman Lands 1480–1820*. Istanbul: Isis Press, 1995.

Fawzi, Mahmud. *al-Baba Shenuda wa tarikh al-kanisa al-qibtiya*. Cairo: Dar El-Nashr Hatier, 1992.

Gershoni, Israel, and James P. Jankowski. *Egypt, Islam and the Arabs: The Search for Egyptian Nationhood, 1900–1930*. New York: Oxford University Press, 1986.

Gran, Peter. *al-Judhur al-islamiya li-l rasmaliya, Misr 1760–1840.* Translated by Mahrus Suliman. Cairo: Supreme Council of Culture, 1993.

Gruber, Mark Francis. "Coping with God: Coptic Monasticism in Egyptian Culture." In *Between Desert and City: The Coptic Orthodox Church Today*, edited by Nelly van Doorn-Harder and Kari Vogt, 52–66. Oslo: Novus Forlag, 1997 and Portland, Ore.: Wipf and Stock Publishers, 2004.

———. "The Monastery as the Nexus of Coptic Cosmology." In *Between Desert and City: The Coptic Orthodox Church Today*, edited by Nelly van Doorn-Harder and Kari Vogt, 67–82. Oslo: Novus Forlag, 1997 and Portland, Ore.: Wipf and Stock Publishers, 2004.

Guirguis (Girgis), Magdi. "al-Adraj al-babawiya al-kanisa al-qibtiya dirasa wa nashr li adraj al-baba Dimitriyus." *al-Majalla al-tarikhiya al-misriya* 41 (2001–2002): 63–87.

———. *An Armenian Artist in Ottoman Egypt: Yuhanna al-Armani and His Coptic Icons.* Cairo and New York: American University in Cairo Press, 2008.

———. "The Financial Resources of Coptic Priests in Nineteenth-century Egypt." In *Money, Land and Trade: An Economic History of the Muslim Mediterranean*, edited by Nelly Hanna, 223–43. London: I.B. Tauris, 2002.

———. "Ibrahim al-Nasikh et la culture copte au XVIIIème siècle." In *Proceedings of the Seventh International Congress of Coptic Studies, Leiden, 27 August–2 September 2000*, edited by Mat Immerzel and Jacques Van Der Vliet. Louvain and Paris: Orientalia Lovaniensia Analecta 133 (collection), 2004.

———. "Idarat al-azamat fi tarikh al-qibt, namudhaj min al-qarn al-thamin 'ashar." *Annales islamologiques* 33 (1999): 45–59.

———. "Marginalization within the Coptic Community." In *The Marginalized and Society.* Annual Seminar of the American University in Cairo, Department of Arabic Studies, February 2003.

———. "Observations on the Churches and Monasteries of Fayoum during the Mamluk and Ottoman Periods." Paper delivered at the Second International Symposium on Monasticism in Egypt, "Monasticism in Fayoum," Fayoum, February 5–10, 2004.

———. *al-Qada' al-qibti fi Misr: dirasa tarikhiya.* Cairo: Mirit Publishing, 1999.

———. "al-Watha'iq al-mufrada al-mahfuzha bibatriarqiyat al-qibt al-urthuduks bi-l-Qahira." PhD diss., Cairo University, Beni Soueif Branch, 2004.

Habib el-Masri, Iris. *Qissat al-kanisa al-qibtiya.* Vol. 4. Alexandria: Maktabat Kanisat Mari Girgis, 1975.

———. *Qissat al-kanisa al-qibtiya.* Vols. 4, 5, 6. Cairo: Maktabat al-Mahabba, 1984–88.

——. *Qissat al-kanisa al-qibtiya*. Vol. 7. Cairo: Maktabat al-Mahabba, 1988.

——. *The Story of the Copts*. Cairo: Middle East Council of Churches, 1978.

Hamilton, Alastair. *The Copts and the West, 1439–1822: The European Discovery of the Egyptian Church*. Oxford and New York: Oxford University Press, 2006.

Hanna, Nelly. *Habiter au Caire: Les maisons moyennes et leurs habitants aux XVIIe et XVIIIe siècles*. Cairo: Institut français d'archéologie orientale, 1991.

——. *In Praise of Books: A Cultural History of Cairo's Middle Class, Sixteenth to Eighteenth Centuries*. Cairo: American University in Cairo Press, 2004.

Hasan, S.S. *Christians versus Muslims in Modern Egypt: The Century-long Struggle for Coptic Equality*. Oxford and New York: Oxford University Press, 2003.

Hathaway, Jane. *The Politics of Households in Ottoman Egypt*. Cambridge, U.K.: Cambridge University Press, 1997. Translated into Arabic by 'Abd al-Rahman al-Shaykh under the title *Siyasat al-zumar al-hakima fi Misr al-'uthmaniya*. Cairo: Supreme Council for Culture, 2003.

Heikal, Mohamed. *Autumn of Fury: The Assassination of Sadat*. London: Andre Deutsch, 1983.

Ibn Isma'il al-Nabulsi, 'Abd al-Ghani. *al-Haqiqa wa-l-majaz fi-l-rihla ila bilad al-sham wa-l-hijaz*. Cairo: al-Hay'a al-Misriya al-'Amma li-l-Kitab, 1986.

Ibn Khaldun Center for Development Studies. http://www.eicds.org/english/introduction/about.htm.

Ibrahim, Vivian. *The Copts of Egypt: Challenges of Modernisation and Identity*. London and New York: I.B. Tauris, 2010.

Immerzeel, Mat. "Coptic Icons: A Reader." *Egyptian-Netherlands Cooperation in Coptic Art Preservation*, Series 2 (1992): 1–14.

Iskarus, Tawfiq. *Nawabigh al-aqbat wa mashahirihim fi-l-qarn al-tasi' 'ashr*. Parts 1 and 2. Cairo: Tawfiq Press, 1910.

Isma'il, al-Bayumi. *al-Nuzum al-maliya fi Misr wa-l-sham zaman: al-salatin al-mamalik*. Cairo: al-Hay'a al-Misriya al-'Amma li-l-Kitab, 1998.

James, Laura M. *Nasser at War: Arab Images of the Enemy*. New York: Palgrave, Macmillan, 2006.

Jean-Marie, Détré. "Contribution à l'étude des relations du Patriarche Copte Jean XVII avec Rome de 1735 à 1738." *Studia Orientalia Christiana* 50 (1960): 123–69.

Kamil, Nabih, and Yuhanna Nasim. "Two Reports on Relations between the Coptic and the Roman Catholic Churches." *Annales islamologiques* 37 (2003): 55–68.

"El-Keraza in English." Coptic Papal Residence: His Holiness Pope Shenouda III. http://www.copticpope.org/modules.php?name=Sections&op=listarticles&secid=7.

Khalil, Elhamy. *The Making of a Diocese: The Early Years of the Coptic Orthodox Diocese of Los Angeles, Southern California, and Hawaii*. Los Angeles: The Coptic Orthodox Diocese, 2008.

el-Khawaga, Dina. "Le débat sur les Coptes: Le dit et le non-dit." *Egypte/Monde Arabe* 20 (4th trimester 1994): 67–90.

———. "The Laity at the Heart of the Coptic Clerical Reform." In *Between Desert and City: The Coptic Orthodox Church Today*, edited by Nelly van Doorn-Harder and Kari Vogt, 142–66. Oslo: Novus Forlag, 1997 and Portland,Ore.: Wipf and Stock Publishers, 2004.

———. "Political Dynamics of the Copts: Giving the Community an Active Role." In *Christian Communities in the Arab Middle East: The Challenge of the Future*, edited by Andrea Pacini, 172–90. Oxford: Clarendon Press, 1998.

———. "Le renouveau copte: La communauté comme acteur politique." PhD diss., Institut d'études politiques de Paris, 1993.

Lane, E.W. *Manners and Customs of the Modern Egyptians*. 1836. Reprint: Cairo: Livres de France, 1981.

Leeder, S.H. *Modern Sons of the Pharaohs*. Reprint: New York: Arno Press, 1973.

Makari, Peter E. *Conflict and Cooperation: Christian–Muslim Relations in Contemporary Egypt*. Syracuse, N.Y.: Syracuse University Press, 2007.

Makdisi, Ussama. "Reclaiming the Land of the Bible: Missionaries, Secularism, and Evangelical Modernity." *American Historical Review* 102 (1997): 680–713.

Malaty, Tadros Y. *Anba Abraam, the Friend of the Poor, 1829–1914*. Santa Monica, Calif.: St. Peter and St. Paul Coptic Orthodox Cathedral, 1995.

Markos, Bishop Antonius. *Come Across . . . and Help Us: The Story of the Coptic Orthodox Church in Africa in Our Present Time*. Part 1. Cairo: Bishopric for African Affairs, 1983.

Masson, Jacques. "La divinisation de l'homme: Les raisons de l'opposition de Shenouda III." *Proche-Orient chrétien* 57, nos. 3–4 (2007): 279–90.

———. "Histoire des causes du divorce dans la tradition canonique copte (des origins au XIIIe siècle)." *Studia Orientalia Christiana Collectanea* (1973): 183–293.

———. "La mission copte en Afrique du Nord." *Proche-Orient chrétien* 55 (2005): 294–308.

———. "Trente ans de règne de Shenouda III." *Proche-Orient chrétien* 51, nos. 3–4 (2001): 317–22.

Masters, Bruce A. *Christians and Jews in the Ottoman Arab World: The Roots of Sectarianism*. Cambridge, U.K.: Cambridge University Press, 2001.

Mataus, al-Anba. *Silsilat tarikh al-batariqa*. Part 5: From the 104th to the 111th Patriarch (1718–1906). 2nd printing. Dayr al-Suryan, 2001.

al-Mati'i, Lam'i. *Ha'ula'i al-rijal min al-aqbat*. Cairo: al-Anglo Bookshop, 1989.

McCallum, Fiona. "The Political Role of the Patriarch in the Contemporary Middle East." *Middle Eastern Studies* 43, no. 6 (November 2007): 923–40.

Medina, Sara, Robert C. Wurmstedt, and Nathaniel Harrison. "Religion: Egypt's Copts in Crisis." *Time*, September 28, 1981. http://www.time.com/time/magazine/article/0,9171,953135-1,00.html

Meeus, Peter. "Herleving Kopties Monnikendom." *Benedictijns Tijdschrift* 1 (1979): 2–20.

Meinardus, Otto F.A. *Christian Egypt, Ancient and Modern*. 2nd rev. ed. Cairo: American University in Cairo Press, 1977.

——. *Christian Egypt, Faith and Life*. Cairo: American University in Cairo Press, 1970.

——. *Christians in Egypt: Orthodox, Catholic, and Protestant Communities Past and Present*. Cairo: American University in Cairo Press, 2006.

——. *Monks and Monasteries of the Egyptian Deserts*. Cairo: American University in Cairo Press, 1961.

——. *Monks and Monasteries of the Egyptian Deserts*. Rev. ed. Cairo: American University in Cairo Press, 2002.

——. *Patriarchen unter Nasser und Sadat*. Hamburg: Deutsche Orient-Institut, 1998.

——. *Two Thousand Years of Coptic Christianity*. Cairo: American University in Cairo Press, 1999.

Mikhail, Kyriakos. *Copts and Moslems under British Control*. Port Washington, N.Y., and London: Kennikat Press, 1911.

Mitchell, Timothy. *Colonising Egypt*. Cambridge, U.K.: Cambridge University Press, 1988.

Moftah, Laurence. "The Coptic Philanthropic Society: Al-Jam'iyyat al-Khayriyyah al-Kibtiyyah Kubra, Founded in 1881, and the Moftah Family." Library of Congress website. http://memory.loc.gov/diglib/ihas/loc.natlib.ihas.200182366/default.html.

Moftah, Ragheb, Margit Toth, and Martha Roy. *The Coptic Orthodox Liturgy of St. Basil: With Complete Musical Transcription*. Cairo: The American University in Cairo Press, 1998.

Mostyn, Trevor. *Egypt's Belle Époque: Cairo and the Age of the Hedonists.* London and New York: Tauris Parke Paperbacks, 2006.

"Movies and Video Clips: Pope Kirellos VI." St. Takla Haymanout Coptic Orthodox Church. http://st-takla.org/Multimedia/09-Videos-Videohat-02-Coptic-Pope_Kyrillos_VI-Al-Baba-Kirellos-Al-Sades-01.html

Naguib, Saphinaz-Amal. "The Era of Martyrs: Texts and Contexts of Religious Memory." In *Between Desert and City: The Coptic Orthodox Church Today*, edited by Nelly van Doorn-Harder and Kari Vogt, 121–41. Oslo: Novus Forlag, 1997 and Portland, Ore.: Wipf and Stock Publishers, 2004.

Nakhla, Kamil Salih. *Silsilat tarikh al-babawat batariqat al-kanisa al-qibtiya.* Fascicles 4 and 5. Cairo: Dayr al-Suryan Publications, 1954.

Nasr, Amir. *Abuna Mina al-Baramusi al-mutawahhid.* Cairo, 1996.

——. *al-Musharaka al-wataniya al-aqbat fi-l-'asr al-hadith: 'ahd al-baba Kyrillos al-khamis.* Cairo: Usqufiya al-Shabab, 1998.

Oram, Elizabeth Edwards. "Constructing Modern Copts: The Production of Coptic Christian Identity in Contemporary Egypt." PhD diss., Princeton University, 2004.

Owen, Roger. "Egypt and Europe: From French Expedition to British Occupation." In *The Modern Middle East*, edited by Albert Hourani, Philip Khoury, and Mary Wilson, 111–23. London and New York: I.B. Tauris, 2005.

Partrick, Theodore H. *Traditional Egyptian Christianity: A History of the Coptic Orthodox Church.* Greensboro, North Carolina: Fisher Park Press, 1996.

Pennington, J.D. "The Copts in Modern Egypt." *Middle Eastern Studies* 18, no. 2 (April 1982): 158–79.

"Pope St. Kyrillos VI Receives the Relics of St. Mark." Pope St. Kyrillos VI Multimedia Web Gallery. http://www.zeitun-eg.org/stcyril6/

Qalada, William Suleiman. "Origins of the Principle of Citizenship in the Tradition of the Copts and the History of Their Country." In *Christianity: A History in the Middle East*, edited by Habib Badr, Suad Abou el-Rousse Slim, and Joseph Abou Nohra, 825–50. Beirut: Middle East Council of Churches, 2005.

Qassim, Qassim 'Abdu. *Ahl al-dhimma fi Misr fi-l-'usur al-wusta.* 2nd ed. Cairo: Dar al-Ma'arif, 1979.

——. *Dirasat fi tarikh Misr al-ijtima'i: 'asr salatin al-mamalik.* 2nd ed. Cairo: Dar al-Ma'arif, 1983.

Rabbath, Antoine. *Documents inédits pour servir à l'histoire du christianisme en Orient.* Vol. 1. Paris: AMS Press, 1910.

Ramzi, Muhammad. *al-Qamus al-jughrafi*. Vol. 2. Cairo: al-Hay'a al-Misriya al-'Amma li-l-Kitab, 1994.

Raymond, André. *Artisans et commerçants au Caire au XVIIIe siècle*. Damascus: Institut français de Damas, 1973.

——. "al-Misriyun wa-l-faransiyun fi-l-Qahira, 1789–1801." Translated by Bashir al-Siba'i. 1st ed. Cairo: 'Ayin for Humanitarian and Social Studies and Research, 2001.

——. "The Role of the Communities *(Tawa'if)* in the Administration of Cairo in the Ottoman Period." In *The State and Its Servants*, edited by Nelly Hanna, 32–43. Cairo: American University in Cairo Press, 1995.

Reedijk, Rachel. *Roots and Routes: Identity Construction and the Jewish-Christian-Muslim Dialogue*. Amsterdam and New York: Rodopi, 2010.

Reid, Donald Malcolm. *Whose Pharaohs? Archaeology, Museums, and Egyptian National Identity from Napoleon to World War I*. Berkeley, Los Angeles, and London: University of California Press, 2002.

Reiss, Wolfram. *Erneuerung in der Koptisch-Orthodoxen Kirche: Die Geschichte der koptisch-orthodoxen Sonntagsschulbewegung und die Aufnahme ihrer Reformansätze in den Erneuerungsbewegungen der Koptisch-Orthodoxen Kirche der Gegenwart*. Hamburg: Lit Verlag, 1998.

Rowe, Paul. "Building Coptic Civil Society: Christian Groups and the State in Mubarak's Egypt." *Middle Eastern Studies* 45, no. 1 (January 2009): 111–26.

Rubinson, Samuel. "Tradition and Renewal in Coptic Theology." In *Between Desert and City: The Coptic Orthodox Church Today*, edited by Nelly van Doorn-Harder and Kari Vogt, 35–51. Oslo: Novus Forlag, 1997 and Portland, Ore.: Wipf and Stock Publishers, 2004.

Rufayla, Ya'qub Nakhla. *Tarikh al-umma al-qibtiya*. 1898. Reprint: Cairo: Metropole Printing, 2000.

——. *Tarikh al-umma al-qibtiya*. 2nd ed. Cairo: St. Mark Foundation for Coptic History Studies, 2000.

Rustum, Rasmi 'Abd el-Malik, and Ishaq Ibrahim 'Agban. *al-Baba Shenuda al-thalith wa hisad al-sinin*. Cairo: Institute for Coptic Studies, 2003.

——. *Qadasa al-baba Shenuda al-thalith wa hisad al-sinin*. Vol. 2. Cairo: Institute for Coptic Studies, 2008.

Sabella, Bernard. "The Emigration of Christian Arabs: Dimensions and Causes of the Phenomenon." In *Christian Communities in the Arab Middle East: The Challenge of the Future*, edited by Andrea Pacini, 111–27. Oxford: Clarendon Press, 1998.

Salama, Magdi. *al-Baba Kyrillos al-sadis: rajul fawq al-kalimat*. Monastery of St. Mina, 1998.

Salib, al-Qummus Mikha'il Girgis. *al-Sijill al-tarikhi li-l-qadasat al-baba Shenuda al-thalith*. Vols. 1–11. Cairo and Damanhur: Maktabat Ra'is al-Mala'ika Mikha'il, 1995–2006.

Sedra, Paul. "Class Cleavage and Ethnic Conflict: Coptic Christian Communities in Modern Egyptian Politics." *Islam and Christian-Muslim Relations* 10, no. 2 (July 1999): 219–35.

——. "Ecclesiastical Warfare: Patriarch, Presbyterian, and Peasant in Nineteenth-century Asyut." http://opus.macmillan.yale.edu/workpaper/pdfs/MESV5-10.pdf

——. "John Lieder and His Mission in Egypt: The Evangelical Ethos at Work among the Nineteenth-century Copts." *Journal of Religious History* 28, no. 3 (October 2004): 219–39.

——. "Writing the History of the Modern Copts: From Victors and Symbols to Actors." *History Compass* 7, no. 3 (2009): 1049–63.

Seikaly, Samir. "Coptic Communal Reform: 1860–1914." *Middle Eastern Studies* 6 (1970): 247–74.

Seraphim, Abba, Metropolitan of Glastonbury. "The Renewal of Coptic Orthodoxy in the Twentieth Century." Lecture, Manchester Metropolitan University, May 30, 1995. *The Glastonbury Bulletin* no. 92 (March 1996).

Shafi'i, Sallam. *Ahl al-dhimma fi Misr fi-l-'asr al-fatimi al-awwal*. Cairo: al-Hay'a al-Misriya al-'Amma li-l-Kitab, 1995.

Shaham, Ron. "Communal Identity, Political Islam and Family Law: Copts and the Debate over the Grounds for Dissolution of Marriage in Twentieth-Century Egypt." *Islam and Christian–Muslim Relations* 21, no. 4 (2010): 409–22.

Sharkey, Heather J. *American Evangelicals in Egypt: Missionary Encounters in an Age of Empire*. Princeton, N.J.: Princeton University Press, 2008.

Sharubim, Mikhail. *al-Kafi fi tarikh Misr al-qadim wa-l-hadith*. Vol. 4. Cairo: al-Matba' al-Kubra al-Amiriya, 1898–1900.

Shenoda, Anthony. "Cultivating Mystery: Miracles and a Coptic Moral Imaginary." PhD diss., Harvard University, 2010.

Shoucri, Mounir. "Mark VIII." In *The Coptic Encyclopedia*, edited by Aziz Suryal Atiya, vol. 5, 1538. New York and Toronto: Macmillan Publishing Company, 1991.

——. "Peter VII." In *The Coptic Encyclopedia*, edited by Aziz Suryal Atiya, vol. 6, 1950–51. New York and Toronto: Macmillan Publishing Company, 1991.

Stene, Nora. "Into the Lands of Immigration." In *Between Desert and City: The Coptic Orthodox Church Today*, edited by Nelly van Doorn-Harder and Kari Vogt, 254–64. Oslo: Novus Forlag, 1997 and Portland, Ore.: Wipf and Stock Publishers, 2004.

Stern, S.M. *Fatimid Decrees: Original Documents from the Fatimid Chancery.* London: Faber and Faber, 1964.

Subhi, Magid. "Shakhsiyat min tarikhina: Fadl Allah al-Ibyari wa Fadl Allah al-Dimirdashi." *al-Karma al-jadida* 1 (2004): 164–70.

Suryal, Riyad. *al-Mujtama' al-qibti fi Misr fi-l-qarn 19.* Cairo: Maktabat al-Mahabba, 1981.

Swanson, Mark N. *The Coptic Papacy in Islamic Egypt.* Cairo and New York: American University in Cairo Press, 2010.

Tadros, Mariz. "The Non-Muslim 'Other': Gender and Contestation of Hierarchy of Rights." *Hawwa: Journal of Women of the Middle East and the Islamic World* 7, no. 2 (2009): 111–43.

——. "The Sectarian Incident That Won't Go Away." Middle East Report Online. http://www.merip.org/mero/mero030510.html (March 5, 2010).

——. "Vicissitudes in the Entente between the Coptic Orthodox Church and the State in Egypt (1952–2007)." *International Journal of Middle East Studies* 41 (2009): 269–87.

Toledano, Ehud. "Social and Economic Change in the Long Nineteenth Century." In *Modern Egypt, from 1517 to the End of the Twentieth Century*, ed. M.W. Daly. Vol. 2 of *The Cambridge History of Egypt.* Cambridge, U.K.: Cambridge University Press, 1998, 252–82.

Tritton, A.S. *Ahl al-dhimma fi al-islam.* Translation and commentary by Hassan Habashi. 3rd ed. Cairo: al-Hay'a al-Misriya al-'Amma li-l-Kitab, 1994.

Trossen, Jean-Pierre. "Les relations du patriarche copte Jean XVI avec Rome (1676–1718)." PhD diss., Luxembourg, 1948.

Valognes, J.-P. *Vie et mort des chrétiens d'Orient.* Mesnil-sur-l'Estrée: Fayard, 1994.

van Doorn-Harder, Pieternella (Nelly). *Contemporary Coptic Nuns.* Columbia: University of South Carolina Press, 1995.

——. "Discovering New Roles: Coptic Nuns and Church Revival." In *Between Desert and City: The Coptic Orthodox Church Today*, edited by Nelly van Doorn-Harder and Kari Vogt, 83–98. Oslo: Novus Forlag, 1997 and Portland, Ore.: Wipf and Stock Publishers, 2004.

——. "Kyrillos VI (1902–1971): Planner, Patriarch and Saint." In *Between Desert and City: The Coptic Orthodox Church Today*, edited by Nelly van Doorn-Harder and Kari Vogt, 230–42. Oslo: Novus Forlag, 1997 and Portland, ore.: Wipf and Stock Publishers, 2004.

——. "Practical and Mystical: Patriarch Kyrillos VI (1959–1971)." *Currents in Theology and Mission* 33, no. 3 (June 2006): 223–32.

van Doorn-Harder, Nelly, and Kari Vogt, eds. *Between Desert and City: The Coptic Orthodox Church Today*. Oslo: Novus Forlag, 1997 and Portland, Ore.: Wipf and Stock Publishers, 2004.

Vatin, Nicolas. "L'ascension des Ottomans (1415–1512)." In *Histoire de l'empire ottoman*, edited by Robert Mantran, 81–116. Paris: Fayard, 2003.

Veinstein, Gilles. "Les provinces balkaniques." In *Histoire de l'empire ottoman*, edited by Robert Mantran, 287–340. Paris: Fayard, 2003.

"Violence against Christians in Al Kosheh, Egypt." Islamic Studies in Christian Perspective. http://www.rim.org/muslim/egypt.htm

Voile, Brigitte. *Les Coptes d'Egypte sous Nasser: Sainteté, miracles, apparitions*. Paris: CNRS Editions, 2004.

Wakin, Edward. *A Lonely Minority: The Modern Story of Egypt's Copts*. New York: William Morrow and Company, 1963.

Waterworth, J., ed. and trans. *The Council of Trent: The Canons and Decrees of the Sacred Oecumenical Council of Trent*. London: Dolman, 1848.

Watson, Andrew. *The American Mission in Egypt 1854–1896*. Pittsburgh, Pa.: United Presbyterian Board of Publication, 1898.

Watson, John. "Abba Kyrillos, Patriarch and Solitary." *Coptic Church Review* 17, nos. 1 and 2 (1996): 3–48.

——. "Abouna Matta el-Miskin, Contemporary Desert Mystic." *Coptic Church Review* 27, nos. 3, 4 (Fall/Winter 2006): 66–92.

——. *Among the Copts*. Brighton and Portland: Sussex Academic Press, 2000.

Youth Bishopric website. http://www.youthbishopric.com

Yusab, Bishop of Fuwwa. "Tarikh al-aba' al-batariqa." Edited by Samu'il al-Suryani and Nabih Kamil, p. 205. Cairo, n.d.

Notes

Introduction to Part One: The Coptic Papacy under Ottoman Rule (1517–1798)

1. Anton Khater and O.H.E. Khs-Burmester, ed. and trans., *History of the Patriarchs of the Coptic Church of Alexandria* (Cairo: Société d'Archéologie Copte, 1970), vol. 3, part 3: 274–303.
2. Kamil Salih Nakhla, *Silsilat tarikh al-babawat: batariqat al-kanisa al-qibtiya*, iv (Cairo: Dayr al-Suryan Publications, 1954).
3. Ya'qub Nakhla Rufayla, *Tarikh al-umma al-qibtiya*, 2nd ed. (Cairo: St. Mark Foundation for Coptic History Studies, 2000).
4. Rufayla, *Tarikh* (2000), 244.
5. These are the dates for which I found related documents: 1508, 1512, 1514, 1522, 1523, 1526, 1543, 1546, 1548, 1555, 1557, and 1563.
6. Otto Meinardus, *Monks and Monasteries of the Egyptian Deserts*, rev. ed. (Cairo: The American University in Cairo Press, 2002), 13–14.
7. Perhaps the most widely circulated errors are the dates of the appointment and death of the patriarchs, and the unfortunate confusion created by the dating for these periods. A case in point is the information mentioned in the available lists of the patriarchs. Most lists indicate that pope number 99 died in 1629, and pope number 100 was appointed in 1630 or 1631. Both dates are wrong, as the decision to appoint Hegumen Tadrus (Pope Matthew II, number 100) as pope of the community of Jacobite Copts in Egypt was issued on 17 Muharram 1038 (September 16, 1628), which precedes the date on which pope number 99 died (Dar al-Watha'iq al-Qawmiya [DWQ] [Egyptian National Archives], Dasht Boxes, 145, p. 360).
8. The term *ahl al-dhimma*, often translated "protected people," is a broad term governed by specific criteria and denotes certain

categories of non-Muslims living in Islamic countries, but we shall use it to indicate the Coptic community.

9. I have dealt with this subject in detail in Magdi Guirguis, *al-Qada' al-qibti fi Misr, dirasa tarikhiya* (Cairo: Mirit Publishing, 1999).

10. *Tawqi'* means basically "the act of adding a note, or affixing a signature, emblem, or motto, at the foot of an official document." As S.M. Stern notes in *Fatimid Decrees, Original Documents from the Fatimid Chancery* (London: Faber and Faber, 1964), 127, the term *'alima* for "emblem, signature," was favored in the Muslim west and in Fatimid Egypt, whereas *tawqi'* was used farther east. Gradually, the use of *tawqi'* became generalized, and among its meanings there developed that of "a general administrative decree emanating from the sultan and requiring his signature and/or emblem." Al-Qalqashandi, *Subh al-a'asha fi sina'at al-insha'* (Cairo: Dar al-Kutub, 1978), 1:52, says that *tawqi'* originally meant the writing on a petition or on its back by the ruler or official to whom the petition has been addressed, but that in his own time, the masses of the people used *tawqi'* as a general term synonymous with *insha',* "the inditing of official correspondence." C.E. Bosworth, "Christian and Jewish Religious Dignitaries in Mamluk Egypt and Syria: Qalqashandi's Information on Their Hierarchy, Titulature, and Appointment (II)," *International Journal of Middle East Studies* 3 (April 1972): 199, fn 1.

11. "Kitab yahtawi mukatabat yahtaju ilayhum al-aba' al-batariqa wa-l-matarina wa-l-asaqifa" (Coptic Patriarchate Library, MS 291/301 Theology, folio 295 r).

12. al-Qalqashandi, *Subh*, 398–404.

13. Nicolas Vatin, "L'ascension des Ottoman (1415–1512)," in *Histoire de l'empire ottoman*, ed. Robert Mantran (Paris: Fayard, 1989), 88.

14. Gilles Veinstein, "Les provinces balkaniques," in *Histoire de l'empire ottoman*, ed. Robert Mantran (Paris: Fayard, 2003), 338.

15. *Qanun-name-i Misr*, trans. Ahmad Fu'ad Mitwalli (n.p., n.d.), 76.

16. Nicoara Beldiceanu, "L'organisation de l'empire ottoman," in *Histoire de l'empire ottoman*, ed. Robert Mantran (Paris: Fayard, 2003), 117.

17. Dar al-Watha'iq, Dasht, 145, p. 360, decree for appointment of Hegumen Tadrus (Pope Matthew II, number 100) as patriarch of the Jacobite Coptic community in Egypt on 17 Muharram 1038 (September 16, 1628).

18. André Raymond, "The Role of the Communities *(Tawa'if)* in the Administration of Cairo in the Ottoman Period," in *The State and Its Servants*, ed. Nelly Hanna (Cairo: The American University in Cairo Press, 1995), 33.

Chapter 1: Exercising Authority: Patriarchs and Public Policy

1. Coptic Patriarchate Library, MS 291/301 Theology, folio 133 r.
2. Coptic Patriarchate Library, MS 291/301 Theology, folio 296 r.–297 r. The following is a list of Egyptian Church bishops in 1509 under Pope John XIII, found in Manuscript 301 (Theology), Coptic Patriarchate Library in Cairo, and not included in the lists of Jacob Muyser.
    1. Anba Isaak (Isaac), archbishop of Ethiopia
    2. Anba Mark, resident bishop in Ethiopia
    3. Anba Ghrigurius (Gregory), bishop of Esna
    4. Anba Basilius (Basil), bishop of Qus and Niqada
    5. Anba Kyrillos (Cyril), bishop of Akhmim and Ibsay
    6. Anba Athnasius (Athanasius), bishop of Asyut
    7. Anba Gabriel, bishop of East al-Khusus
    8. Anba Mikha'il (Michael), bishop of Qisqam
    9. Anba Samwil (Samuel), bishop of al-Ashmunin (al-Urashi)
    10. Anba Mikha'il (Michael), bishop of al-Qays
    11. Anba Mikha'il (Michael), bishop of Atfih
    12. Anba Mikha'il (Michael), bishop of Fayyum
    13. Anba Filutaus (Philotheus), bishop of Mona al-Amir
    14. Anba Mark, bishop of Qalyub
    15. Anba Mataus (Matthew), bishop of Minyat Sard
    16. Anba Isaak (Isaac), bishop of Atrib
    17. Anba Gabriel, bishop of Sahrigt
    18. Anba Yusab, bishop of Samanud
    19. Anba Mikha'il (Michael), bishop of Dafra
    20. Anba John, bishop of Sandafa
    21. Anba Mikha'il (Michael) al-Qubrusi, archbishop of Cyprus, then Rhodes, then retired at present
    22. Anba Kiriakūs, archbishop of the Five Cities (Pentapolis), who presently resides in his monastery in Shayhat mountain, is now called Sawiris
3. Coptic Patriarchate Library, MS 291/301 Theology, folio 246 v.
4. This man reached a very high position at the beginning of the Ottoman period, causing a contemporary historian to marvel at his high standing, the great number of gifts he received at Easter 1522, and the great amounts of money he spent on banquets held on this occasion, to the extent that Khayir Bey, *malik al-umara'*, on his deathbed, urged the new ruler to take care of his children and of Sheikh Yunis. Ibn Iyas, *Badai' al-zuhur fi waqa'i' al-duhur*, ed. M. Mustafa (Wiesbaden: Franz Steiner, 1931), 5:448, 481.

5. Coptic Patriarchate Library, MS 291/301 Theology, folio 233 r. Samanud was one of the old cities in the province of Gharbiya, presently the principal city in the district of Samanud, governorate of Gharbiya: Muhammad Ramzi, *al-Qamus al-jughrafi* (Cairo: al-Hay'a al-Misriya al-'Amma li-l-Kitab, 1994), 2:71.
6. Coptic Patriarchate Library, MS 291/301 Theology, folio 268 r.–269 v. For the biblical quotation, see Mark 12:13–17; Matthew 22:15–22; Luke 20:20–26.
7. al-Qisma al-'Arabiya Court, *Sijill* 45, case 566, p. 398 (AH 1066). This obligation is also mentioned in the biography of Pope Mark al-Manfaluti (96th pope), as the sultan required him to collect the *jizya* of the Copts (Nakhla, *Silsilat*, 4:77).
8. Tukh al-Nasara, or Tukh Delka, presently in the Governorate of Munufiya.
9. Coptic Patriarchate Library, MS 291/301 Theology, folio 119 r. It should be pointed out that this kind of social punishment was meted out by Pope John XIII for prostitution and concubinage.
10. Guirguis, *al-Qada' al-qibti*, 12.
11. Tracing the effectiveness and feasibility of the penalties is fraught with many practical difficulties: the nature of the composition of Coptic sources does not reveal the people's reaction to the pope's decisions. They are mostly sources formulated by the church institution and therefore express its views, with no room for those of dissenters. We therefore had to trace reactions to church orders through other avenues and other sources whose composition and framework give room for the emergence of a different category of people. Fortunately, the registers of shari'a courts were the natural source in which to find such people, because their deviation from the church emanated from their resorting to the shari'a courts in matters of marriage and divorce. Magdi Guirguis, "Marginalization within the Coptic Community," in *The Marginalized and Society* (Annual Seminar of the American University in Cairo, Department of Arabic Studies, February 2003).
12. Sa'id 'Ashur, *al-Mujtama' al-misri fi salatin al-mamalik* (Cairo: Dar al-Nahda al-'Arabiya, 1987), 113, 139, 226–29; Ahmad 'Abd al-Raziq, *al-Mar'a fi Misr al-mamlukiya* (Cairo: al-Hay'a al-Misriya al-'Amma li-l-Kitab, 1992), 91–122. Both tracked down testimonials by contemporary historians.
13. al-Bayumi Isma'il, *al-Nuzum al-maliya fi Misr wa-l-sham: zaman al-salatin al-mamalik* (Cairo: al-Hay'a al-Misriya al-'Amma li-l-Kitab, 1998), 199–201.

14. Qassim 'Abdu Qassim, *Dirasat fi tarikh Misr al-ijtima'i, 'asr salatin al-mamalik*, 2nd ed. (Cairo: Dar al-Ma'arif, 1983), 139.
15. Qassim 'Abdu Qassim, *Ahl al-dhimma fi Misr fi-l-'usur al-wusta*, 2nd ed. (Cairo: Dar al-Ma'arif, 1979), 153.
16. Qassim, *Ahl al-dhimma*, 153.
17. Magdi Guirguis, "Observations on the Churches and Monasteries of Fayoum during the Mamluk and Ottoman Periods," paper delivered at the Second International Symposium on Monasticism in Egypt, "Monasticism in Fayoum," Fayoum, 5–10 February 2004.
18. Melkite (Greek Orthodox) laws prevent intermarriage between third-generation cousins: Ibn al-'Assal, *al-Majmu' al-safawi*, ed. Girgis Filuthaus 'Awad (Cairo, n.d.), 2:229. It appears that objectors were influenced by the views of the Melkites.
19. Coptic Patriarchate Library, MS 291/301 Theology, folio 197 r.–198 v.
20. Ibn al-'Assal, *al-Majmu' al-safawi*, 2:241.
21. Coptic Patriarchate Library, MS 291/301 Theology, folio 66 r.–68 v.
22. Coptic Patriarchate Library, MS 291/301 Theology, folio 66 r.–68 v.
23. Concubinage is the state in which a man cohabited with his slave girl, and if she became pregnant she was named as the mother of his child.
24. It appears that the Copts envied the Muslims their polygamy, divorce, and concubinage, and before long, after Copts had mixed with Muslims, the Copts also practiced polygamy during the rule of Caliph 'Abd al-Malik ibn Marwan. When the bishops forbade them, they complained to the wali against the bishops. Likewise, concubinage was a constant source of disturbance for the patriarchs; in fact, two of them lost their lives because of this problem. Pope Ibram ibn Zar'a (975–78) forbade concubinage that had spread among the Copts at the time. One of the Coptic notables would not comply, so the pope excommunicated him. It was said that this notable poisoned the pope. The same thing happened with Pope John (the 99th pope) (1619–29) at the hands of one of the notables of Abnub, while his predecessor, Pope Mark (the 98th pope, 1603–19), was sent to jail because he forbade the Copts of Lower Egypt to practice polygamy. Despite the efforts of the patriarchs in opposing these practices, witnesses point to their ongoing existence. Al-Jabarti mentions that the Copts practiced concubinage, and one of the estates brought before the patriarch in 1868 mentions among the legacy of the deceased "six slave girls, one of whom was the concubine of the deceased" (Guirguis, *al-Qada' al-qibti*, 61).

25. Coptic Patriarchate Library, MS 291/301 Theology, folio 22 r.
26. This phenomenon reappeared in the eighteenth century. However, this time the church was not able even to censure such behavior, because the Coptic notables were in control of all matters. We shall discuss this issue later when we come to the eighteenth century (see the section in chapter two entitled "Elections and the Erosion of Papal Authority").
27. Mentioned by Kamil Salih Nakhla, who quoted it from footnotes written on a manuscript by one of the monks at the Monastery of St. Anthony (*Silsila*, 4:70).
28. His official name is on many documents, such as Coptic Patriarchate Archives, D416, al-Salih Court (6 Dhu al-Hijja 970/July 27, 1563).
29. Coptic Patriarchate Archives, A3079 (28 Jumada al-Ula 927/1521).
30. There are four bishops by the name Mikha'il in the list of Pope John XIII, in the sees of Qisqam, al-Qays, Atfih, and Dafra, so we cannot determine the diocese of this bishop.
31. Coptic Patriarchate Archives, margin of document G 440 (17 Rabi' al-Awwal 925/1519).
32. Coptic Patriarchate Archives, G423 al-Salih court (9 Rajab 981/ December 1573).
33. Many researchers have been curious about non-Muslims—especially Christians—resorting to Islamic shari'a courts in matters of marriage and divorce. Many interpreted it as a desire by some Christians to solemnize their marriages before shari'a courts so as to benefit from the Islamic marriage contract as regards the right to divorce, and the possibility of adding certain conditions to the contract. The principal problem these researchers fall into is that they depend on references issued in the twentieth century to understand marriage legislation and apply them to the period under study; however, legislation governing divorce for the Copts during the sixteenth century was very flexible, and granted divorce even in cases of simple disputes between couples who refused to be reconciled. Thus there was no need to resort to shari'a courts to obtain a divorce; but they did resort to them for the purpose of bigamy, or for reasons that might prevent the marriage according to church canons, but which were not regarded as a hindrance to marriage by Islamic laws.
34. Here, I have depended on the records of the Court of Misr al-Qadima at Dar al-Watha'iq al-Qawmiya: after making a detailed account of marriages and related matters, I then studied specific cases of Copts.

35. J. Waterworth, ed. and trans., *The Council of Trent: The Canons and Decrees of the Sacred Oecumenical Council of Trent* (London: Dolman, 1848), 2.
36. Détré Jean-Marie, "Contribution à l'étude des relations du Patriarche Copte Jean XVII avec Rome de 1735 à 1738," *Studia Orientalia Christiana* 50 (1960): 132.
37. V. Buri, "L'unione della Chiesa copta con Roma sotto Clemente VIII," *Orientalia Christiana* 23 (1931): 101–264.
38. Antoine Rabbath, *Documents inédits pour servir à l'histoire du christianisme en Orient*, vol. 1 (Paris: AMS Press, 1910).
39. Jean-Pierre Trossen, "Les relations du patriarche copte Jean XVI avec Rome (1676–1718)" (PhD diss., Luxembourg, 1948).
40. Buri published many of these messages.
41. Message of Pope John XIV to Pope Gregory, Bibliothèque Nationale de Strasbourg, Ms. 4314, folio 12.
42. There are many differences between the Coptic and Catholic sources concerning this point.
43. Nakhla, *Silsila,* 4:79; *History of the Coptic Catholic Church*, ed. Coptic Catholic Patriarchate (Cairo: Matba'at Sayidat al-Karmil, 2001), 55.
44. The text of this agreement was edited in Buri, "L'unione," 147.
45. Bab 'Ali Court, 60, p. 209, case 826, 3 Safar 1003/October 18, 1594.
46. Bab 'Ali Court, 60, p. 209, case 826.
47. Alexandria Court, 13, p. 448, case 1068. Some sources claim that this dispute was followed by certain procedures that ended with the deposition of Pope Gabriel VIII. However, Cairo notables intervened and procured an order from the wali for his reinstatement (Nakhla, *Silsilat,* 4:85). There seems to be a mix-up between the biographies of this pope and Pope Mark V who succeeded him, because we have found no evidence regarding the deposition of Pope Gabriel. There were many intimations about this incident in the footnotes of Coptic manuscripts, but none mentioned the deposition of the patriarch.
48. Nabih Kamil and Yuhanna Nasim, "Two Reports on Relations between the Coptic and the Roman Catholic Churches," *Annales islamologiques* 37 (2003): 59–61.
49. Coptic Patriarchate Library, MS 301 Theology, folio 238 r.
50. Nakhla, *Silsila*, 4:85.
51. Coptic Patriarchate Library, MS 512/134 Theology, folio 218 r.
52. Yusab, Bishop of Fuwwa, "Tarikh al-aba' al-batariqa," ed. Samwil al-Suryani and Nabih Kamil (Cairo, n.d.), 205.

53. Footnotes of manuscript number 283 Arabic, National Library, Paris, ed. Magid Subhi, "Shakhsiyat min tarikhina: Fadlallah al-Ibyari wa Fadl Allah al-Dimirdashi," *al-Karma al-jadida* 1 (2004): 167.
54. Footnotes of manuscript number 283 Arabic, National Library, Paris, ed. Magid Subhi, "Shakhsiyat min tarikhina: Fadl Allah al-Ibyari wa Fadl Allah al-Dimirdashi," *al-Karma al-jadida* 1 (2004): 167.
55. Muhammad ibn Abu Surur al-Bakri, *al-Rawda al-manusa fi Misr al-mahrusa*, ed. 'Abd al-Raziq 'Isa (Cairo: Maktabat al-Thaqafa al-Diniya, undated), 112–16.
56. Edith Butcher, *The Story of the Church of Egypt* (London: Smith, Elder and Co., 1897), 2:270.
57. This opinion was also adopted by Muhammad Afifi, *al-Aqbat fi Misr fi-l-'asr al-'uthmani* (Cairo: al-Hay'a al-Misriya al-'Amma li-l-Kitab, 1992), 275.
58. Misr al-Qadima Court 98, case 444, p. 127 (22 Dhu al-Qa'da 1018/February 16, 1610); case 1095, p. 309 (18 Dhu al-Hijja 1019/March 3, 1611).
59. Misr al-Qadima Court 98, case 444, p. 127.
60. Misr al-Qadima Court 98, cases 1328, 1329, p. 368 (Jumada al-Ula 1020/July 1611).
61. Misr al-Qadima Court 98, cases 701, 702, 817 (28 Rabi' al-Thani–21 Jumada al-Thaniya 1019/July 20–September 10, 1610).
62. Misr al-Qadima Court 100, case 2205, p. 577 (20 Sha'ban 1021/October 16, 1612).
63. Misr al-Qadima Court 100, case 431, p. 45 (15 Jumada al-Ula 1026/July 20, 1617). The papers of the register are loose and therefore are not in chronological order, as page numbering took place during restoration of the registers.
64. Misr al-Qadima Court 100, case 431, p. 45.
65. Yusab, "Tarikh al-aba' al-batariqa," 206.
66. Dar al-Watha'iq, Dasht, 144, p. 155 (15 Jumada al-Ula 1035/February 12, 1626).
67. Dar al-Watha'iq, Dasht, 142, pp. 346–47 (Muharram 1034/October 1624). There are many other such examples.
68. For example, Dar al-Watha'iq, Dasht, 142 (Bab 'Ali Court, Cairo), p. 91 (6 Shawwal 1031/August 14, 1622).
69. Dar al-Watha'iq, Dasht, 145 (Bab 'Ali Court), p. 360 (17 Muharram 1038/September 16, 1628). This document reveals the errors in the date of the death of Pope John XV and the appointment of Pope Matthew III as shown in Coptic sources.
70. Nakhla, *Silsila*, 4:97.

Chapter 2: Contesting Authority: Patriarchs and Coptic Notables

1. Jane Hathaway, *The Politics of Households in Ottoman Egypt* (Cambridge, U.K.: Cambridge University Press, 1997), translated into Arabic by 'Abd al-Rahman al-Shaykh under the title *Siyasat al-zumar al-hakima fi Misr al-'uthmaniya* (Cairo: Supreme Council for Culture, 2003), 39.
2. Nelly Hanna, *Habiter au Caire: Les maisons moyennes et leurs habitants aux XVIIe et XVIIIe siècles* (Cairo: Institut français d'archéologie orientale, 1991), 15.
3. Hanna, *Habiter au Caire*, 17–18.
4. Suraya Faruqi, "Ottoman Guilds in the Late Eighteenth Century: The Bursa Case," in *Making a Living in the Ottoman Lands 1480–1820* (Istanbul: Isis Press, 1995), 95; André Raymond, *Artisans et commerçants au Caire au XVIIIe siècle* (Damascus: Institut français de Damas, 1973), 659–71.
5. Nakhla, *Silsila*, 4:107.
6. Yusab, "Tarikh al-aba' al-batariqa," 207.
7. al-Qisma al-'Arabiya Court 45, case 566, p. 398 (26 Rajab 1066/May 20, 1656).
8. al-Qisma al-'Arabiya Court 45, case 567, p. 399 (26 Rajab 1066/May 20, 1656).
9. Coptic Patriarchate Archives, D397, Bab al-'Ali Court (10 Rajab 1113/December 11, 1701).
10. Coptic Patriarchate Archives, D286, Tulun Court (4 Muharram 1121/March 3, 1709).
11. Coptic Patriarchate Archives, D216, al-Salih Court (8 Sha'ban 1133/June 3, 1721); D217, al-Salih Court (13 Jumada al-Ula 1133/March 12, 1721); D225, al-Qisma al-'Arabiya Court (7 Rabi' al-Akhar 1163/March 16, 1750); al-Qisma al-'Askariya Court, register 147, p. 86.
12. Coptic Patriarchate Archives, D8, al-Salih Court (Rabi' al-Awwal 1146/August 1733).
13. Coptic Patriarchate Archives, Z518, Bab al-Sha'riya Court (1 Muharram 1097/November 28, 1685); Ahmad al-Dimirdash, *al-Durra al-musana fi akhbar al-kinana*, ed. Daniel Crecelius and 'Abd al-Wahhab Bakr (Cairo: Dar al-Zahra, 1992), 62–63, 73, in which he mentions the important role of Yuhanna Abu Masri, *mubashir* for Ruznama.
14. Magdi Guirguis, "Idarat al-azamat fi tarikh al-qibt, namudha min al-qarn al-thamin 'ashar," *Annales islamologiques* 33 (1999): 45–59.

15. For more details of high-ranking posts of *arakhina* during the eighteenth century, see Guirguis, "Idarat al-azamat," 52–56.
16. Coptic Patriarchate Archives, G11, Bab 'Ali Court (26 Dhu al-Qa'da 1160/November 1747); D474, al-Zahed Court (Sha'ban 1178/January 1765).
17. Coptic Patriarchate Archives, Z361, al-Salih Court (3 Safar 1141/September 8, 1728).
18. Grand Sheikh of al-Azhar, 1137–71/1724–58.
19. 'Abd al-Rahman al-Jabarti, *Aja'ib al-athar fi-l-tarajim wa l-akhbar* (Cairo: al-Anwar al-Muhamadiya Press, 1297/1897), 2:133. I shall mention other examples when referring to the restoration and renovation of churches.
20. The system applied by the shari'a courts does not reveal the real value of inheritance components, as Copts, like the rest of the Egyptians, used various methods to conceal a large part of their inheritances from the eyes of the officers of Bayt al-Mal and other institutions. These offices investigated estates left with no heirs, those whose heirs were not entitled to the entire inheritance according to Islamic shari'a, or those with an heir who was still a minor. The large number of legacies left by Coptic *arakhina*, which we found in the al-Qisma al-'Arabiya Court registers, reveals the extent of their wealth.
21. Guirguis, "Idarat al-azamat," 48.
22. Nakhla, *Silsila*, 4:137.
23. Coptic Patriarchate Archives, Z518, Bab al-Sha'riya Court (1 Muharram 1097/November 28, 1685; G286, Bab 'Ali Court (14 Rajab 1116/November 12, 1704).
24. al-Dimirdash, *al-Durra al-musana*, 62–63, 73.
25. Nakhla, *Silsila*, 4:138.
26. Coptic Museum in Cairo, *Tarikh 'amal al-mayrun*, MS 128, Liturgy 839, 30 r.
27. Coptic Patriarchate Archives, D397, Bab 'Ali Court (10 Rajab 1113/December 11, 1701).
28. Coptic Patriarchate Archives, D41, al-Salih Court (1 Muharram 1131/November 24, 1718).
29. *Book of the Sinaksar* (a collection of information on prophets, apostles, martyrs, and saints) (Cairo: Maktabat al-Mahabba, 1972), 2:72.
30. Nakhla, *Silsila*, 5:10.
31. Coptic Patriarchate Archives, D103, Bab 'Ali Court (28 Jumada al-Akhar 1146/December 6, 1733).
32. St. Paul Monastery Library, MS 117 History, folio 143 r.

33. al-Qisma al-ʻAskariya Court, register 147, case 163, p. 142.
34. For details on his position and influence, see Guirguis, "Idarat al-azamat," 54.
35. Coptic Patriarchate Archives, G416, Bab al-Shaʻriya Court (16 Dhu al-Hijja 1168/September 23, 1755).
36. al-Qisma al-ʻArabiya Court, register 115, case 654, p. 350 (Rabiʻ al-Awwal 1173/19 November, 1759).
37. al-Jabarti, *Aja'ib al-athar,* 2:393–94.
38. This title was used by most of the Coptic sources I have consulted, but I have insisted on using the Coptic Synaxarion version, which is an official text recited during the liturgy. *Sinaksar*, 2:201.
39. al-Jabarti, *Aja'ib al-athar,* 4:180–81.
40. I have followed the selection of popes through biographies compiled by Nakhla, *Silsila,* 5. I believe it is the most accurate and dependable Coptic source available because of the author's wide knowledge, his meticulousness regarding dates, and his dependence on manuscripts of various monasteries, although I may have observations to offer concerning his interpretation of events.
41. Nakhla, *Silsila*, 4:106.
42. Nakhla, *Silsila*, 4:134.
43. Nakhla, *Silsila*, 5:6.
44. A case in point is the discussions that occurred regarding the unification of the Coptic Church and the Church of Rome, and how Pope John XIV (number 96 of the patriarchs, 1571–86) confined the discussion of this matter to the bishops alone.
45. St. Paul Monastery, MS 117, folio 27 r.
46. Magdi Guirguis, "The Financial Resources of Coptic Priests in Nineteenth-century Egypt," in *Money, Land and Trade: An Economic History of the Muslim Mediterranean*, ed. Nelly Hanna (London: I.B. Tauris, 2002), 223–43.
47. Tawfiq Iskarus, *Nawabigh al-aqbat wa mashahirihim fi-l-qarn al-tasiʻ ʻashr* (Cairo: Tawfiq Press, 1910), 1:263–64.
48. Ahmad Shalabi ʻAbd al-Ghani, *Awdat al-isharat fi man tawala Misr al-Qahira min al-wuzara wa-l-bashawat*, ed. ʻAbd al-Rahim ʻAbd al-Rahman ʻAbd al-Rahim (Cairo: al-Khangi Library, 1978), 590–91.
49. Coptic Patriarchate Library, MS 390, Liturgy/886, folio 191 v.
50. Coptic Patriarchate Library, MS 390, Liturgy/886, folio 192 r.
51. Coptic Patriarchate Library, "Adraj al-baba Mark al-thamin" (1796–1806), MS 972/345 Theology.
52. Coptic Patriarchate Library, "Adraj al-baba Mark al-thamin," folio 24 r.

53. Guirguis, *al-Qada' al-qibti*, 61–62.
54. See the section "Legislation and New Social Circumstances" at the beginning of chapter 1.
55. Sawiris ibn al-Muqafa', *Tarikh batariqat al-kanisa al-misriya*, ed. Yassa 'Abd al-Massih and Aziz Suryal (Cairo: Publications de la Société d'archéologie copte, 1959), 2:173.
56. Coptic Patriarchate Library, sermons and messages of Pope Butrus al-Gawli, MS 259, Theology/447, folio 10 r.
57. Nakhla, *Silsila,* 4:117.
58. Nakhla, *Silsila,* 4:135.
59. Nakhla, *Silsila*, 5:8.
60. 'Abd al-Ghani ibn Isma'il al-Nabulsi, *al-Haqiqa wa-l-majaz fi-l-rihla ila bilad al-sham wa-l-hijaz* (Cairo: al-Hay'a al-Misriya al-'Amma li-l-Kitab, 1986), 252. Laylat al-Qadr (Night of Power) is a night near the end of the fasting month of Ramadan when Muslims celebrate the revelation of the Qur'an.
61. Nakhla, *Silsila*, 4:153–54.
62. This is confirmed by the contracts concluded in Jerusalem by prominent notables now preserved in manuscripts of the Coptic Orthodox Patriarchate, by the honorary titles mentioned in the documents of the shari'a courts that were bestowed on the *mubashirin* in the eighteenth century and that refer to notables who made the pilgrimage to Jerusalem, as well as to Copts who died during the pilgrimage, and by the great number of icons in the churches that were brought back from Jerusalem by the pilgrims.
63. al-Jabarti, *Aja'ib al-athar*, 194; see also André Raymond, "al-Misriyun wa-l-faransiyun fi al-Qahira, 1789–1801," trans. Bashir al-Siba'i, 1st ed. (Cairo: 'Ayin for Humanitarian and Social Studies and Research, 2001), 57–58.
64. Coptic Patriarchate Library, MS 414/350 Theology, folio 212 v.
65. Al-Jabarti records the preparations made by Mu'allim Girgis al-Gawhari to travel with Sheikh al-Sharqawi to attend the *mawlid* of al-Sayyid al-Badawi in Tanta.
66. One church source declares that "throughout this period [the Copts] lived with their Muslim brethren on the best of terms, sharing with them their joys and sorrows" (Nakhla, *Silsila*, 5:21).
67. Many studies have dealt with this matter, including A.S. Tritton, *Ahl al-dhimma fi-l-islam*, trans. and commentary by Hassan Habashi, 3rd ed. (Cairo: al-Hay'a al-Misriya al-'Amma li-l-Kitab, 1994), 70; Qassim, *Ahl al-dhimma*; Afifi, *al-Aqbat fi Misr*, 54.

68. Ibn Taghribirdi (d. AH 874), *al-Nujum al-zahira fi muluk Misr wa-l-Qahira* (Cairo: Dar al-Kutub, n.d.), 2:66.
69. There is no denying that there were those who opposed church renovation and restoration, but the tide was against them and they could not stop it.
70. Nakhla, *Silsila*, 4:146–47.
71. Full details of the construction of the church and its consecration ceremony are recorded in MS 117 History, in the monastery library. The name of Mu'allim Girgis Yusuf al-Suruji and the date on which the church was built are inscribed on the door to the altar of the church. The church was named after the angel Michael and John the Baptist.
72. The name of Mu'allim Ibrahim al-Gawhari and the church's construction date are inscribed on the arch of its outer door.
73. To date we have been able to track down 842 *waqf* deeds from the eighteenth century in the patriarchate archives in Cairo, which cover all the churches and monasteries in Egypt.
74. Mu'allim Yuhanna Abu Masri restored the church of the Virgin in Harit Zuwayla, Mu'allim Girgis al-Tukhi the two churches of Mu'allaqa and the Virgin in Harit al-Rum; Nakhla, *Silsila*, 4:136–37.
75. Nakhla, *Silsila*, 5:10. Paid reconciliation was the order of the day during that period, not only with rulers but also with *faqih*s: to obtain a fatwa entitling someone to a certain right, or to change the gist of an adverse fatwa, was possible for anyone who could pay. Al-Jabarti cites many examples: *Aja'ib al-athar* (Beirut: Dar al-Jil, undated), 1:589–90; 2:46.
76. Coptic Patriarchate Archives, S21, Bab 'Ali Court (25 Rajab 1133/May 22, 1721).
77. Coptic Patriarchate Archives, S16, al-Salihiya al-Najmiya Court (15 Sha'ban 1165/June 28, 1752).
78. Coptic Patriarchate Archives, M4, al-Salih Court (13 Ramadan 1191/October 15, 1777).
79. Iskarus, *Nawabigh al-aqbat*, 1:332ff., where he mentions other examples of fatwas.
80. Coptic Patriarchate Archives, U7 (15 Shawwal 1193/October 26, 1779).
81. All *madhahib* (Islamic schools of law) imposed restrictions on *waqf*s established directly for churches, as they also restricted any apparent intent of the endower that contradicted Islamic shari'a, and there is no doubt that the teachings of Christianity fall within this sphere. All *faqih*s, without exception, approved *waqf*s endowed by Copts to

the poor from among their faith. Although it is well known that monks are Christians devoted to practicing their worship according to non-Islamic religious rites, monks have been accorded special appreciation in the Islamic heritage. This could be an extension of the affection they received from the Prophet Muhammad, as it is said that he gave to the monks from *sadaqat al-fitr*, which is purely Islamic money. Qur'an interpreters also tell the story of the origins of monasticism with great respect and appreciation, as related in verse 27 of Surat al-Hadid (57): "Then, We sent after them Our Messengers, and We sent 'Isa [Jesus], son of Maryam, and gave him the Injil [gospel]. And We placed in the hearts of those who followed him compassion and mercy. But monasticism they invented—We did not prescribe it for them—only seeking to please God, but they did not observe it with the right observance. So We gave those among them who believed their reward; but many of them are *fasiqun* [people who live evil lives]." The early interpreters claimed that "those who did not observe it with the right observance" came after those who "invented" it, and the fact that God says, "We gave those among them who believed their reward," is proof that there were among them those who rightly observed monasticism. As the monks lived in monasteries, the *faqih*s therefore saw no disgrace whatever in permitting *waqf*s to the isolated residents of monasteries. This tradition, understood to have been initiated by the Prophet, was emulated by the caliphs and other rulers. So we find that many rulers would endow *waqf*s (or, more accurately, make bequests) to monasteries. Because of this special treatment given to monasteries and their residents, the Copts called their other religious institutions 'monasteries.' So all churches came to be called 'monasteries,' even though they had no relationship whatsoever with the monastic institution in which monks live. The customary expression used in the Coptic *waqf* documents when mentioning the beneficiaries on which the *waqf* is bestowed became: "On the poor who visit, frequent and live in the monastery of . . ." This deliberate intermingling between the two terms 'monastery' and 'church' was clear to the judges and *faqih*s. It was even known that the expressions used in the *waqf* documents, describing those endowed as the isolated poor and the frequenters of those places, were a matter of formality not related to the actual situation. Muhammad Muhammad Amin, *al-Awqaf wa-l-hayat al-ijtima'iya fi Misr*, 1st ed. (Cairo: Dar al-Nahda al-'Arabiya, 1980), 30–31; Muhammad ibn Idris al-Shafi'i, *al-Umm*, ed.

Muhammad Zahri al-Najjar, 2nd ed. (Beirut: Dar al-Ma'rifa, 1973), 4:213; Abu 'Abayd, *Kitab al-amwal*, ed. Muhammad Hamid al-Fiqa (Cairo, 1353/1934–35), 613; Ibn Qayyim al-Jawziya, *Ahkam ahl al-dhimma*, ed. Subhi al-Salih, 1st ed. (Damascus, 1961), 302; Abu Ja'afar Muhammad ibn Jarir al-Tabari, *Jami' al-bayan fi tafsir al-Qur'an* (Egypt: al-Maymaniya Press, n.d.), 26:123–25; Ibn Kathir, *Tafsir al-Qur'an al-'azim* (Lebanon: Dar al-Jil, 1990), 4:316–17; Sallam Shafi'i, *Ahl al-dhimma fi Misr fi-l-'asr al-fatimi al-awwal* (Cairo: al-Hay'a al-Misriya al-'Amma li-l-Kitab, 1995), 98–99; Hassan al-Wafa'i al-Hanafi al-Sharanbalali, "al-tahqiqat al-qudsiya wa-l-nafahat al-rahmaniya fi-l-rasa'il al-hasaniya" (manuscript at Dar al-Kutub al-Masriya, *fiqh* Hanafi Tala'at no. 622/microfilm 9222, folio 450 v, 451 r).

82. Nakhla, *Silsila*, 4:136. This claim was mentioned in subsequent published studies.
83. Coptic Patriarchate Archives, G278, Bab 'Ali Court (1077/1666); D340, Babi Sa'dah wa-l-Kharq Court (1086/1675).
84. Coptic Patriarchate Archives, D384, Qanatir al-Seba' Court (1186/1762).
85. Coptic Patriarchate Archives, D331, al-Zahed Court (1206/1791).
86. See note 82 above. We have seen the difficulties involved in finding a way to allow endowments or *waqfs* for churches, so it is inconceivable that the endowers would be allowed to mention details about the activities for which the *waqf* was intended. The declared intent of the endower, which was drafted into the documents, could not contradict Islamic shari'a. This necessity in shari'a documents in Coptic *waqfs* deprives us of meaningful information about Coptic religious and educational institutions and the manner in which they were run. (In contrast, we are able to obtain much more information about Islamic institutions from these documents.) However, this does not mean that Coptic religious and educational institutions did not exist or that the endowers did not provide for them.
87. Nelly Hanna describes the book industry in Egypt in the Ottoman period and the popularity of reading among various social classes: Nelly Hanna, *In Praise of Books: A Cultural History of Cairo's Middle Class, Sixteenth to Eighteenth Centuries* (Cairo: American University in Cairo Press, 2004), 93–94.
88. This same percentage applies to manuscript catalogs of the Coptic Patriarchate Library in Cairo, the Coptic Museum Library in Cairo, and the library of St. Paul Monastery near the Red Sea.
89. Magdi Guirguis, "Ibrahim al-Nasikh et la culture copte au XVIIIème siècle," in *Proceedings of the Seventh International Congress of Coptic*

Studies, Leiden, 27 August–2 September 2000, ed. Mat Immerzel and Jacques Van Der Vliet (Louvain and Paris: Orientalia Lovaniensia Analecta 133 (collection), 2004), 939–52.

90. Iskarus, *Nawabigh al-aqbat*, 1:274–75. There is a copy in the Coptic Patriarchate Library, MS 436/61 Theology, and another copy, MS 437/77 Theology, which concludes with: "Taken from the Greek by Mus'ad Ikumunus of the See of St. Mark."

91. The Synaxarion book was translated from Amharic to Arabic in three volumes in 1734: Coptic Museum Library, MSS 220/155 Liturgy, 221/155B Liturgy, 222/155C Liturgy.

92. The book entitled *Manarit al-aqdas* was translated from the Syriac by a priest named Hindi at the request of Pope Mark VIII (1796–1809): Coptic Patriarchate Library, MS 434/337 Theology, as well as *Murshid al-kahin,* Coptic Patriarchate Library, MS 493/161 Theology.

93. I researched the inheritances of Coptic *arakhina* from the eighteenth century in the records of al-Qisma al-'Askariya Court in the National Archives in Cairo, and found no titles of the books left behind, so I was unable to assess the situation from court registers. This matter is related to the nature of work in Ottoman courts and the manner in which documents were created and registered. However, through her excellent study of the middle-class culture of Cairo in Ottoman Egypt, Nelly Hanna was able to track down and analyze inheritances containing books and came out with very informative results concerning the history of culture during that period: Hanna, *In Praise of Books*, 83–86.

94. Coptic Patriarchate Archives, U22 (end of Safar 1195/February 15, 1781).

95. Peter Gran, *al-Judhur al-islamiya li-l-ra'smaliya, Misr 1760–1840*, trans. Mahrus Suliman (Cairo: Supreme Council of Culture, 1993), 103.

96. For example, Coptic Patriarchate Library, MSS 68/94 Biblical, 74/147 Biblical, 76/77 Biblical, 85/140 Biblical.

97. For example, Coptic Patriarchate Library, MSS 70/118 Biblical, 79/124 Sacred, 82/7 Biblical.

98. Guirguis, "Ibrahim al-Nasikh."

99. Coptic Museum Library, MS 231/137 Liturgy (1758).

100. Mat Immerzeel, "Coptic Icons: A Reader," *Egyptian-Netherlands Cooperation in Coptic Art Preservation*, series 2 (1992): 10–14.

101. For a study of Yuhanna the Armenian and his works, see Magdi Guirguis, *An Armenian Artist in Ottoman Egypt: Yuhanna al-Armani and His Coptic Icons* (Cairo and New York: American University in Cairo Press, 2008).

102. Ibn al-'Assal, *al-Majmu' al-safawi*, 1:32.
103. Coptic Patriarchate Archives, D189, Bab 'Ali Court (29 Jumada al-Ula 1181/October 23, 1767); D466, Babi Sa'dah wa-l-Kharq Court (2 Dhu al-Hijja 1181/May 10, 1768).
104. Coptic Patriarchate Archives, D364, Qusun Court (12 Shawwal 1182/February 19, 1769).
105. Coptic Patriarchate Archives, D260, al-Salih Court (10 Shawwal 1192/November 1, 1778).
106. Coptic Patriarchate Archives, Z108, al-Salih Court (15 Safar 1165/January 3, 1752).
107. al-Qisma al-'Arabiya Court, register 123, p. 348 (12 Rabi' al-Awwal 1186/June 13, 1772).
108. al-Qisma al-'Arabiya Court, register 122, p. 361 (20 Rabi' al-Thani 1184/August 13, 1770).
109. For example, Dar al-Watha'iq al-Qawmiya, Dasht, 293, p. 53 (7 Sha'ban 1190/September 21, 1776).
110. Coptic Patriarchate Archives, Z25, Qanatir al-Seba' Court (14 Rabi' al-Thani 1192/May 12, 1778).
111. Court of Jami' al-Salih, register 346, case 1295, p. 528 (9 Rabi' al-Thani 1136/January 6, 1724).
112. On the relationship between the general public and the shari'a courts, and the Copts in particular, see Magdi Guirguis, "al-Qibt wa-l-mahakim al-islamiya," in "al-Watha'iq al-mufrada al-mahfuzha bi-batriarqiyat al-qibt al-orthudux bi-l-Qahira" (PhD diss., Cairo University, Beni Soueif Branch, 2004), 1–37.
113. Cited by Tawfiq Iskarus, *Nawabigh al-aqbat wa mashahirihim fi-l-qarn al-tasi' 'ashr* (Cairo: Tawfiq Press, 1910), 1:224.
114. Iskarus devoted 162 pages to the life of Ibrahim al-Gawhari in *Nawabigh al-aqbat* (1:206–367), which is a comprehensive biography compiled from various archives.
115. Iskarus, *Nawabigh al-aqbat*. It is worth mentioning that this historian was very knowledgeable: he had a prominent position in the Khedival Kutubkhana (library) and was the first to use the patriarchal archives for purposes of dating.
116. Iskarus, part 2.
117. See note 118.
118. Nineteenth-century documents related to the management of church affairs reveal the presence of bishops and certain priests in Cairo as legal representatives of the church, whereas such details are rarely found in similar eighteenth-century documents.

Introduction to Part Two: The Modern Coptic Papacy (1798–2010)

1. The number of Copts is disputed and estimates range from 6 percent to 20 percent. The number given here relies on the entry about Egypt in the *CIA Factbook*, https://www.cia.gov/library/publications/the-world-factbook/geos/eg.html
2. *al-Kiraza* 12, no. 41 (2001).
3. J.-P. Valognes, *Vie et mort des chrétiens d'Orient* (Mesnil-sur-l'Estrée: Fayard, 1994), 533–34.
4. Ehud Toledano, "Social and Economic Change in the Long Nineteenth Century," in *Modern Egypt, from 1517 to the End of the Twentieth Century*, ed. M.W. Daly, vol. 2 of *The Cambridge History of Egypt* (Cambridge, U.K.: Cambridge University Press, 1998), 255.
5. Although biased against the Coptic Church and pope, Andrew Watson, *The American Mission in Egypt 1854–1896* (Pittsburgh, Pa.: United Presbyterian Board of Publication, 1898) provides interesting details about the reign of Pope Demetrius II.
6. Al-Jabarti made different versions of his work on the French occupation. His magnum opus, entitled *'Aja'ib al-athar fi-l-tarajim wa-l-akhbar,* covers Egypt's history between 1688 and 1821. I have used the French edition that covers Napoleon's occupation: 'Abd-al-Rahman al-Jabarti, *Journal d'un notable du Caire durant l'expédition française 1798–1801,* trans. Joseph Cuoq (Paris: Albin Michel, 1979).
7. Doris Behrens-Abouseif, *Die Kopten in der ägyptischen Gesellschaft–von der Mitte der 19. Jahrhundert bis 1923* (Freiburg im Breisgau: Klaus Schwarz Verlag, 1972).
8. Iris Habib al-Masri, *Qissat al-kanisa al-qibtiya* (Cairo: Maktabat al-Mahabba, 1984–88).
9. Paul Sedra, "Class Cleavage and Ethnic Conflict: Coptic Christian Communities in Modern Egyptian Politics," *Islam and Christian-Muslim Relations* 10, no. 2 (July 1999): 219–35; "Ecclesiastical Warfare: Patriarch, Presbyterian, and Peasant in Nineteenth-century Asyut," http:opus.macmillan.yale.edu/workpaper/pdfs/MESV5-10.pdf; "John Lieder and His Mission in Egypt: The Evangelical Ethos at Work among the Nineteenth-century Copts," *Journal of Religious History* 28, no. 3 (October 2004): 219–39; "Writing the History of the Modern Copts: From Victors and Symbols to Actors," *History Compass* 7, no. 3 (2009): 1049–63.
10. Samir Seikaly, "Coptic Communal Reform: 1860–1914," *Middle Eastern Studies* 6 (1970): 247–74.

11. The decisions during Shenouda's papacy have been systematically published: Secretary of the Holy Synod, *al-Qararat al-mujammaʿiyat fi ʿahd sahib al-ghibta wa-l-qadasa al-baba Shenuda al-thalith (117)* (Cairo: Coptic Orthodox Patriarchate, 2001).
12. Vivian Ibrahim, *The Copts of Egypt: Challenges of Modernisation and Identity* (London and New York: I.B. Tauris, 2010).
13. Wolfram Reiss, *Erneuerung in der Koptisch-Orthodoxen Kirche: Die Geschichte der koptisch-orthodoxen Sonntagsschulbewegung und die Aufnahme ihrer Reformansätze in den Erneuerungsbewegungen der Koptisch-Orthodoxen Kirche der Gegenwart* (Hamburg: Lit Verlag, 1998).
14. Mariz Tadros, "Vicissitudes in the Entente between the Coptic Orthodox Church and the State in Egypt (1952–2007)," *International Journal of Middle East Studies* 41 (2009): 269–87; "The Sectarian Incident that Won't Go Away," http://www.merip.org/mero/mero030510.html (March 5, 2010); and Anthony Shenoda, "Cultivating Mystery: Miracles and a Coptic Moral Imaginary" (PhD diss., Harvard University, 2010).
15. Brigitte Voile, *Les Coptes d'Egypte sous Nasser: Sainteté, miracles, apparitions* (Paris: CNRS Editions, 2004).
16. Among others: Dina el-Khawaga, "Le renouveau copte: La communauté comme acteur politique" (PhD diss., Institut d'études politiques de Paris, 1993); S.S. Hasan, *Christians versus Muslims in Modern Egypt: The Century-long Struggle for Coptic Equality* (Oxford and New York: Oxford University Press, 2003); and John Watson, *Among the Copts* (Brighton and Portland: Sussex Academic Press, 2000).

Chapter 3: Preparing for Reformation

1. Behrens-Abouseif, *Die Kopten*, 10.
2. Fred Lawson, "Egypt's Forgotten Revolution," *Al-Ahram Weekly*, no. 762 (September 29–October 5, 2005, http://weekly.ahram.org.eg/2005/750/special.htm).
3. al-Jabarti, *Journal,* 21.
4. al-Jabarti, *Journal,* 21.
5. Yaʿqub Nakhla Rufayla, *Tarikh al-umma al-qibtiya* (1898; repr., Cairo: Metropole Printing, 2000), 281.
6. Theodore H. Partrick, *Traditional Egyptian Christianity: A History of the Coptic Orthodox Church* (Greensboro, North Carolina: Fisher Park Press, 1996), 123. About Napoleon's attitude toward the Christians, see, among others, the description in Trevor Mostyn, *Egypt's Belle*

Époque: Cairo and the Age of the Hedonists (London and New York: Tauris Parke Paperbacks, 2006), 17.

7. For examples of the chaos, see Khaled Fahmy, "The Era of Muhammad 'Ali Pasha, 1805–1848," in *Modern Egypt, from 1517 to the End of the Twentieth Century*, ed. M.W. Daly, vol. 2 of *The Cambridge History of Egypt* (Cambridge, U.K.: Cambridge University Press, 1998), 140–41.
8. Butcher, *The Story of the Church of Egypt*, 2:398. The burning of the *mayrun* is mentioned in al-Anba Mataus, *Silsilat tarikh al-batariqa*, Part 5: From the 104th to the 111th Patriarch (1718–1906), 2nd printing (Dayr al-Suryan, 2001), 59.
9. Iris Habib al-Masri, *The Story of the Copts* (Cairo: Middle East Council of Churches, 1978), 499.
10. Habib al-Masri, *The Story of the Copts*, 497. Also see the entry "Mark VIII" by Mounir Shoucri in *The Coptic Encyclopedia*, 5:1538.
11. al-Anba Mataus, *Silsilat tarikh*, 61–62. Bible translation from the Revised Standard Version, 1953.
12. Febe Armanios, *Coptic Christianity in Ottoman Egypt* (New York: Oxford University Press, 2011), ch. 6, "Weapons of the Faithful: The Coptic Retort to Catholics and Muslims."
13. Armanios, *Coptic Christianity*, 138–41. Armanios provides examples of sermons by Pope John XVIII that specifically address the drinking habits of priests.
14. al-Jabarti, *Journal*, 178–79.
15. Armanios, *Coptic Christianity*, 131. Bishop Yusab's sermons have been saved in a collection called *Silat al-Mu'minin*, which circulated widely throughout Egypt and of which several copies still exist in Egypt and in Paris.
16. al-Anba Mataus, *Silsilat tarikh*, 63–64.
17. Habib al-Masri, *The Story of the Copts*, 499–500, and Partrick, *Traditional Egyptian Christianity*, 122.
18. Habib al-Masri, *The Story of the Copts*, 501–502, and Aziz Suryal Atiya, *A History of Eastern Christianity* (London: Methuen, 1968), 101–103.
19. Habib al-Masri, *The Story of the Copts*, 501.
20. Roger Owen, "Muhammad Ali: A View from the New World," *Al-Ahram Weekly*, no. 750 (July 7–13, 2005), http://weekly.ahram.org.eg/2005/750/special.htm
21. Roger Owen, "Egypt and Europe: From French Expedition to British Occupation," in *The Modern Middle East*, ed. Albert Hourani, Philip Khoury, and Mary Wilson (London and New York: I.B. Tauris, 2005), 114, 115.

22. Mostyn, *Egypt's Belle Époque*, 25.
23. Owen, "Egypt and Europe," 118.
24. Magdi Guirguis, "Restructuring Egyptian Society," *Al-Ahram Weekly*, no. 760 (September 15–21, 2005), http://weekly.ahram.org.eg/2005/760/special.htm
25. Partrick, *Traditional Egyptian Christianity*, 127.
26. al-Jabarti, quoted in Guirguis, "Restructuring Egyptian Society."
27. Guirguis, "Restructuring Egyptian Society."
28. For example, see al-Anba Mataus, *Silsilat tarikh*, 92.
29. al-Anba Mataus, *Silsilat tarikh*, 81.
30. Riyad Suryal, *al-Mujtama' al-qibti fi Misr fi-l-qarn 19* (Cairo: Maktabat al-Mahabba, 1981), 22.
31. al-Anba Mataus, *Silsilat tarikh*, 99.
32. al-Anba Mataus, *Silsilat tarikh*, 98.
33. Mounir Shoucri, "Peter VII," *The Coptic Encyclopedia,* 6:1950–51.
34. See, for example, ch. 3, on theological controversies, in vol. 1 of this series: Stephen J. Davis, *The Early Coptic Papacy: The Egyptian Church and Its Leadership in Late Antiquity* (Cairo and New York: American University in Cairo Press, 2004).
35. Habib al-Masri, *The Story of the Copts*, 509–10.
36. Suryal, *al-Mujtama' al-qibti*, 22.
37. al-Anba Mataus, *Silsilat tarikh*, 97–98.
38. al-Anba Mataus, *Silsilat tarikh*, 92–93; Habib al-Masri, *The Story of the Copts*, 509.
39. al-Anba Mataus, *Silsilat tarikh*, 87–89; Habib al-Masri, *The Story of the Copts*, 509.
40. Alastair Hamilton, *The Copts and the West, 1439–1822: The European Discovery of the Egyptian Church* (Oxford and New York: Oxford University Press, 2006); see ch. 4, "The First Jesuit Mission," 58–73.
41. al-Anba Mataus, *Silsilat tarikh*, 87.
42. Sedra, "John Lieder," 223.
43. Partrick, *Traditional Egyptian Christianity*, 125.
44. A summary of the first missionary activities can be found in Partrick, *Traditional Egyptian Christianity*, 125–26; and in Reiss, *Erneuerung*, 19–20.
45. Sedra, "John Lieder," 222, 226; the latter part of the quote is in reference to Ussama Makdisi, "Reclaiming the Land of the Bible: Missionaries, Secularism, and Evangelical Modernity," *American Historical Review* 102 (1997): 683.
46. Sedra, "John Lieder," 222.
47. Sedra, "John Lieder," 235.

48. Sedra, "John Lieder," 235, quoting from CMS Archives, Lieder to the Secretaries, March 14, 1845, C/M/S 48/121.
49. Sedra, "John Lieder," 233.
50. Seikaly, "Coptic Communal Reform," 247.
51. Abdel Moneim el-Gemeiy, "Educating Egypt," *Al-Ahram Weekly* no. 766 (October 27–November 2, 2005).
52. Guirguis, "Restructuring Egyptian Society."
53. Behrens-Abouseif, *Die Kopten*, 7.
54. Bruce A. Masters, *Christians and Jews in the Ottoman Arab World: The Roots of Sectarianism* (Cambridge, U.K.: Cambridge University Press, 2001), 140.
55. Partrick, *Traditional Egyptian Christianity*, 128.
56. Behrens-Abouseif, *Die Kopten*, 22.
57. Butcher, *The Story of the Church of Egypt*, 2:380.
58. William Suleiman Qalada, "Origins of the Principle of Citizenship in the Tradition of the Copts and the History of Their Country," in *Christianity: A History in the Middle East*, ed. Habib Badr, Suad Abou el-Rousse Slim, and Joseph Abou Nohra (Beirut: Middle East Council of Churches, 2005), 837.
59. Qalada, "Origins of the Principle of Citizenship," 837. Qalada refers to Mikhail Sharubim, *al-Kafi fi tarikh Misr al-qadim wa-l-hadith* (Cairo: al-Matba'a al-Kubra al-Amiriya, 1898–1900), 4:111–12. In "Writing the History," Paul Sedra refers for the quote to Iris Habib al-Masri, *Qissat al-kanisa al-qibtiya* (Alexandria: Maktabat Kanisat Mari Girgis, 1975), 4:335.

Chapter 4: Educating Egypt

1. Suryal, *al-Mujtama' al-qibti*, 26; Sedra, "John Lieder," 236.
2. Sedra, "John Lieder," 236.
3. Sedra, "Ecclesiastical Warfare," 292; Habib al-Masri, *Qissat al-kanisa*, 4:334.
4. Habib al-Masri, *The Story of the Copts*, 514.
5. Laurence Moftah, quoting Coptic historian Girgis Philothaous Awad's book *Bawarik al-isla: Kyrollos al-Rabi' 'Abu-al-isla al-qibtiya*, 86–87 in "The Coptic Philanthropic Society: Al-Jam'iyyat al-Khayriyyah al-Kibtiyyah Kubra, Founded in 1881, and the Moftah Family," Library of Congress website, http://memory.loc.gov/diglib/ihas/loc.natlib.ihas.200182366/default.html
6. Seikaly, "Coptic Communal Reform," 248; Sedra, "John Lieder," 236.
7. Sedra, "John Lieder," 236.

8. Behrens-Abouseif, *Die Kopten*, 15.
9. For a comprehensive list of the administrative entries, see Magdi Guirguis, "al-Adraj al-babawiya al-kanisa al-qibtiya dirasa wa nashr li adraj al-baba Dimitriyus," *al-Majalla al-tarikhiya al-misriya* 41 (2001–2002): 70–71.
10. Habib al-Masri, *Qissat al-kanisa*, 4:326–27; Aziz Suryal Atiya, *A History of Eastern Christianity* (1968; repr., Millwood, N.Y: Kraus, 1980), 105; Seikaly, "Coptic Communal Reform," 248–49.
11. For a detailed account of the priests' income, see Guirguis, "Financial Resources."
12. Guirguis, "Financial Resources," 227–36.
13. Ibrahim, *The Copts,* 23.
14. Guirguis, "Financial Resources," 224, 231.
15. Sedra, "John Lieder," 237, referring to the study of Gabriel Baer, *A History of Landownership in Modern Egypt, 1800–1950* (London: Oxford University Press, 1962).
16. Seikaly, "Coptic Communal Reform," 251.
17. Reiss, *Erneuerung*, 21–22.
18. Behrens-Abouseif, *Die Kopten*, 15.
19. Timothy Mitchell, *Colonising Egypt* (Cambridge, U.K.: Cambridge University Press, 1988), 7, 34 describes the process of colonizing Egypt whereby exhibitions, museums, and later Muhammad 'Ali's army and the entire system of educational and industrial services it generated, served as a means of producing culture and empire. Cyril IV jump-started this process for the Copts, who later in the century would build their own museum.
20. Behrens-Abouseif, *Die Kopten*, 22.
21. Benedict Anderson, *Imagined Communities: Reflections on the Origin and Spread of Nationalism,* 2nd ed. (London: Verso, 1992).
22. Butcher, *The Story of the Church of Egypt*, 2:398–99. The claim that he had the icons burned is questioned, for example, by Paul Sedra in "John Lieder," 236. Sedra also refers to Iris Habib al-Masri, *Qissat al-kanisa*, 4:335–36 as another source contesting the icon burning.
23. Behrens-Abouseif, *Die Kopten*,19.
24. Behrens-Abouseif, *Die Kopten*, 20.
25. Otto Meinardus, *Christians in Egypt: Orthodox, Catholic, and Protestant Communities Past and Present* (Cairo: The American University in Cairo Press, 2006), 70–74.
26. Behrens-Abouseif, *Die Kopten,* 20.

27. For example, S.H. Leeder, *Modern Sons of the Pharaohs* (repr., New York: Arno Press, 1973) wrote just before the First World War that Cyril IV had "aroused the suspicions of the Moslem authorities, so that the traditional cup of coffee is said to have ended a noble life" (257).
28. Behrens-Abouseif, *Die Kopten*, 21.
29. Lady Lucie Duff Gordon, *Letters from Egypt (1862–1869)* (New York: Praeger, 1969).
30. Habib al-Masri, *The Story of the Copts*, 524.
31. See, for example, Seikaly, "Coptic Communal Reform," 248–50.
32. Guirguis, "Financial Resources," 229; Guirguis, "al-Adraj al-babawiya," 80.
33. See Sedra, "Ecclesiastical Warfare," 290–314.
34. Heather J. Sharkey, *American Evangelicals in Egypt: Missionary Encounters in an Age of Empire* (Princeton, N.J.: Princeton University Press, 2008), 32, 35, 45.
35. A. Watson, *The American Mission*, 155.
36. Armanios, *Coptic Christianity in Ottoman Egypt,* ch. 6.
37. Meinardus, *Christians in Egypt*, 85.
38. Meinardus, *Christians in Egypt*, 74–86.
39. Behrens-Abouseif, *Die Kopten*, 38.
40. B.L. Carter, *The Copts in Egyptian Politics, 1918–1952* (London, Sydney, and Dover, New Hampshire: Croom Helm, 1986), 8; Hamilton, *The Copts and the West,* 279.
41. A. Watson, *The American Mission*, 187.
42. A. Watson, *The American Mission*, 187.
43. A. Watson, *The American Mission*, 188.
44. Sharkey, *American Evangelicals*, 76.
45. Sharkey, *American Evangelicals*, 38.
46. A. Watson, *The American Mission*, 201.
47. A. Watson, *The American Mission*, 202–11; Behrens-Abouseif, *Die Kopten*, 39.
48. A. Watson, *The American Mission,* 202, 207; Sharkey, *American Evangelicals*, 38.
49. Behrens-Abouseif, *Die Kopten*, 40; Sharkey, *American Evangelicals*, 18, 39.
50. Zakhariyyas al-Antuni, *al-Baba Kyrillos al-rabi' (abu al-isla)* (Cairo: Dar al-Taba'a al-Qawmiya bi-l-Fajjala, 1994), 155.
51. al-Antuni, *al-Baba Kyrillos*, 155.
52. al-Antuni, *al-Baba Kyrillos*, 157. See also Meinardus, *Christians in Egypt*, 85.

53. Habib al-Masri, *The Story of the Copts*, 521.
54. Partrick, *Traditional Egyptian Christianity*, 125.
55. Mostyn, *Egypt's Belle Époque*, 43.
56. Mostyn, *Egypt's Belle Époque*, 45.
57. Mitchell, *Colonising Egypt*, 29.
58. Hamilton, *The Copts and the West*—for example, the visitor described on p. 69.
59. Sedra, "Ecclesiastical Warfare," 296.
60. Hamilton, *The Copts and the West*, 279, 289.
61. Duff Gordon, *Letters*, 256–57.
62. al-Anba Mataus, *Silsilat tarikh*, 164; Habib al-Masri, *The Story of the Copts*, 524.
63. Sedra, "Ecclesiastical Warfare," 307.
64. Sedra, "Ecclesiastical Warfare," 303.
65. Mostyn, *Egypt's Belle Époque*, 109.
66. The French historian Brigitte Voile identifies three defining developments: the activities of the missionaries, the lifting of the *dhimma* status, and the migration from the countryside to the cities (*Les Coptes d'Egypte sous Nasser*, 33–35).

Chapter 5: Redefining Authority

1. Yunan Labib Rizk, "The Selfless Patriot: A Diwan of Contemporary Life," *Al-Ahram Weekly* no. 408 (September 20–26, 2001), http://weekly.ahram.org.eg/2001/552/chrncls.htm/. Pope Cyril V had died on August 7.
2. Seikaly, "Coptic Communal Reform."
3. Donald Malcolm Reid, *Whose Pharaohs? Archaeology, Museums, and Egyptian National Identity from Napoleon to World War I* (Berkeley, Los Angeles, and London: University of California Press, 2002), 261.
4. Sedra, "Writing the History," 1056.
5. Rufayla, *Tarikh al-umma al-qibtiya*, 329.
6. Ibrahim, *The Copts*, 34.
7. Seikaly, "Coptic Communal Reform," 251.
8. Seikaly, "Coptic Communal Reform," 262.
9. Rizk, "The Selfless Patriot."
10. Rizk, "The Selfless Patriot."
11. Rufayla, *Tarikh al-umma al-qibtiya*, 337.
12. Rizk, "The Selfless Patriot."
13. Seikaly, "Coptic Communal Reform," 256.
14. Seikaly, "Coptic Communal Reform," 256–58.

15. Among others, see Rufayla, *Tarikh al-umma al-qibtiya*, 362.
16. Leeder, *Modern Sons of the Pharaohs*. Also see Rufayla, *Tarikh al-umma al-qibtiya*, 363–64, and Habib al-Masri, *Qissat al-kanisa al-qibtiya*, 5:36–37.
17. Otto F.A. Meinardus, *Two Thousand Years of Coptic Christianity* (Cairo: American University in Cairo Press, 1999), 72.
18. Carter, *The Copts in Egyptian Politics*, 29, referring to an article in *Misr*.
19. Leeder, *Modern Sons of the Pharaohs*, 259.
20. Sharkey, *American Evangelicals*, 45.
21. Seikaly, "Coptic Communal Reform," 266–67.
22. Partrick, *Traditional Egyptian Christianity*, 132.
23. Atiya, *A History of Eastern Christianity* (repr. 1980), 108.
24. Seikaly, "Coptic Communal Reform," 263.
25. For more details about the initial launching of the society, see Moftah, "The Coptic Philanthropic Society."
26. Lam'i al-Mati'i, *Ha'ula' al-rijal min al-aqbat* (Cairo: al-Anglo Bookshop, 1989), 100.
27. Rufayla, *Tarikh al-umma al-qibtiya*, 333–34.
28. For more detailed information about the charitable societies, see Ibrahim, *The Copts*, ch. 4.
29. Behrens-Abouseif, *Die Kopten*, 44, 47.
30. Carter, *The Copts in Egyptian Politics*, 43–44; Behrens-Abouseif, *Die Kopten*, 44.
31. Seikaly, "Coptic Communal Reform," 264.
32. Seikaly, "Coptic Communal Reform," 265.
33. Butcher, *The Story of the Church of Egypt*, 2:403–404; Meinardus, *Two Thousand Years of Coptic Christianity*, 71–72.
34. Atiya, *A History of Eastern Christianity* (repr. 1980), 107.
35. Metropolitan Bishoy, "Revival of the Egyptian Church since the Middle of the Nineteenth Century," in *Christianity: A History in the Middle East*, ed. Habib Badr, Suad Abou el-Rousse Slim, and Joseph Abou Nohra (Beirut: Middle East Council of Churches, 2005), 778.
36. Metropolitan Bishoy, "Revival of the Egyptian Church," 782. The periodicals were: *Marma al-naga*, 1892; *al-Rawi*, 1892; *al-Haqq*, 1895; *al-Ikhlas*, 1896; *al-Karma*, 1904; *al-Rabita al-masihiya*, 1907; and *'Ain Shams*, 1907.
37. Reiss, *Erneuerung*, 54.
38. Reiss, *Erneuerung*, 52.
39. Seikaly, "Coptic Communal Reform," 267.

40. Reiss, *Erneuerung*, 45.
41. Suryal, *al-Mujtama' al-qibti*, 279–80.
42. Reiss, *Erneuerung*, 55.
43. Juan R.I. Cole, *Colonialism and Revolution in the Middle East: Social and Cultural Origins of Egypt's 'Urabi Movement* (Princeton, N.J.: Princeton University Press, 1993), 275.
44. Cole, *Colonialism*, 240, explains that the main charge against Tawfiq was apostasy from Islam. According to Cole, this was "a subtle way of declaring him deposed."
45. Cole, *Colonialism*, 247.
46. Amir Nasr, *al-Musharaka al-wataniya al-aqbat fi-l-'asr al-hadith: 'ahd al-baba Kyrillos al-khamis* (Cairo: Usqufiyat al-Shabab, 1998), 47, proudly shows the document with signatures.
47. Israel Gershoni and James P. Jankowski, *Egypt, Islam and the Arabs: The Search for Egyptian Nationhood 1900–1930* (New York: Oxford University Press, 1986), 8.
48. Doris Behrens-Abouseif, "Nationalist Party (Hizb al-Watani)," *The Coptic Encyclopedia*, 6:1987–88.
49. Behrens-Abouseif, *Die Kopten*, 59.
50. Behrens-Abouseif, *Die Kopten*, 70.
51. Translation based on Rizk, "The Selfless Patriot," and Samirah Bahr, "Coptic Congress of Asyut," *The Coptic Encyclopedia*, 2:602.
52. Kyriakos Michael, *Copts and Moslims under British Control* (Port Washington, N.Y., and London: Kennikat Press, 1911), 26–27.
53. Bahr, "Coptic Congress of Asyut," 602.
54. Behrens-Abouseif, *Die Kopten*, 74.
55. Carter, *The Copts in Egyptian Politics*, 62.
56. Carter, *The Copts in Egyptian Politics*, 143, 146. The Wafd won the elections of 1924, 1929, 1936, and 1942.
57. Carter, *The Copts in Egyptian Politics*, 114. For a description of Sergius' activities and position in the Church, see Ibrahim, *The Copts*, 59–67.
58. Rizk, "The Selfless Patriot."
59. Carter, *The Copts in Egyptian Politics*, 72.
60. For more detailed figures on Coptic participation in the Egyptian bureaucracy during the British occupation, see Ibrahim, *The Copts*, 44–47.
61. E.W. Lane, *Manners and Customs of the Modern Egyptians* (1836; repr., Cairo: Livres de France, 1981), 524.
62. Behrens-Abouseif, *Die Kopten*, 48.
63. Ibrahim, *The Copts*, 48–49.
64. The Earl of Cromer, *Modern Egypt* (London: Macmillan, 1908), 2:210.

65. The Earl of Cromer, *Modern Egypt*, 2:202, 210.
66. See the article by *al-Liwa*'s Tunisian editor-in-chief, Sheikh 'Abd al-'Aziz Gawish, in Behrens-Abouseif, *Die Kopten*, 58–59.
67. Nasr, *al-Musharaka al-wataniya*, 67.
68. Nasr, *al-Musharaka al-wataniya*, 66.
69. Leeder, *Modern Sons of the Pharaohs*.
70. Atiya, *A History of Eastern Christianity*, 108.
71. Lane, *Manners and Customs*, 525.
72. Ibrahim, *The Copts*, 123.
73. Ibrahim, *The Copts*, 125.
74. Leeder, *Modern Sons of the Pharaohs*, 248.
75. Leeder, *Modern Sons of the Pharaohs*, 251.
76. See the reflection honoring the day of Cyril's death (August 7, 1927) at http://www.copticchurch.net/classes/synex.php?day=1&month=12.
77. Leeder, *Modern Sons of the Pharaohs*, 265–66.
78. Tadros Y. Malaty, *Anba Abraam, the Friend of the Poor, 1829–1914* (Santa Monica, Cal.: St. Peter and St. Paul Coptic Orthodox Cathedral, 1995), 26–27. Also accessible at http://www.saint-mary.net/books/Anba%20Abraam%20the%20Friend%20of%20the%20Poor.pdf
79. Nasr, *al-Musharaka al-wataniya*, 38–39.
80. The Arabic title of the history is *al-Kafi fi tarikh Misr al-qadim wa-l-hadith* (1898–1900), in Reid, *Whose Pharaohs?*, 283.
81. Reid, *Whose Pharaohs?*, 22.
82. Carter, *The Copts in Egyptian Politics*, 96.
83. Reid, *Whose Pharaohs?*, 267–68 provides a succinct overview of the founders of Coptic studies: Emile Amélineau, Oskar von Lemm, and Walter Crum worked on language and literature; George Steindorff published his Coptic grammar in 1894; and in 1884 Alfred J. Butler published *Ancient Churches of Egypt*, in which he closely studies Coptic art and architecture.
84. Reid, *Whose Pharaohs?*, 269–70.
85. Reid, *Whose Pharaohs?*, 258.
86. Reid, *Whose Pharaohs?*, 271.
87. Reid, *Whose Pharaohs?*, 258.
88. Reid, *Whose Pharaohs?*, 275.
89. Reid, *Whose Pharaohs?*, 279.
90. Reid, *Whose Pharaohs?*, 278.
91. Carter, *The Copts in Egyptian Politics*, 41.

Chapter 6: Leading in the Midst of Political Change

1. This year is taken from *The Coptic Encyclopedia*, 4:1351. Iris Habib al-Masri, *Qissat al-kanisa*, 6:31, states that the year of Pope John's birth was 1858.
2. Habib al-Masri, *Qissat al-kanisa*, 6:38.
3. *The Coptic Encyclopedia*, 6:1911.
4. Habib al-Masri, *Qissat al-kanisa*, 6:24.
5. Carter, *The Copts in Egyptian Politics*, 31.
6. Carter, *The Copts in Egyptian Politics*, 31–32.
7. Carter, *The Copts in Egyptian Politics*, 29–30.
8. Bernard Botiveau, "The Law of the Nation-State and the Status of Non-Muslims in Egypt and Syria," in *Christian Communities in the Arab Middle East: The Challenge of the Future*, ed. Andrea Pacini (Oxford: Clarendon Press, 1998), 116–20.
9. Jacques Masson, "Histoire des causes du divorce dans la tradition canonique copte (des origins au XIIIe siècle)," *Studia Orientalia Christiana Collectanea* (1973): 214; Ron Shaham, "Communal Identity, Political Islam and Family Law: Copts and the Debate over the Grounds for Dissolution of Marriage in Twentieth-Century Egypt," *Islam and Christian-Muslim Relations* 21, no. 4 (2010): 409–22.
10. Habib al-Masri, *Qissat al-kanisa*, 6:40–41.
11. Habib al-Masri, *Qissat al-kanisa*, 6:34.
12. Habib al-Masri, *Qissat al-kanisa*, 6:35, 70.
13. Reiss, *Erneuerung*, 82.
14. For this development, see Reiss, *Erneuerung*, 77–133, and S.S. Hasan, *Christians versus Muslims in Modern Egypt*, 57–102.
15. Reiss, *Erneuerung*, 87.
16. Reiss, *Erneuerung*, 71.
17. Copts count the two ceremonies of Anba John as the twenty-fourth and twenty-fifth in the history of the Coptic Church. Pope Cyril VI (1959–71) celebrated the twenty-sixth occasion. Since then, Pope Shenouda III has presided over this ceremony seven times, which brings the number of ceremonies to thirty-three.
18. Habib al-Masri, *Qissat al-kanisa*, 6:42.
19. Habib al-Masri, *Qissat al-kanisa*, 6:43.
20. Haggai Ehrlich, "Identity and Church: Ethiopian–Egyptian Dialogue, 1924–1959," *International Journal of Middle Eastern Studies* 32, no. 1 (February 2000): 26–27.
21. *The Coptic Encyclopedia*, 3:980.

22. Yunan Labib Rizk, "Separate Ways," *Al-Ahram Weekly* (September 15–21, 2005): 19.
23. Rizk, "Separate Ways," 19.
24. Jacques Masson, "La mission copte en Afrique du Nord," *Proche-Orient chrétien* 55 (2005): 295–96.
25. Habib al-Masri, *Qissat al-kanisa*, 6:50–60 provides a detailed account of the visit.
26. Habib al-Masri, *Qissat al-kanisa*, 58.
27. Habib al-Masri, *Qissat al-kanisa*, 59.
28. Ehrlich, "Identity and Church," 36–37.
29. Reiss, *Erneuerung*, 78–79.
30. Rizk, "Separate Ways," 19.
31. Rizk, "Separate Ways," 19.
32. Ehrlich, "Identity and Church," 35.
33. Ehrlich, "Identity and Church," 37.
34. Carter, *The Copts in Egyptian Politics*, 266–78; Peter E. Makari, *Conflict and Cooperation: Christian–Muslim Relations in Contemporary Egypt* (Syracuse, N.Y.: Syracuse University Press, 2007), 50–53.
35. Carter, *The Copts in Egyptian Politics*, 262 (the note was dated December 1, 1937).
36. Carter, *The Copts in Egyptian Politics*, 269.
37. Carter, *The Copts in Egyptian Politics*, 226–27.
38. Reiss, *Erneuerung*, 69–73.
39. Reiss, *Erneuerung*, 75.
40. Carter, *The Copts in Egyptian Politics*, 34–35.
41. Habib al-Masri, *Qissat al-kanisa*, 6:119.
42. Habib al-Masri, *Qissat al-kanisa*, 6:120–27, 208–209.
43. Habib al-Masri, *Qissat al-kanisa*, 6:125.
44. Habib al-Masri, *Qissat al-kanisa*, 6:126.
45. *The Coptic Encyclopedia*, 5:1489; Ibrahim, *The Copts,* 145–46.
46. Carter, *The Copts in Egyptian Politics*, 36.
47. Habib al-Masri, *Qissat al-kanisa*, 6:214–15.
48. Carter, *The Copts in Egyptian Politics*, 36–37.
49. *The Coptic Encyclopedia*, 7:2363; Edward Wakin, *A Lonely Minority: The Modern Story of Egypt's Copts* (New York: William Morrow and Company, 1963), 93–94.
50. Carter, *The Copts in Egyptian Politics*, 230–39.
51. Reiss, *Erneuerung*, 153.
52. Reiss, *Erneuerung*, 154.
53. Reiss, *Erneuerung*, 153.

54. Reiss, *Erneuerung*, 167.
55. When Metropolitan Abram, who was in charge of the district of Giza where the Sunday School Movement had a strong presence, passed away, the pope experienced the power of the movement at first hand. When several lay and clerical leaders, including the famous priest Salib Suryal, found out that an unpopular cleric had already bought the position via the pope's servant Milik, they decided to protest in public. At the time of the new bishop's ordination, they shouted that it went against the wishes of the people and the teachings of the early Church (Reiss, *Erneuerung*, 156–57).
56. Carter, *The Copts in Egyptian Politics*, 37.
57. Carter, *The Copts in Egyptian Politics*, 38; Wakin, *A Lonely Minority*, 94–95.
58. Ibrahim, *The Copts,* 161–62, 168–69.
59. Wakin, *A Lonely Minority*, 98.

Chapter 7: Reviving Tradition, Reviving the Church

1. Wakin, *A Lonely Minority*, 107.
2. For the 1957 regulations of the state and the Holy Synod, see Otto Meinardus, *Christian Egypt, Faith and Life* (Cairo: The American University in Cairo Press, 1970), 129–40.
3. Some of the information in this chapter can be found in two articles I published earlier on Pope Cyril VI: Nelly van Doorn-Harder, "Practical and Mystical: Patriarch Kyrillos VI (1959–1971)," *Currents in Theology and Mission* 33, no. 3 (June 2006): 223–32; and "Kyrillos VI (1902–1971): Planner, Patriarch and Saint," in *Between Desert and City: The Coptic Orthodox Church Today*, ed. Nelly van Doorn-Harder and Kari Vogt (Oslo: Novus Forlag, 1997 and Portland, Ore.: Wipf and Stock Publishers, 2004), 230–42.
4. Magdi Salama, *al-Baba Kyrillos al-sadis: rajul fawq al-kalimat* (Monastery of St. Menas, 1998).
5. van Doorn-Harder, "Practical and Mystical."
6. John Watson, "Abba Kyrillos, Patriarch and Solitary," *Coptic Church Review* (Society of Coptic Church Studies) 17, nos. 1, 2 (1996): 3–48.
7. Voile, *Les Coptes d'Égypte sous Nasser*, 58.
8. J. Watson, "Abba Kyrillos," 20.
9. Hanna Yusuf 'Ata, Rafa'il Ava Mina, and Rufa'il Subhi, *Mudhakkirat 'an hayat al-baba Kyrillos al-sadis* (Cairo: Abna' al-Baba Kyrillos al-Sadis, 1985), 155.

10. Iris Habib al-Masri's biography is published as the seventh volume in her series on the history of the Coptic Church: *Qissat al-kanisa al-qibtiya*, vol. 7 (Cairo: Maktabat al-Mahabba, 1988). Anba Cyril's brother, Hanna Yusuf 'Ata, wrote a biography that has been translated into English: *The Life of the Saint Pope Kyrollos the Sixth*, 2nd ed. (Cairo: The Sons of Pope Kyrillos VI, 2002). This text is also widely available via the Internet at www.zeitun-eg.org/stcyril6/. Hanna Yusuf 'Ata also co-wrote a biography with Abuna Rafa'il Ava Mina (of the Monastery of St. Menas) and Rufa'il Subhi: *Mudhakkirat 'an hayat al-baba Kyrillos al-sadis* (Cairo: Abna' al-Baba Kyrillos al-Sadis, 1985). Amir Nasr's *Abuna Mina al-Baramusi al-mutawahhid* (Cairo, 1996) is highly regarded as a source of information. The famous observer of the Coptic Church, Otto Meinardus, mentions Anba Cyril in several of his books. His *Patriarchen unter Nasser und Sadat* (Hamburg: Deutsche Orient-Institut, 1998) especially addresses Cyril's political relationships, mostly with President Nasser.
11. Voile, *Les Coptes d'Égypte sous Nasser*, 190. Most biographies do not mention these regular visits of Pope John, but they make sense when considering the attention he paid to Cyril during the latter's time as a monk and hermit.
12. Most of the information about Cyril's childhood is from the books his brother wrote and co-wrote.
13. Little is known about this hermit apart from what Meinardus wrote about him in the original edition of his book, *Monks and Monasteries of the Egyptian Deserts* (Cairo: American University in Cairo Press, 1961), 157. Also see Meinardus' personal communication to me about how he tried to meet with al-Habashi, arriving in a small plane which he landed in front of the hermit's cave: van Doorn-Harder, "Practical and Mystical," 228. Al-Habashi wanted neither to talk to him, nor to accept his gifts of canned tuna, which he called "Satan's lure."
14. Voile, *Les Coptes d'Égypte sous Nasser*, 195.
15. 'Ata, *The Life of the Saint*, 37–38.
16. Abna' al-Baba Kirullus al-Sadis (Sons of Pope Cyril VI), ed., *Service and Humility in the Life of the Saint Pope Kyrollos the Sixth* (Cairo, 1999), 13.
17. Abna' al-Baba Kirullus, *Service and Humility*, 15–16.
18. About similar strategies used by holy figures in antiquity, see, for example, Peter Brown, "The Rise and Function of the Holy Man in Late Antiquity," *Journal of Roman Studies* 61 (1971): 80–101.

19. According to Meinardus, the British suspected Cyril of spying: *Christian Egypt: Faith and Life*, 44.
20. ʿAta, *The Life of the Saint*, 48.
21. Reiss, *Erneuerung*, 238.
22. Meinardus, *Patriarchen unter Nasser und Sadat*, 15.
23. Wakin, *A Lonely Minority*, 151.
24. Meinardus, *Patriarchen unter Nasser und Sadat*, 34.
25. Meinardus, *Patriarchen unter Nasser und Sadat*, 35.
26. Wakin, *A Lonely Minority*, 51.
27. Meinardus, *Patriarchen unter Nasser und Sadat*, 27.
28. Meinardus, *Patriarchen unter Nasser und Sadat*, 43–46.
29. Wakin, *A Lonely Minority*, 55.
30. Meinardus, *Patriarchen unter Nasser und Sadat*, 56.
31. Laura M. James, *Nasser at War: Arab Images of the Enemy* (New York: Palgrave, Macmillan, 2006), 102.
32. Meinardus, *Patriarchen unter Nasser und Sadat*, 52.
33. Mohamed Heikal, *Autumn of Fury: The Assassination of Sadat* (London: Andre Deutsch, 1983), 158.
34. Meinardus, *Two Thousand Years of Coptic Christianity*, 34. Video clips of Pope Cyril meeting the delegation at the airport and the enshrinement of the relic in the new cathedral are available at http://www.zeitun-eg.org/stcyril6/ and at http://st-takla.org/Multimedia/09-Videos-Videohat-02-Coptic-Pope_Kyrillos_VI-Al-Baba-Kirellos-Al-Sades-01.html
35. Wakin, *A Lonely Minority*, 151.
36. *The Coptic Encyclopedia*, 2:582. This board was called the Coptic Orthodox Waqfs Organization. See also Wakin, *A Lonely Minority*, 151.
37. Voile, *Les Coptes d'Égypte sous Nasser*, 210.
38. *The Coptic Encyclopedia,* 2:582.
39. Ehrlich, "Identity and Church," 41–42.
40. Habib al-Masri, *Qissat al-kanisa*, 7:31.
41. Ehrlich, "Identity and Church," 43.
42. Reiss, *Erneuerung*, 215.
43. For a summary of information about the Syrian and Armenian churches in Egypt, see Otto F.A. Meinardus, *Christian Egypt, Ancient and Modern*, 2nd rev. ed. (Cairo: American University in Cairo Press, 1977), 552–56.
44. Abna' al-Baba Kirullus al-Sadis (Sons of Pope Cyril VI), ed., *al-Baba Kirullus al-sadis tarikh . . . wa Amjad* (Cairo, 2002), 6.
45. Habib al-Masri, *Qissat al-kanisa*, 7:43.

46. Abna' al-baba Kirullus al-Sadis (Sons of Pope Cyril VI), ed., *Jami'at al-ruh al-muqaddas* (Cairo, 1991), 26.
47. Reiss, *Erneuerung*, 216. For the decisions taken during the two meetings, see Habib al-Masri, *Qissat al-kanisa*, 7:44–45.
48. Masson, "La mission copte en Afrique du Nord," 296.
49. For the Copts it was problematic that the pharaonic heritage that had become a cultural marker during the early 1900s was not included as one of these circles. Peter E. Makari also discusses Egypt's Mediterranean identity as another potential sphere of influence and identity, one which would have added a greater geographic and cultural range to Nasser's vision (*Conflict and Cooperation*, 61).
50. Meinardus, *Patriarchen unter Nasser und Sadat*, 42.
51. Meinardus, *Patriarchen unter Nasser und Sadat*, 42.
52. Christine Chaillot, *The Coptic Orthodox Church: A Brief Introduction to Its Life and Spirituality* (Paris: Inter-Orthodox Dialogue, 2005), 49.
53. *The Coptic Encyclopedia*, "Migration," 5:1620–24.
54. See Nora Stene, "Into the Lands of Immigration," in *Between Desert and City*, ed. van Doorn-Harder and Vogt, 254–64. For more general information on emigration trends in the Middle East, see Bernard Sabella, "The Emigration of Christian Arabs: Dimensions and Causes of the Phenomenon," in *Christian Communities in the Arab Middle East: The Challenge of the Future*, ed. Andrea Pacini (Oxford: Clarendon Press, 1998), 111–27.
55. Abna' al-Baba Kirullus al-Sadis (Sons of Pope Cyril VI), ed., *The Fruits of Love: The Saint Pope Kyrollos the Sixth* (Cairo, 1999), 6–7; Meinardus, *Christian Egypt, Faith and Life*, 141.
56. The American journalist Edward Wakin was baffled, and wrote that the Coptic community "was besieged, the minority anxious, the hierarchy, the clergy and monks in disarray, the church wounded by turmoil, and the Patriarch lays a foundational stone in a deserted place for another monastery" (*A Lonely Minority,* 112).
57. Abna' al-Baba Kirullus al-Sadis (Sons of Pope Kyrollos VI), ed., *Christian Behaviour According to the Saint Pope Kyrollos the Sixth* (Cairo: 2000), 20–21.
58. See Mark Francis Gruber, "Coping with God: Coptic Monasticism in Egyptian Culture," and "The Monastery as the Nexus of Coptic Cosmology," in *Between Desert and City*, ed. van Doorn-Harder and Vogt, 52–66 and 67–82.
59. This video clip and most of the others available from the time of Pope Cyril can be found at "Movies and Video Clips: Pope Kirellos VI," St. Takla Haymanout Coptic Orthodox Church, http://

st-takla.org/Multimedia/09-Videos-Videohat-02-Coptic-Pope_Kyrillos_VI-Al-Baba-Kirellos-Al-Sades-01.html. The website Pope St. Kyrillos VI Multimedia Web Gallery, http://www.zeitun-eg.org/stcyril6/, provides even more clips, among others showing the windmill where Anba Cyril stayed before moving into the church complex near Old Cairo.

60. el-Khawaga, "Le renouveau copte," 169.
61. Abna' al-Baba Kirullus, *Christian Behaviour*, 12.
62. Abna' al-Baba Kirullus, *Christian Behaviour*, 40.
63. Voile, *Les Coptes d'Égypte sous Nasser*, 95.
64. For the precise numbers, see Voile, *Les Coptes d'Égypte sous Nasser*, 77–86.
65. Voile, *Les Coptes d'Égypte sous Nasser*, 73.
66. For the names of individuals added to the Synaxarium in 1951, see Voile, *Les Coptes d'Égypte sous Nasser*, 125–28.
67. Saphinaz-Amal Naguib, "The Era of Martyrs: Texts and Contexts of Religious Memory," in *Between Desert and City*, ed. van Doorn-Harder and Vogt, 136.
68. Mutraniya Beni Soueif, ed., *Bustan al-ruhban* (Beni Soueif, 1968).
69. John Watson, "Abouna Matta el-Miskin, Contemporary Desert Mystic," *Coptic Church Review* 27, nos. 3, 4 (Fall/Winter 2006): 73, 77.
70. Matta al-Miskin, *The Communion of Love* (New York: St. Vladimir's Seminary Press, 2004). For an extensive list and description of some of Father Matta al-Miskin's most important works, see Samuel Rubinson, "Tradition and Renewal in Coptic Theology," in *Between Desert and City*, ed. van Doorn-Harder and Vogt, 40–41.
71. Dayr al-Qadis Anba Maqar, ed., *Abuna al-qummus Matta al-Miskin* (Dayr al-Qadis, 2006), 7.
72. Habib al-Masri, *Qissat al-kanisa*, 7:24.
73. Meinardus, *Christian Egypt, Faith and Life*, 44–45; Maurice Assad, "Prägung der koptischen Identität," in *Koptisches Christentum*, ed. P. Verghese (Stuttgart: Evangelisches Verlagswerk, 1973), 114–16.
74. Meinardus, *Christian Egypt, Faith and Life*, 46.
75. Reiss, *Erneuerung*, 250–51, fn 179, provides an extensive bibliography of the books published by the Bait al-Takris and the Patristic Center.
76. Reiss, *Erneuerung*, 221, fn 79, provides this information, which is seldom mentioned. As a fourth area of governance the report indicated matters concerning "rites and consecration."
77. For more detailed information, about Anba Samuel's activities, see, among others, Maurice Assad, *al-Anba Samu'il fi dhikrihi al-'ishrin (6 October 1981–2001)* (Cairo: Asdiqa' al-Anba Samu'il, 2001).

78. Reiss, *Erneuerung*, 224.
79. Reiss, *Erneuerung*, 224–26.
80. Ragheb Moftah, Margit Toth, and Martha Roy, *The Coptic Orthodox Liturgy of St. Basil: With Complete Musical Transcription* (Cairo: American University in Cairo Press, 1998).
81. Meinardus, *Two Thousand Years of Coptic Christianity*, 253.
82. Dayr al-Qadis 'Anba Maqar, *'Abuna al-qummus Matta al-Miskin*, 35.
83. Dayr al-Qadis 'Anba Maqar, *'Abuna al-qummus Matta al-Miskin*, 36.
84. Dayr al-Qadis 'Anba Maqar, *'Abuna al-qummus Matta al-Miskin*, 34.
85. As early as 1979, monastic journals outside Egypt described the project at St. Macarius in great detail. See, for example, Peter Meeus, "Herleving Kopties Monnikendom," *Benedictijns Tijdschrift* 1 (1979): 2–20.
86. For the story of the purchase of the land, see Nelly van Doorn-Harder, "Discovering New Roles: Coptic Nuns and Church Revival," in *Between Desert and City*, ed. van Doorn-Harder and Vogt, 94–95.
87. Convent of the Great Martyr St. Philopater Mercurius "Abu Seifein" for Nuns, ed., *Tamav Erene: The Jewel of Heaven and the Beacon of Monasticism* (Cairo: Convent of Abu Seifein, 2007), 108–11; Pieternella van Doorn-Harder, *Contemporary Coptic Nuns* (Columbia: University of South Carolina Press, 1995), 54–59.
88. Convent of the Great Martyr, *Tamav Erene*, 96.
89. For some observations about how Ummina Irini related the stories of St. Abu al-Sayfayn to the Coptic public, see van Doorn-Harder, *Contemporary Coptic Nuns*, 168–69.
90. For the story of the building of the church, see van Doorn-Harder, *Contemporary Coptic Nuns*, 172.
91. In some cases, sudden death removed his detractors from the scene: 'Ata, *The Life of the Saint*, 113–16.
92. "Death of Pope Kirullos VI," http://www.youtube.com/watch?v=zdOUnbXgPak&feature=PlayList&p=F058CF13B38CE97B&playnext=1&playnext_from=PL&index=55.
93. 'Ata, *The Life of the Saint*, 120.
94. Habib al-Masri, *Qissat al-kanisa*, 7:149.
95. Dina el-Khawaga, "Political Dynamics of the Copts: Giving the Community an Active Role," in *Christian Communities in the Arab Middle East: The Challenge of the Future*, ed. Andrea Pacini (Oxford: Clarendon Press, 1998), 181.

Chapter 8: Negotiating Political Landscapes

1. Hasan, *Christians versus Muslims in Modern Egypt,* 234 compares Shenouda to an enlightened absolutist monarch from eighteenth-century Europe.
2. "Chroniques," *Proche-Orient chrétien* 54, nos. 1–2 (2004): 132.
3. al-Qummus Mikha'il Girgis Salib, *al-Sijill al-tarikhi li-l-qadasat al-baba Shenuda al-thalith*, vols. 1–11 (Cairo and Damanhur: Maktabat Ra'is al-Mala'ika Mikha'il, 1995–2006).
4. Rasmi 'Abd el-Malik Rustum and Ishaq Ibrahim 'Agban, *al-Baba Shenuda al-thalith wa hisad al-sinin* (Cairo: Institute for Coptic Studies, 2003) and *Qadasa al-baba Shenuda al-thalith wa hisad al-sinin*, vol. 2 (Cairo: Institute for Coptic Studies, 2008). The second, updated volume will be used for quotations.
5. "El-Keraza in English," on the website Coptic Papal Residence: His Holiness Pope Shenouda III, http://www.copticpope.org/modules.php?name=Sections&op=listarticles&secid=7
6. Fiona McCallum, "The Political Role of the Patriarch in the Contemporary Middle East," *Middle Eastern Studies* 43, no. 6 (2007): 930.
7. Among others, see Maurits Berger, "Apostasy and Public Policy in Contemporary Egypt: An Evaluation of Recent Cases from Egypt's Highest Courts," *Human Rights Quarterly* 25 (2003): 720–40.
8. Among others, see "When the Social Becomes Political," http://weekly.ahram.org.eg/2004/721/eg7.htm
9. For example, see the report on the state of religion in Egypt published by Al-Ahram Center for Political and Strategic Studies: Nabil 'Abd al-Fattah, ed., *Taqrir al-hala al-diniya fi Misr* (Cairo, 1995).
10. Mahmud Fawzi, *al-Baba Shanuda wa tarikh al-kanisa al-qibtiya* (Cairo: Dar al-Nashr Hatier, 1992), 123–25.
11. For more details on the *jama'at* and their relationships with other constituencies in society see, among others, Hamied Ansari, "Sectarian Conflict in Egypt and the Political Expediency of Religion," *Middle East Journal* 38, no. 3 (Summer 1984): 402.
12. For an analysis of this process, see Ansari, "Sectarian Conflict," 410–16.
13. Hasan, *Christians versus Muslims in Modern Egypt*, 106–107.
14. Heikal, *Autumn of Fury*, 163.
15. Ansari, "Sectarian Conflict," 407.
16. Hasan, *Christians versus Muslims in Modern Egypt*, 108.
17. Heikal, *Autumn of Fury*, 220–21.
18. J.D. Pennington, "The Copts in Modern Egypt," *Middle Eastern Studies* 18, no. 2 (April 1982): 174.

19. Nadia Ramsis Farah, *Religious Strife in Egypt: Crisis and Ideological Conflict in the Seventies* (Montreux and New York: Gordon and Breach Science Publishers, 1986), 3, 10. According to Mohamed Heikal, Sadat had wanted to "make a direct attack on the leadership of the Coptic Church" as early as 1972 when Pope Shenouda sent a delegation of bishops and priests to Khanqa: *Autumn of Fury,* 163.
20. Farah, *Religious Strife in Egypt*, 13.
21. Ansari, "Sectarian Conflict," 413.
22. Pennington, "The Copts in Modern Egypt," 176.
23. J. Watson, *Among the Copts*, 96–97.
24. Hasan, *Christians versus Muslims in Modern Egypt*, 113.
25. Dayr al-Qadis Anba Maqar, *Abuna al-qummus Matta al-Miskin*, 58.
26. Dayr al-Qadis Anba Maqar, *Abuna al-qummus Matta al-Miskin*, 57.
27. Sara Medina, Robert C. Wurmstedt, and Nathaniel Harrison, "Religion: Egypt's Copts in Crisis," *Time*, September 28, 1981, http://www.time.com/time/magazine/article/0,9171,953135-1,00.html
28. Medina et al., "Religion: Egypt's Copts in Crisis."
29. One year later Father Markus was brutally murdered. For the full story about Father Markus, see J. Watson, *Among the Copts,* 72–92. For a copy of the committee's decision to defrock Father Markus and Pope Shenouda's rebuttal, see Reiss, *Erneuerung*, 304–306.
30. Interview with Bishop Athanasius, Beni Soueif, February 19, 1998.
31. Beni Soueif Bishopric, ed., *al-Anba Athanasiyus, ayquna hubb wa 'ata'* (Beni Soueif: Beni Soueif Bishopric, 2000), 11–17.
32. Interview with Bishop Athanasius, Beni Soueif, February 19, 1998.
33. Tadros, "Vicissitudes in the Entente," 276.
34. Hasan, *Christians versus Muslims in Modern Egypt*, 116.
35. For an analysis of this phenomenon, see, among others, Rachel Reedijk, *Roots and Routes: Identity Construction and the Jewish-Christian-Muslim Dialogue* (Amsterdam and New York: Rodopi, 2010), 45–48.
36. Makari, *Conflict and Cooperation*, 69–81.
37. Makari, *Conflict and Cooperation*, 85.
38. Makari, *Conflict and Cooperation*, 179–82, analyzes Pope Shenouda's reaction to the violence in al-Kusheh as published in *al-Kiraza* of January 21, 2000 ("Violence against Christians in Al Kosheh, Egypt," available at the website Islamic Studies in Christian Perspective, http://www.rim.org/muslim/egypt.htm
39. *al-Kiraza*, January 21, 2000, http://www.rim.org/muslim/egypt.htm

40. Quoted on the website of the Ibn Khaldun Center for Development Studies, http://www.eicds.org/english/introduction/about.htm. For further analysis of the conference, see Ami Ayalon, "Egypt's Coptic Pandora's Box," in *Minorities and the State in the Arab World*, ed. O. Bengio and Ben-Dor (Boulder: Lynne Rienner, 1999), 53–73.
41. Dina el-Khawaga analyzed the debate surrounding the conference as one between the competing models of Copts as equal citizens and Copts in the status of *dhimmis*, in "Le débat sur les Coptes: Le dit et le non-dit," *Egypte/Monde Arabe* 20 (4th trimester 1994): 67–90. For a discussion about the debates regarding Coptic identity at the conference, see Elizabeth Edwards Oram, "Constructing Modern Copts: The Production of Coptic Christian Identity in Contemporary Egypt" (PhD diss., Princeton University, 2004), 53–76.
42. Makari, *Conflict and Cooperation*, 164.
43. *Proche-Orient chrétien* 50, nos. 1, 2 (2000): 336 and *al-Kiraza* (November 24, 2000).
44. For an extensive discussion of the formation of Coptic civil society, see Paul Rowe, "Building Coptic Civil Society: Christian Groups and the State in Mubarak's Egypt," *Middle Eastern Studies* 45, no. 1 (January 2009): 111–26.
45. Tadros, "Vicissitudes in the Entente," 278.
46. Tadros, "The Sectarian Incident."
47. Aladdin Elaasar, *The Last Pharaoh: Mubarak and the Uncertain Future of Egypt in the Obama Age* (Missoula, Montana: Beacon Press, 2009), 291.
48. Tadros, "The Sectarian Incident."
49. Dina Ezzat, "A Moment of Recognition," *Al-Ahram Weekly*, January 6–12, 2011.
50. Tadros, "Vicissitudes in the Entente," 282.
51. On the website of the British Orthodox Church within the Coptic Patriarchate, see "Pope Shenouda Comments on the Egyptian Revolution," http://britishorthodox.org/1676/pope-shenouda-comments-on-the-egyptian-revolution/, and "H.H. Pope Shenouda Issues Statement on the Egyptian Revolution," http://britishorthodox.org/1653/pope-shenouda-issues-statement-on-the-egyptian-revolution/

Chapter 9: Reforming the Church for the Twenty-first Century

1. One of the best studies analyzing the clericalization process is Dina el-Khawaga's PhD thesis, "Le renouveau copte: La communauté comme acteur politique" (Institut d'études politiques de Paris, 1993). She summarized her main arguments in "The Laity at the Heart of the Coptic Clerical Reform," in *Between Desert and City*, ed. van Doorn-Harder and Vogt, 142–66. The field notes presented by Hasan in *Christians versus Muslims in Modern Egypt* have much illustrative material about how this reform operates at the diocesan level. On the Holy Synod's important role in this process of restructuring, see Secretary of the Holy Synod, *al-Qararat al-mujamma'iyat*, 4–14.
2. Salib, *al-Sijill al-tarikhi*, 9:104.
3. For more information on the revival within the convents, see van Doorn-Harder, *Contemporary Coptic Nuns*.
4. Rustum and 'Agban, *Qadasat al-baba Shenuda*, 137–47. Several of the current bishops are general; they are not connected to a diocese, and instead are in charge of youth or the papal printing shop, serve as the pope's secretaries, or assist diocesan bishops.
5. Rustum and 'Agban, *Qadasat al-baba Shenuda*, 148–49.
6. Jacques Masson, "Trente ans de règne de Shenouda III," *Proche-Orient chrétien* 51, nos. 3–4 (2001): 319.
7. Abba Seraphim, Metropolitan of Glastonbury, "The Renewal of Coptic Orthodoxy in the Twentieth Century" (lecture, Manchester Metropolitan University, May 30, 1995), *The Glastonbury Bulletin*, no. 92 (March 1996).
8. See Hasan, *Christians versus Muslims in Modern Egypt*, ch. 9, "Haraka wa Baraka: Arsanios, a Model Bishop," 137–52.
9. Hasan, *Christians versus Muslims in Modern Egypt*, 162–66.
10. Hasan, *Christians versus Muslims in Modern Egypt*, 130.
11. el-Khawaga, "The Laity," 147; "Le renouveau copte, " 234–36.
12. el-Khawaga, "Le renouveau copte," 241–46. As is the case with the church councils, the names of those elected are published in *al-Kiraza* as well. For an example, see *al-Kiraza*, April 21, 2006.
13. Chaillot, *The Coptic Orthodox Church*, 38.
14. Secretary of the Holy Synod, *al-Qararat*, 82–83.
15. In 2004, Christine Chaillot estimated that there were more than four hundred consecrated women: *The Coptic Orthodox Church*, 39.
16. For example, see *al-Kiraza*, November 26, 2006, which mentions the third conference on people with special needs, held in the Diocese of Ismailiya.

17. For analyses of the Bishopric of Youth until the early 1990s and the rationale for creating it, see el-Khawaga, "Le renouveau copte," 247–56; el-Khawaga, "The Laity," 154–58; and Hasan, *Christians versus Muslims in Modern Egypt*, ch. 12, "The Glorious and the Sacred," 183–98. Especially after dioceses were established in the United Kingdom and North America, the work of the Bishopric of Youth was adapted to the needs of youth growing up in the west. Most of the material for this period can be found on the websites of individual dioceses, in *al-Kiraza*, on the website of the Bishopric of Youth, and in the various writings about developments in these new churches. This section is also based on several interviews I had over the years with *mukarrasat* working in the bishopric and with Bishop Musa himself.
18. Father Matthew Attia, "Thirty Glorious Years: Anba Moussa, Bishop of Youth . . . The Three S's, Four P's, and the H Club," *Watani International* (May 23, 2010), available at http://youthbishopricsite.blogspot.com/2010/05/glorious-years30.html
19. Attia, "Thirty Glorious Years."
20. Youth Bishopric website, http://www.youthbishopric.com
21. Interview with Bishop Musa, February 18, 1998.
22. Rustum and 'Agban, *Qadasat al-baba Shenuda*, 18. The dissertation of Ghada Botros examines the challenges of the church in North America: "Competing for the Future: Adaptation and the Accommodation of Difference in Coptic Immigrant Churches" (PhD diss., University of Toronto, 2005). She summarized some of her findings in "Religious Identity as an Historical Narrative: Coptic Orthodox Immigrant Churches and the Representation of History," *Journal of Historical Sociology* 19, no. 2 (June 2006): 175.
23. Botros, "Religious Identity as an Historical Narrative," 195, n. 3.
24. It is almost impossible to keep up with the number, since churches continue to be established in countries around the world and the number of bishops serving as general bishop or in charge of a diocese keeps growing. See Masson, "Trente ans de règne de Shenouda III," 321–23. For the list of bishops ordained between 1971 and 2008, see Rustum and 'Agban, *Qadasat al-baba Shenuda*, 137–47.
25. Rustum and 'Agban, *Qadasat al-baba Shenuda*, 16, list as places that have a seminary: New Jersey and Los Angeles in the United States, Melbourne and Sydney in Australia, Stevenage near London, and Kroffelback in Germany.
26. See the theoretical considerations in Botros, "Religious Identity as an Historical Narrative," 19–22.

27. Botros, "Religious Identity as an Historical Narrative," 75.
28. Botros, "Religious Identity as an Historical Narrative," 66–68.
29. Elhamy Khalil, *The Making of a Diocese: The Early Years of the Coptic Orthodox Diocese of Los Angeles, Southern California, and Hawaii* (Los Angeles: The Coptic Orthodox Diocese, 2008), 4.
30. Botros, "Religious Identity as an Historical Narrative," 64.
31. Khalil, *The Making of a Diocese*, 21–50.
32. Khalil, *The Making of a Diocese*, 8.
33. Masson, "La mission copte en Afrique du Nord," 299.
34. Bishop Antonius Markos, *Come Across . . . and Help Us: The Story of the Coptic Orthodox Church in Africa in Our Present Time*, Part 1 (Cairo: Bishopric for African Affairs, 1983), ch. 14.
35. The Wikipedia article "Coptic Orthodox Church in Africa," http://en.wikipedia.org/wiki/Coptic_Orthodox_Church_in_Africa, provides links to the documents on which the count of churches in Africa is based.
36. "Agreement on Interchurch Marriages between the Catholic Church and the Malankara Syrian Orthodox Church," Syrian Orthdox Resources, http://sor.cua.edu/Ecumenism/19940125SOCRCMarriageAgmt.html
37. Masson, "Trente ans de règne de Shenouda III," 326.
38. See, for example, Mariz Tadros, "The Non-Muslim 'Other': Gender and Contestation of Hierarchy of Rights," *Hawwa: Journal of Women of the Middle East and the Islamic World* 7, no. 2 (2009): 111–43.
39. *The Coptic Encyclopedia*, 6:1943. The astonishing reality is that most documents mention adultery committed by the woman, not by the man.
40. Tadros, "The Non-Muslim 'Other,'" 120–21.
41. *al-Kiraza*, January 22, 1999, and "Chroniques des Pays," *Proche-Orient chrétien* 49, nos. 1–2 (1999): 168–69.
42. "Coptic Pope Rejects Egyptian Court Ruling on Remarriage of Divorcees," Assyrian International News Agency, http://www.aina.org/news/20100608192647.htm
43. Pope Shenouda III, *The Release of the Spirit* (Rockville, Md.: St. Mark's Orthodox Fellowship, 1990), 25.
44. Pope Shenouda III, *The Release of the Spirit*, 27.
45. Jacques Masson, "La divinisation de l'homme: Les raisons de l'opposition de Shenouda III," *Proche-Orient chrétien* 57, nos. 3–4 (2007): 280.
46. Stephen J. Davis, *Coptic Christology in Practice: Incarnation and Divine Participation in Late Antique and Medieval Egypt* (Oxford: Oxford University Press, 2008), 273.

47. *al-Kiraza*, March 23, 2006.
48. Davis, *Coptic Christology*, 277–78. Masson ("La divinisation de l'homme," 286) sees Pope Shenouda's view of human sinfulness as another reason—that is to say, that he considers people too impaired by sin to participate in divine attributes.
49. Davis, *Coptic Christology*, 274.
50. *al-Kiraza*, February 23, 2007: 11.
51. "Chroniques," *Proche-Orient chrétien* 48, nos. 1–2 (1998): 381.
52. "Chroniques," *Proche-Orient chrétien* 54, nos. 1–2 (2004): 131.
53. Tadros, "Vicissitudes in the Entente," 279–81, details the story of Maximos.
54. Tadros, "Vicissitudes in the Entente," 281.
55. Interview with Marie Assaad, May 16, 2004.
56. Khalil, *The Making of a Diocese*, 6, relates that when Bishop Serapion of the Diocese of Los Angeles, Southern California, and Hawaii was chosen, churches signed a petition accepting or rejecting the pope's suggestion.

Index

'Abbas I, 76–77, 87
'Abbas II, 87, 91
'Abdallah al-Shabrawi, Sheikh, 35
'Abd al-Rahim al-Sharif, Sheikh, 42
'Abduh, Muhammad, 98
Abraam, bishop of Fayoum, 104–105, 144, 151
Adultery, 16, 114, 184, 185
al-Afghani, Jamal al-Din, 97, 98
Ahl al-dhimma/ dhimmi (protected peoples), 6, 9, 10, 37, 57, 69–70, 167
    Coptic papacy, 65
    dhimmi status, 58, 69–70, 92, 163, 169
    education, 69, 70
    lifting of status, 58, 70, 73, 86
All Africa Council of Churches, 139, 156, 166, 182
Antunius, bishop of Jirja, 25
Apostasy, 114, 162
'Aqd al-dhimma (Covenant of Protection), 7, 9
    'Umar ibn al-Khattab, Caliph, 7
Arabic language, 47, 61, 69, 75, 79, 80, 98, 106, 144, 156–57, 179
Archives, ix, 6, 59, 104
    Coptic Orthodox Patriarchate, Cairo, 5, 48
    Egyptian, vii, 3, 4–5
    Ottoman, 3
Armenian Orthodox Church/Christians, 8, 48, 66, 77, 102, 105, 139, 182, 184
al-Askity, Father Markus, 165–66
Assaad, Marie, 188
'Ata, Hanna Yusuf, 130
Athanasius, bishop of Beni Soueif, 125, 140, 147, 149, 164, 166–67, 174, 176, 184
Athanasius of Sanabu, bishop, 91
Athanasius, Pope, 18
Atiya, Aziz Suryal, vii, 149
Awakening *(al-nahda)*, 58, 86, 88–91, 94
    lay involvement in, 89
al-Azhar University, 59, 98, 101, 120
    'ulama, 35

Baghdadi, Father Philotheos Ibrahim, 82
Bayt al-Takris, 144, 146, 147
Behrens-Abouseif, Doris, 59, 60, 77
Benjamin II, pope, 8
Bibawi, George Habib, 186–87
Bible, 48, 68, 69, 74, 105, 106, 117, 121, 130, 186, 187
    divorce, 114, 184
    Gospel/New Testament, 8, 12, 69, 106, 136, 127, 184
    marriage, 16
    reading, 69, 79, 80–81, 131
    study of, 84, 115, 120, 134, 149, 163, 175, 176, 179
    translations, 79, 81, 116
Bigamy
    Tukh al-Nasara, 13
Bishara, Mu'allim, 33, 34, 38, 49
Black Death/Great Annihilation, 14
Boulos, Father Boulos, 146

Britain, 57, 98
  British occupation, 55–56, 83, 87, 94, 97, 98, 100, 101, 102–103
  British withdrawal, 135
  colonialism, 58, 98
  Copts/British relationship, 102–103
  Cromer, Lord, British consul general, 103
  Egyptian independence from, 58, 71, 97, 101, 106
  Gorst, Sir Eldon, British consul general, 100
  Kitchener, Lord, British consul general, 103
Bustan al-ruhban (The Garden of the Monks), 145
Butrus wild Yusuf, 35

Canon law, 89, 166
  marriage, 15–17, 18, 28, 184
  marriage between relatives, 15–16
  number of times marriage is permitted, 16
  papal election, 112, 164
  al-Safi ibn al-'Assal, 15, 48, 89
Capitulations, 70
Carter, B.L., 60
Catholic Church, *see* Coptic Catholic Church; Roman Catholic Church
Charitable societies, 94–95, 96, 108, 120, 144
  Great Benevolent Coptic Society, 95
  Tawfiq/Reconciliation Society, 95
Churches, 5, 104, 106, 137
  Abu Sarga, Old Cairo, 45–46
  Abu al-Sayfayn, Harit Zuwayla, 38
  Abu al-Sayfayn, Monastery of St. Paul, 43
  Angel Gabriel, al-Saqaqqin, 104
  Babylon al-Daraj, Old Cairo, 44
  building of, 42, 66, 70, 104, 120, 137, 159–60, 162, 168
  Church of the Holy Virgin, Faggala, 146
  Church of the Holy Virgin, Muharram Bey, Alexandria, 144
  Church of the Holy Virgin, Qasriyat al-Rihan, Old Cairo, 44
  Church of the Holy Virgin, Sammanud, 145
  Church of the Holy Virgin, Zaytun, 153
  Church of the Virgin, al-Damshiriya, Old Cairo, 44
  Lower Egypt churches, 24
  manuscripts of, 5
  Mu'allaqa, Old Cairo, 115, 123
  number, 6
  al-Qiddisayn, Alexandria, 170–71
  restoration, 36–37, 42–46, 47, 104, 122
  St. Antonius, Shubra, 147, 157
  St. George, Alexandria, 144
  St. Mark's Cathedral, Abbasiya, 137, 138, 139, 153
  St. Mark's Cathedral, Ezbekiya, 56, 66, 67, 76
  St. Mark's, Giza, 104, 146, 148, 176
  St. Mena, Cairo, 131
  waqf, 29
Church Fathers, 17, 125, 142–46, 147, 186
  Athanasius of Alexandria, 84, 145, 186
  Cyril of Alexandria, 145, 183, 186
  marriage, 15, 16
Citizenship, 101, 134, 159, 169, 170, 178
Clergy/priest, 93, 96, 108
  corruption, 75, 92, 107, 114, 124, 125, 126, 143
  education, 73–74, 75, 80, 92, 95, 96, 114, 148, 153, 175
  income, 74–75, 81, 92
  nazir, 45–46
  salary, 75, 78, 92, 175
  Shenouda III, 173, 174–75, 188
  see also Seminary
Cole, Juan, 97
Colonialism, 58, 84, 98, 141
Community Council, *see* Majlis al-Milli
Concubinage, 14, 17, 18, 28, 39
  children of concubines, 18, 28
  penalties, 18, 28
  slave girls, 14, 17, 18, 28
Constantinople, *see* Istanbul
Convents, 45, 145, 151–52, 174
  Abu al-Sayfayn (St. Mercurius), Old Cairo, 151–52, 174
  (Ummina Irini, Mother Superior, 150, 151–52, 174)

al-Banat, Old Cairo: Mariam bint Yusuf ibn Yuhanna, Mother Superior, 28
Banat Maryam, Beni Soueif, 176–77
(Rauth, Sister, viii, 177)
Community of the Daughters of St. Mary, Beni Soueif, 147
Harit Zuwayla, 45
(Irani bint Yuhanna ibn Mikha'il, Mother Superior, 28)
Ifrusiya: Rifqa bint Ma'tuk ibn Mansur, Mother Superior, 28
Mari Girgis (St. George), Old Cairo, 174
number of nuns and convents, 56, 173
St. Dimiana, Damietta, 174, 177
waqfs, 28
Conversion, 159, 160, 185
to Catholicism, 25, 68, 79–80
to Islam, 36, 159, 162
to Protestantism, 78, 81, 82, 84
Coptic Catholic Church, 51, 68, 80
Coptic Center for Social Studies, 178
Coptic Church/government relationship, 98, 108–109, 112–13, 119–20, 122, 125
Cyril VI, 128, 129, 134–42
National Church, 128, 135–37
new regime, 134–35, 138
St. Mark's Cathedral, Abbasiya, 137, 138
see also Shenouda III, political role
Coptic Congress, Asyut, 99–100, 108, 120
Macarius of Asyut, bishop, 100, 108, 120
Coptic identity, 58, 75–76, 84, 107–108, 142, 145, 185
Pharaonic roots, 106–108
Coptic Institute for Higher Studies, 149, 158
Coptic language, 75, 76, 93, 95, 106, 107, 122, 144
Coptic script, 61
translation into other languages, 130, 140, 142, 180, 182
Coptic liturgy, 80, 116, 137, 149, 166, 186
Moftah, Ragheb, Coptic Orthodox Liturgy of St. Basil, 149
see also Rites/festivals
Coptic Museum, 107
manuscripts, 41, 46
nationalization, 115
Simaika, Marcus, 107–108
Coptic Nation, *see* Jama'at al-Umma al-Qibtiya
Coptic papacy, 4, 11, 23, 56, 62
authority of, x, 7–9, 10, 12, 22, 28, 38–40, 56, 57, 63, 80–81, 86, 90, 92, 108–109, 187, 188
leadership, ix, x, 11, 22, 31, 33, 34, 51, 65
papacy/lay leadership conflict, ix, 10, 22–23, 24, 25, 28, 33, 58, 86, 91, 93, 95, 96, 111, 138, 153
rebellion against, 23, 24, 25
role vis-à-vis the government, 65, 67, 129, 138, 156, 158
tawqi' (decree of appointment), 7–8, 23
see also Coptic papal election
Coptic papal election, 9, 34, 37–40, 89, 112–13, 116, 121, 122, 123, 127
by altar lot, 127, 152, 155
Holy Synod, 89, 112, 121, 125, 127
Majlis al-Milli, 89, 112, 121, 125, 127
al-Toukhy, Rafik Bassili, 127
Coptic Patriarchate Archives, 48
Coptic reform, 67, 88, 114
administrative reform, 74–75
Cyril IV, 57, 74–76, 78, 88
Cyril VI, 57, 58, 146–52
educational reform, 75–76
lay reform movement, 58, 59, 60, 88–92, 93, 94–95, 96, 108, 128, 155
Macarius III, 113, 120–21, 122
reforming bishops, 147–49
reforming churches, 146–47
reforming monks and nuns, 133–34, 145, 149–52
Shenouda III, 155, 173, 175
see also Cyril VI; Lay leadership; Sunday School Movement
Coptic Synaxarion, 36, 40, 50, 144
Copts outside Egypt, x, 56, 67, 141, 148
Africa, 140–41, 179, 181–82
Australia, x, 156, 179, 184
Bishopric for Youth, 178–79
bishops, 174, 179

Canada, 141, 184
Europe, x, 156, 179
Kuwait, 141
national unity, 169
North America, x, 141, 156, 179, 180–81
population, 179, 182
Shenouda III, 155, 156, 159, 162, 164, 165, 179–82
sub-Saharan Africa, 141, 181–82
"theologizing experience," 180
United States, 141, 162, 165, 169, 184
see also Los Angeles, Diocese of

Council of Chalcedon, 68, 140, 183
Council of Florence, 21
Council of Nicea, 15
Cyril IV, pope, 55, 73–78, 140
"Abu al-Islah," 73
administrative reform, 74–75
clergy's education, 73–74, 75, 82
educational reform, 75–76
Ezbekiya, cathedral, 76
international relations, 76–78
military conscription, 71
reform, 57, 74–76, 78, 88

Cyril V, pope, 55, 60, 80, 86, 87–109, 117
awakening *(al-nahda)*, 58, 86, 88–91, 94, 105–108
charitable societies and press, 94–95, 108
Coptic Congress, Asyut, 99–100
Copts/British relationship, 102–103
exile/return, 91, 112
lay reform movement, 58, 59, 60, 88–92, 93, 94–95, 96, 108
monastic ideals, 104–105
renewal of the church, 56–57, 108
seminary, 92, 95–96, 108
Sunday School Movement, 59, 96–97, 108
see also Majlis al-Milli

Cyril VI, pope, 55, 60, 86, 114, 115, 117, 126, 127–54, 155, 184, 186
ascetic/spiritual practices, 57, 126, 128, 129, 135, 149
'Atta, Azer Yusuf, 115, 130
biographical information, 129–34
Church and Egyptian state, 128, 129, 134–42
Copts outside Egypt, 141–42
ecumenical relations, 138, 139–40
election by altar lot, 127, 152
Ethiopian Church, 128, 138–39, 140
foreign politics, 136
hagiographies and Holy Fathers, 143–46
Majlis al-Milli, 138, 142
miracle, 60, 129, 130, 153
mission to Africa, 140–41
Nasser relationship, 135, 136, 137, 138, 160
National Church, 128, 135–37
nationalism, 135, 136
reform, 57, 58, 146–52
reforming bishops, 147–49
reforming churches, 146–47
reforming monks and nuns, 133–34, 145, 149–52
renewal of monasteries, 133–34, 142–43, 151, 152
reviving traditions, 128, 129, 133, 142
St. Mark's Cathedral, Abbasiya, 137, 138
Sunday School Movement, 129–30, 133–34, 146
Virgin Mary, 152, 153

Daftardar (chief financial officer), 32
Daniel, Abuna, 187
Dar al-Watha'iq al-Qawmiya, 5
Diwan al-Ruznama, records of, 5
al-Jayshiya, records of, 5
Rizq (Rizaq) Ihbasa (Ihbasiya), 5
Shari'a Courts, records of, 5
Deaconess, *see* Women
Demetrius II, pope, 75, 78–86, 108
Orientalist gaze, 83–85
sainthood, 85–86
Western missions, 78–79, 80–82, 84–85, 86
Dhimmi, *see Ahl al-dhimma*
al-Dimirdashi, Fadlallah, 25–26
Divorce, 63, 124, 138, 184–85, 188
1938 Code, 113–14, 184
punishment, 39
Diwan, 38, 74
Diwan of al-Jawali, 12, 33
Diwan al-Ruznama, 35, 36
mubashir to, 35
Drinking and intoxication, 63, 74, 93

Duff Gordon, Lucie, 84–85

Easter, 101, 132, 143, 162, 163
 date of, 23, 24
 Holy Saturday, 41
'Ebeid, Makram, 101, 119
Ecumenical relations, 56, 77, 102, 124, 137, 153
 All Africa Council of Churches, 139, 156, 166, 182
 Anglican Church, 77
 Armenian Orthodox Church, 77
 Chalcedonian Orthodox Churches, 140, 183
 Christian reunification, 21–25, 68, 79, 183
 Christology, 183
 Cyril VI, 138, 139–40
 Greek Orthodox Church, 77, 183
 marriage and divorce, 184–85
 Middle East Council of Churches, 156, 182
 non-Chalcedonian Churches, 139, 140, 182
 Peter VII, pope, 67–69
 Russian Orthodox Church, 67, 77, 183
 Second Vatican Council, 136, 140, 179
 Shenouda III, 155, 156, 166, 182–84
 World Alliance of Reformed Churches, 184
 World Council of Churches (WCC), 124, 136, 139, 148, 156, 166, 182
 see also Ethiopia; Protestants; Roman Catholic Church/Coptic Church relationship

Education, 64, 69–70, 86, 94–95, 102, 105, 114–15, 120, 122, 144, 158, 173, 175
 "Arabization" of curricula, 119, 134
 charitable societies, 94–95
 children and youth, 95, 96, 120, 129, 144
 clergy/priest, 73–74, 75, 80, 92, 95, 96, 114, 148, 153, 175
 compulsory education, 119
 Coptic access to, 69, 71, 73, 86, 88, 108, 135
 girls' school, 68, 75, 90, 95, 120, 175
 Muhammad 'Ali, 69–70
 reform, 46–48, 75–76
 religious education, 96–97, 119, 122, 144, 148, 158
 theological education, 73, 74, 81, 82, 175, 178, 187
 see also Schools; Seminary; Sunday School Movement
Egypt
 "Belle Epoque," 83, 85
 changes toward a modern society, 55, 57, 65, 68, 71, 86
 civil war, 62
 cotton export, 57, 65, 66
 independence, 58, 71, 97, 101, 106, 118
 independence from Ottoman Empire, 55, 57, 64
Egyptian Parliament, 100, 111, 113, 124, 134, 163
Eritrean Church, 117–18, 174
Ethiopia, 11, 73, 76–77
 autonomous status, 118, 139, 181
 Basilios, Bishop, 117, 118, 139
 Church of, 38, 63–64, 68, 76, 115, 116–18, 123, 128, 138–39, 140
 Haile Selassie, Emperor, 116, 117, 118, 123, 137, 139, 140
 Italian invasion of, 115, 117–18
 Macarius, archbishop, 63–64
 Nasser, Gamal 'Abd-al, 138
Excommunication, 13, 17, 18, 91, 112, 150, 165–66, 186, 187

Fanous, Isaac, 149
Faqih (expert in Islamic jurisprudence), 35, 43, 44
Farouk, King, 111, 119
Fasting, 22, 25, 26, 62, 84, 128, 133, 142, 162, 168
Fatwa, 22, 23, 35, 44
Fiqh (Islamic jurisprudence), 4, 46
 church and monastery restoration, 42–43
First World War, 58, 79, 97, 100, 117
Freedom of religion, 70, 159
French Expedition 3, 50, 61–62, 63, 64
 Bonaparte, Napoleon, 55, 56, 58, 62, 64

Gabriel VII, pope, 18–20, 38

- marriage, 18–20
- Gabriel VIII, pope
  - rebellion against, 23, 24
  - relations with Church of Rome, 20, 22–25
- Gentry (*mubashirin*), 12, 23, 33, 34, 40, 135, 137, 158
  - Cairo, 24, 25, 29
  - Lower Egypt, 22–23, 24, 25–26, 29
  - papacy/Coptic gentry conflict, 10, 22–23, 24, 25, 28, 33
  - rebellion against papacy, 23, 24, 25–26
  - Upper Egypt, 28
  - *see also* Katkhuda; Notables
- Ghali Pasha, Butrus, 89, 90, 91, 99
- Girgis Abu Mansur al-Tukhi, 36, 41, 42, 44
- Girgis al-Gawhari, 37, 50, 61, 64, 66
- Girgis, Habib, 58, 95, 96, 114, 124, 146
  - *see also* Sunday School Movement
- Girgis ibn Butrus, 26
- Girgis Sidarus, 44
- Girgis Yusuf al-Suruji, 35, 36–37, 43
- Gospel, *see* Bible
- Greek Orthodox Church/Christians, 8–9, 77
  - Greek Orthodox Patriarch, 8, 9
- Gregorian calendar, 22–23, 24
- Gregorius, bishop for Higher Theological Education, Coptic Culture, and Academic Research, 147, 149, 164, 166
- Guirguis, Magdi, vii, viii, ix–x, 3–51, 59

- al-Habashi, 'Abd al-Masih, 131
- Habib al-Masri, 121
- Habib al-Masri, Iris, 59, 82, 112, 121, 123, 130
- Haile Selassie, Emperor, 116, 117, 118, 123, 137, 139, 140
  - Tafari, Ras, Crown Prince, 116, 117
- Hanna, Iskander, 114, 115, 120
- Hanna, Ya'qub, 64
- Harat al-Rum, papal headquarters, 62
- *History of the Patriarchs of the Coptic Church of Alexandria*, 4, 40
- Hizb al-Watani (National Party), 98–99
  - *see also* Nationalism
- Holy Synod, 60, 96, 113, 114, 116, 117, 122, 167, 176, 177, 184, 186–87, 188
  - papal election, 89, 112, 121, 125, 127
- Homosexuality, 17, 180

- Ibn Khaldun Center for Developmental Studies, 169
- Ibrahim al-Gawhari, 37, 38, 42, 43, 44, 47, 48, 50–51, 61, 145
  - sainthood, 50, 145
  - Sultan of the Copts, 37, 50
- Ibrahim, Saad Eddin, 169
- Icon, 47, 48, 76, 145, 149
  - Girgis the Greek, 48
  - Ibrahim Sim'an al-Nasikh, 48
  - of popes, 56–57
  - al-Qiss Kirillos, 48
  - al-Qiss Manqarius Girgis, 48
  - Surial ibn Abu al-Mina, 48
  - Yuhanna the Armenian, 48
- *Infitah*, 161
- Irini, Mother Superior of Dayr Abu Sayfayn, 150, 151–52, 174
- Isaac of Nineveh, 131, 143–44, 145
- Islam
  - Committee of National Unity, 168
  - festivals, 42, 101
  - intercommunal harmony, 101, 103
  - Mecca and Medina, 68
  - mosque, 41, 101, 163
  - Muslim–Coptic relations, 42, 101, 103, 111, 118, 119, 128, 135–36, 168, 178
  - Nasser, Gamal 'Abd-al, 134
  - Qur'an, 6, 119, 134, 136
  - Ramadan, 66, 101, 161, 168
  - *see also* National unity
- Islamists/militant groups, 161–62, 163, 177
  - attacks on Christians, 77, 94, 99, 103, 159, 162, 163, 167–68, 170
  - al-Sadat, Anwar, 161–62, 163, 164
- Isma'il, Khedive, 70, 75, 81, 85–86, 87, 105, 106
  - bankruptcy, 83, 85, 97
  - deposition, 97
  - Egypt's Belle Epoque, 83, 85, 106
- Istanbul, 3, 8, 9, 11, 22, 24, 32, 39, 65

al-Jabarti, 'Abd al-Rahman, 37, 41, 50, 59, 63, 66
Jacobite Christians, 37
Jama'at al-Umma al-Qibtiya (Coptic Nation), 123, 125
Jerusalem, 11, 66, 136
  Dayr al-Sultan Monastery, 116, 139
  pilgrimage to, 41, 163
Jews, 67, 100, 113, 136, 153
Jizya (poll tax), 6, 10, 12, 39, 69, 167
  abolition, 70
John XIII, pope, 11–18, 24, 79
  jizya, 12
  loss of jurisdiction, 11–12
  population crisis and Coptic marriage, 14–18
John XIV, pope, 20, 21–22
John XV, pope, 28–29
John XVI, pope, 38, 45
John XVIII, pope, 58, 62, 63, 79
John XIX, pope, 108, 111, 112–20, 131, 132, 145
  communal solidarity/discord, 118–20
  educational developments, 114–15
  election, 112–13
  Ethiopian Church, 115, 116–18
  Majlis al-Milli, 112, 113
  money and marriage concerns, 113–14
John Chrysostom, St., 47
John of Alexandria, bishop, 91
Jullien, Michel, 84

Kamil, Bishoi, Father, 144, 177, 181
Kamil, Mustafa, 98–99
Katkhuda, 34
  Ahmed Agha Katkhuda Mustahfazan, 34
  Ibrahim Katkhuda Mustahfazan, 34
  katkhuda ta'ifa mustahfazan, 34
  Muhammad Kadak Katkhuda Mustahfazan, 35, 36
  Murad Katkhuda Mustahfazan, 36
  Ridwan Katkhuda 'Azaban, 37
  'Uthman Katkhuda Mustahfazan, 35, 36
Khadim al-kanisa (servant of the church), 115, 121, 177, 180
Khalil, Elhamy, viii, 180–81
Kiraza (celibacy), 146
Kircher, Athanasius, 106
al-Kusheh, *see* Sectarian incidents

Labib, Claudius, 106
Lane, Edward, 102, 104
Lay leadership, ix, 39, 58, 80, 108
  American Mission, 79
  Coptic intellectual elite, 85, 88–92
  education, 80, 82, 90, 106
  lay "clericalization," 156, 173, 175–76, 187, 188
  lay reform movement, 58, 59, 60, 88–92, 93, 94–95, 96, 108, 128, 155
  papacy/lay leadership conflict, ix, 10, 22–23, 24, 25, 28, 33, 58, 86, 91, 93, 95, 96, 111, 138, 153
  see also Coptic reform; Gentry; Majlis al-Milli; Notables; Sunday School Movement
Leeder, S.H., 104, 105
Levantine Christians, 51, 66
Los Angeles, Diocese of, viii, 141, 179, 180–81
  Coptic American Association, 181
  Graduates and Young Professionals Committee, 179
  Henein, Father Antonious, 181
  Serapion, bishop of Los Angeles and Hawaii, viii, 179, 181
Lutfallah Abu Yusuf, 35, 36, 37, 38, 40, 44
Luther, Martin, 21

Macarius III, pope, 108, 120–22, 125, 184
  bishop of Asyut, 100, 108, 112, 113, 114, 120, 122
  church revival, 120, 122
  education revival, 120, 122
  electoral discord, 121
  reform-minded, 113, 120–21, 122
Magic/superstition, 63, 74, 78, 83, 93
Mahabba Bookstore, 144
Majlis al-kanisa (church council), 175
Majlis al-Milli (Community Council), 58, 88–93, 94–95, 96, 107, 108, 112, 122, 158
  1938 Code, 113, 184
  canon law, 89
  papal election, 89, 112, 121, 125,

127, 175
pope/Community Council clashes, 90–91, 92–93, 96, 108, 113, 122, 125, 129, 135, 138, 142
Shenouda III, 173, 175–76
waqf, 113, 122, 125, 138
see also Cyril V
Majlis al-Nuwwab (Chamber of Deputies), 105
Majlis Shurat al-Qawanin (Advisory Council of Laws), 70
Malati, Mu'allim, 64
Malaty, Father Tadros, 181
Mamluk period, 7, 8, 9, 13–14
prostitution, 14
Mamluks, 32, 62, 65, 66
Manqarius, Yusuf, 95
Manuscripts, 144, 145
Coptic Museum, 41, 46
copying, 46–47, 93
illumination, 47–48
Mark, St., the Evangelist, 16, 55, 137, 140
Mark V, pope, 24, 25–27
rebellion against, 24, 25–26
Mark VI, pope, 12, 33, 34, 38
Mark VII, pope, 25
Mark VIII, pope, 55, 57, 58, 61–66, 76
adraj (decrees or letters), 62–63
Ezbekiya, cathedral, 56, 76
notables, 63, 64
pastoral concerns, 62–64
Markus of al-Beheira, Metropolitan, 88
Marriage, 15–20, 25, 93, 124, 138, 175, 180, 184–85
between Copts and Catholics, 39, 63, 79, 183
between Copts and Muslims, 39
between cousins, 16
canon law, 15–17, 18, 28, 184
intermarriage, 15–16, 39, 159, 184
number of times permitted, 16, 185
see also Divorce
Maspero, Gaston, 106
Matthew III, pope, 29, 38
Matthew IV, pope, 34, 38, 40
Maximos, bishop of Benha, 164
Media, x, 57, 129, 143, 157, 161, 164, 165, 167, 178, 187
al-Ahram, 87, 118
al-Ahram Weekly, 87
The Branches, 178
hagiographies, 144
al-Kiraza, 156, 157, 164, 169, 175, 177, 186
al-Liwa', 99
The Message of the Church Youth, 178
Mina' al-khalas, 143
Misr, 95
press, 94, 97, 99, 106, 112, 125, 143, 151
print, 55, 74, 76, 81, 105, 129, 130, 144, 147
radio, 143
Sunday School Magazine, 147, 156, 157
al-Watan, 88, 94, 164
The Word, 178
Meinardus, Otto, 60, 135
Menas, St., 131–32
Michel, Max/Archbishop Maximos, 187–88
Athanasius Association, 187
Middle East Council of Churches, 156, 182
Milik (servant of Pope Yusab II), 125
Military, 39, 40
1952 Free Officers' coup, 56, 111, 134
Coptic legion, 64
Coptic participation in, 69, 71, 73
military conscription, 59, 61, 71
Muhammad 'Ali, 65, 69, 70–71
Ottoman state, 25, 32, 61
ujaq (military official), 32, 34
Minority status debate, 101, 169
Miracle, 60, 129, 130, 143, 145, 153
al-Miskin, Father Matta, 125, 133, 145–6, 147, 150–51
disagreements with Shenouda III, 165, 166, 186
Wadi al-Rayyan, 150
Missionaries, western, 59, 74, 78–82, 84, 86, 92, 102, 120, 139
American Mission, 79, 80–82, 102
Capuchins, 79
Catholics, 63, 79, 102
English Church Missionary Society (CMS), 68–69, 79, 80
Franciscans, 79
missionary schools, 68–69, 80

see also Protestants
Monasteries, 5, 142–43, 145, 152
  al-'Azab, 104–105
  contribution to church renewal, 142, 151, 173–74
  Jaffa, 123
  manuscripts of, 5
  al-Muharraq, 92, 95, 105, 123, 149
  number, 6, 56, 173
  number of monks, 12, 56, 173
  Our Lady of Suryan, 19, 134, 147, 157
  renewal under Cyril VI, 133–34, 142–43, 151, 152
  renewal under Shenouda III, 173–74
  restoration, 5, 36–37, 42–46, 49, 104, 122
  St. Anthony, 4, 18, 38, 66, 73, 122, 123
  St. Baramus, 24, 93, 105, 112, 131, 132, 143, 181
  St. Bishoi, 164, 171, 174, 183
  St. Macarius, 24, 29, 78, 125, 151
  St. Menas, 129, 130, 131–32, 133, 138, 142, 143, 152
  St. Paul, 4, 43, 91
  St. Samuel, 133, 146, 150
  al-Sultan (Jerusalem), 116, 139
  Syrians, 134, 146, 147, 150, 157
  Wadi al-Natrun, 24, 29, 134, 150, 151
  waqf, 4, 28, 29, 92, 95, 104, 113, 122, 125
Morcos, Father Morcos, 180
Morcos, Samir, viii, 169
Mubarak, Hosni, 158, 159, 160, 166, 167–71
  Islamists/militant groups, 167–68
Mubashirin, *see* Gentry
Mufti, 22, 23, 45, 101
Muhammad 'Ali, 3, 50, 51, 64–66, 75, 76, 77, 87, 102, 106, 140
  army, 65, 69, 70–71
  education, 69–70
  military conscription, 71
  modern Egypt, 65, 71
  tax collection, 64, 65, 66
  territorial expansion, 68
Muhammad al-Fatih (the Conqueror), Sultan, 8
Mukarrasin, 147, 149
Murqus Sergius, 101, 120
Musa, bishop for Youth, viii, 178
Musa ibn 'Issa, 43
Muslim Brotherhood, 101, 111, 118, 119, 136, 160, 161
  al-Banna, Hassan, 119
  suppression, 134, 136
al-Muttawahid, Mina, 115

Nag Hammadi, *see* Sectarian incidents
al-Nahda, *see* Awakening
Nakhla, Kamil Salih, 4
Nasser, Gamal 'Abd-al, 113, 123, 127, 159
  1952 Free Officers' coup, 56, 111, 134
  Cyril VI relationship, 135, 136, 137, 138, 160
  nationalization policies, 124, 134, 135, 141
  new regime, 134–35
  reforms, 129, 139
  "three circles of interest," 140–41
National identity, 99, 106, 108
Nationalism, 58, 59, 71, 76, 87, 98–102, 106, 128, 136, 163
  1919 Nationalist Revolution, 56, 58, 87, 97, 100–101, 120
  Cyril VI, 135, 136
  Hizb al-Watani (National Party), 98–99
  Husayn, Ahmad, 132
  National Church, 128, 135–37
  Shenouda III, 160
  'Urabi Revolt, 98
  see also Cyril VI; Nasser, Gamal 'Abd-al; Wafd Party
National unity, 101, 111, 113, 118, 168–69, 171
  Committee of National Unity, 168
  Muslim–Coptic relations, 42, 101, 103, 111, 118, 119, 128, 135–36, 168, 178
Nayruz Abu Nawwar, 37, 41
Nazir (notable or church administrator), 37, 44, 45–46
Newspaper, *see* Media
Notables *(arakhina)*, 12, 28, 31, 33–51, 57, 63, 64, 66, 88
  appointment/election of popes, 33, 34, 37–40
  attendance at Islamic festivals, 42

church and monastery restoration, 36–37, 42–46, 47
consecration of new patriarch, 40
decline of power, 64, 65
educational/cultural reform, 46–48
financial management, 34–35, 38
Holy Saturday, 41
leadership role, 31, 33, 36–37, 40, 49, 50, 63, 65
pilgrimage, 41
preparation of holy oil *(mayrun)*, 41–42
relations with Islamic religious leaders, 35
relations with prestigious, politically connected families, 34
ritual life, 40–42
sainthood, 40, 50
secular bishops, 48–49
selection of lay leaders, 36–37
wealth, 34, 35–36, 42, 43, 63, 65

October War, 160, 168
Old Cairo
Copts of, 19, 20, 26, 44, 45–46, 107, 151
marriage issues, 19–20
Orientalists, 3, 83–85
Ottoman Empire, 3, 9, 57, 98
annexation of Egypt, 9, 11
Christian communities, 77
Ottoman pasha, *see Wali al-amr*
Ottoman reforms, 70
Hatt-i Humayun decree, 70, 137
Hatt-i Sherif of Gülhane decree, 70
Tanzimat reforms, 70
Ottoman state/government, 6, 9
Coptic Church, 6, 7–10, 11, 13, 22
decentralization of Ottoman authority, 25, 32
decline, 25, 31–32, 57, 70
independence from, 55, 57, 64
military, 25, 32, 61
see also 'Aqd al-dhimma

Palestinian cause, 101, 136, 160, 163
Pan-Islamism, 98–99, 103, 134
Paris Peace Conference, 100
Patriarchal School (Madrasat al-Aqbat al-Kubra), 75, 107
Patristic Studies Center, 147
Penalties, 12–13, 17, 18, 19, 28
bigamy, 12–13
concubinage, 18, 28
polygamy, 19–20
prostitution, 17, 18
see also Excommunication
Pentapolis, 12, 132
Personal status laws, 70, 82, 113, 124, 138, 185
Peter VI, pope, 38, 40
Peter VII, pope, 40, 55, 57, 65, 66–71, 73, 76, 80, 108, 115, 140
Coptic Church reform, 67
holiness, 67
icon of, 56
international church relations, 67–69
notables, 66
seminary, 69, 80
St. Mark's Cathedral, Ezbekiya, 56, 66, 67
Pharaonic roots/heritage, 58, 76, 106–108
Philokalia, 144
Philotheus, scholar-priest, 95
Polygamy, 17, 19–20, 26, 63
penalties, 19–20
Population, 21, 56, 155
Census of 1897, 102
crisis, 14–15
immigration, 141, 180
Poverty, 62, 68, 81, 83, 89, 92, 93, 104, 149, 158
socioeconomic inequality, 83, 111, 161
see also Charitable societies
Print, *see* Media
Prostitution, 14, 17, 18
penalties, 18
taxes on, 14
Protestants, 58, 68, 78, 80–82, 84, 92, 95, 102, 108, 120, 187
American Mission, 79, 80–82, 102
Anglican Church, 77, 103, 184
'Ebeid, Makram, 101, 119
ecumenical relations with, 183–84
English Church Missionary Society (CMS), 68–69, 80
Evangelical Coptic Church, 74, 80, 82
Jowett, William, 80

Lieder, John, 69
missionary schools, 68–69, 80, 102
Watson, Andrew, 79, 80–81

Qadi al-qudah (chief judge), 9, 35, 44, 64
Qanun-name-i Misr, 9
Qasr al-Sham', 26, 27
al-Qiddisayn Church, Alexandria, *see* Sectarian incidents
Qilada, William Sulaiman, 169

Rafa'il, assistant to Pope Cyril VI, 130
Reform, 55, 88
Luther, Martin, 21
wali al-amr, 26
see also Coptic reform
Reid, Donald Malcolm, 88, 107
Reiss, Wolfram, 60
Revolution, 55, 61, 87
1881–82, 'Urabi Revolt, 55–56, 58, 87, 90, 97–98
1919 Nationalist Revolution, 56, 58, 87, 97, 100–101, 120
1952 Free Officers' coup, 56, 111, 134
2011, January 25, 56
Revolutionary Command Council, 123–24
Rites/festivals, 40–42, 74, 91, 92, 174
Christmas, 117, 137, 162, 166, 168, 170
consecration of church, 43
consecration of popes and bishops, 40, 63, 68, 115, 133, 138
Eucharist (mass), 13, 40, 73, 91, 115, 131, 132–33, 146, 150, 162, 180
mawlid, 42, 78, 143, 174
mayrun (holy oil), 41–42, 62, 115, 153
pilgrimage, 41, 105, 131, 136, 143, 152, 163, 174
prayer, 6, 84, 104, 105, 131, 133, 136, 143, 144, 145, 186
retreat, 131, 151, 174, 184
see also Coptic liturgy; Easter
Rizq, Mu'allim, 35, 37
Rizqallah al-Badawi, 35, 39
Roman Catholic Church, 8, 51
Jesuits, viii, 84, 106
John XIV, pope, 20, 21–22
missions, 63, 79
nature of Christ, 183
reform, 21
Second Vatican Council, 136, 140, 179
see also Roman Catholic Church/Coptic Church relationship; Roman Catholic popes
Roman Catholic Church/Coptic Church relationship, 20, 21–25, 136, 137, 183
Christian reunification, 21–25, 68, 79
differing views, 183
hostility, 23, 84
Roman Catholic popes, 68
Gregory XIII, 21
Sixtus V, 22
Rufayla, Ya'qub Nakhla, 4, 62, 88, 89, 91, 94
Rural community, 6, 81–82, 148
Rural Diaconate Project, 146–47, 149, 181
Russian Orthodox Church, 67, 77, 79, 183

al-Sadat, Anwar, 156, 158, 159, 160–64, 170
infitah, 161
Islamic law, 161, 162, 163, 164
Islamists/militant groups, 161–62, 163, 164, 170
al-Safi ibn al-'Assal
canon law, 15, 48, 89
Sa'id, Khedive, 70, 76, 77, 83, 85–86, 87
Samuel, bishop for Public, Ecumenical, and Social Services, 136, 140, 141, 146, 148, 155, 158, 166, 177, 181
Papal Committee, 164, 166, 167
Sarabamun, bishop of al-Munufiya and al-Beheira, 67
Schools, 73, 76, 85, 96, 100, 104, 120
American Mission, 79, 80
charitable societies, 94
Coptic Orthodox, 75, 76, 78, 81, 85, 92, 93, 96, 100, 106, 120, 138
girls' school, 68, 75, 90, 95, 120, 175
government, 69–70, 74, 80, 81, 83, 96, 119
kuttab (elementary schools), 47, 73, 75, 105, 106, 112
Patriarchal School (Madrasat al-Aqbat al-Kubra), 75, 107
Protestant, 68–69, 80, 85, 102
see also Education; Seminary; Sunday School Movement
Scribes, 12, 61, 66

copying/transcription of manuscripts and books, 46–47

Second World War, 3, 111, 133, 135

Sectarian incidents, 159, 162, 163, 167–68, 169, 170–71
- Khanqa, 162
- al-Kusheh, 167, 169
- Nag Hammadi, 168, 170
- al-Qiddisayn Church, Alexandria, 170–71
- al-Zawya al-Hamra', 163

Secular bishops, 48–49
- Athanasius, son of 'Abd al-Massih al-Ghamrawi, 49
- Bishara al-Khanani, 49
- Gadallah, son of Mu'allim Buqtur, 49
- Girgis, son of Buqtur al-Manfaluti, 48
- Makram, son of Mu'allim Bishara, 49
- Yusuf al-Sohagi, 48–49

Sedra, Paul, 59, 68, 74

Seikaly, Samir, 60, 74

Seminary, 69, 80, 92, 108, 125, 175
- Coptic Seminary, Cairo, 95–96, 114, 147, 148, 157, 179
- Coptic Seminary, Helwan, 114, 131

Sexual issues, 13–18, 180
- *see also* Concubinage; Homosexuality; Prostitution

al-Sha'arawi, Sheikh Muhammad Mitwalli, 167

Shari'a Courts, 5, 23, 39
- Alexandria, 23
- Bab 'Ali Court, 22, 23, 29
- Cairo, 5, 19
- Diwan 'Ali, 23
- documents, 5, 28, 29, 46
- Mahalla al-Kubra, 23
- Old Cairo (Misr al-Qadima), 19–20, 27
- al-Qisma al-'Arabiya, 35

Sharubim, Mikha'il, 106

Shenoda, Anthony, 60

Shenouda III, viii, x, 55, 60, 75, 86, 129, 133, 150, 155–71
- biographical information, 157–58
- bishops and priests, 173, 174–75, 188
- deaconesses/consecrated women, 173, 176–77
- ecumenical relations, 155, 156, 166, 182–85
- education, 173, 175
- election, 155
- Gayed, Nazir, 124, 147, 157
- icon of, 56, 57
- keeping and contesting the faith, 185–88
- lay "clericalization," 156, 173, 175–76, 187, 188
- lectures, 148–49, 158, 175, 178
- Majlis al-Milli, 173, 175–76
- marriage and divorce, 184–85
- monasteries, 173–74
- reform and renewal, 155, 173, 175
- Sunday School Movement, 124, 147, 157, 185
- writings of, 185–87
- writings on, 156–57
- youth, 173, 177–79
- *see also* Copts outside Egypt; Shenouda III, political role

Shenouda III, political role, 155–71
- church-based civil society, 156, 170
- Coptic Church/government relationship, 159, 162–63, 166, 167, 188
- exile, 159, 164–66, 167
- Mubarak era, 158, 159, 160, 166, 167–71
- nationalist, 160
- national unity, 168–69, 171
- Papal Committee, 164–67
- Sadat era, 156, 158, 159, 160–64, 170
- sectarian incidents, 162, 163, 167–68, 169, 170–71
- UNESCO–Madanjeet Singh Prize for the Promotion of Tolerance and Non-violence, 169–70

Shenouda, bishop of Christian Education, 140, 148, 155, 158, 182

Six-Day War, 136, 153

Social service, 175
- BLESS, 147

Spirituality, 97, 114, 126, 173–74
- Cyril V, 93, 104
- Cyril VI, 57, 128, 130, 133
- Macarius III, 121
- spiritual revival, 56, 114

St. Menas Association, 144

Sublime Porte, 62, 65

Sub-Saharan Africa, 141, 181–82

Boulos, bishop, East/Central Africa, 182
Morqos, Antonios, bishop, South/West Africa, 181–82
Sudan, 83, 140, 179
Domadius, first bishop to Sudan, 68
Suez Canal, 83, 86, 88, 135
Sunday School Movement (Mashru' Madaris al-Ahad), 58–59, 60, 108, 114, 124–25, 127, 146, 188
children/youth education, 96, 144, 145
Cyril VI, 129–30, 133–34, 146
Girgis, Habib, 58, 95, 96, 114, 124, 146
khadim al-kanisa, 115, 121
lajna 'ulya (Higher Committee), 124
lay reform movement, 58, 59, 60
official status within the church, 124
papacy/lay leadership conflict, 58, 96
Shenouda III, 124, 147, 157, 185
Sunday School Magazine, 147, 156, 157
Suryal, Father Salib, 146, 147, 176
Syrian Christians, 40, 61, 77, 105, 139–40, 181, 183
Monastery of Wadi al-Natrun, 24, 29, 134, 150, 151

Tadros, Mariz, viii, 60, 167, 170
Ta'ifa (denomination, confessional minority), 12
Takris (service to the church), 124–25, 134, 146, 147
Tawa'if (professional/craft guilds), 6
Tawfiq, Khedive, 87, 90–91, 92, 97–98
Tax collection, 61, 64, 65, 66, 83, 97, 100, 102
jizya (poll tax), 6, 10, 12, 39, 69, 70, 167
Turkey, 21, 22, 70, 75, 85
Turkish language, 98, 106

'Ulama (board of legal scholars), 35, 44, 101
Dar al-'Ulum teachers' college, 106
'Urabi, Ahmad, 98
'Urabi Revolt, *see* Revolution

Virgin Mary, 152
appearances of, 153
Voile, Brigitte, 60
Wadi al-Natrun, 24, 29, 134, 150, 151
Wadi al-Rayyan, 150
Wafd Party, 58, 100–101, 108, 118, 119
dissolution, 124
'Ebeid, Makram, 101, 119
Zaghlul, Sa'd, 100–101
see also Nationalism
Wali al-amr (Ottoman pasha/governor), 22, 23, 25, 26, 29, 31–34, 39, 43, 44
authority of, 32
Muhammad Pasha Qul Qaran, 27
Waqf (religious endowment), 4, 5, 26–27, 28–29, 37, 43, 44, 74, 89, 92–93, 95, 104, 113, 122, 125, 135, 138, 159–60
administrator of *(taqrir al-nuzur)*, 26–27, 29
Mikha'il ibn Rafa'il, Mu'allim, 26–27
Watson, John, 130, 157
Wealth, 75, 92, 102–103, 105, 108, 111, 119, 129, 160
notables, 34, 35–36, 42, 43, 63, 65
see also Poverty
Women, 93
American Mission, 79, 82
education, 69, 74, 148, 175
girls' school, 68, 75, 90, 95, 120, 175
leadership, 128
mukarrasat (consecrated virgins), 56, 147, 176–77
role in the church, 56, 79, 128, 158, 180
shammasa (deaconess), 146, 147, 176–77, 178
slave girls and concubinage, 14, 17, 18, 28
World Alliance of Reformed Churches, 184
World Council of Churches (WCC), 124, 136, 139, 148, 156, 166, 182
World War I, *see* First World War
World War II, *see* Second World War

Yuhanna, bishop of Tanta, 164
Youth, 144, 173, 177–79
Bishopric for Youth, 177–79, 180
The Branches, 178
education, 95, 96, 120, 129, 144
Great Britain, 178–79

interfaith activities, 178
Los Angeles, 179
Mahragan al-Kiraza (competition), 179
The Message of the Church Youth, 178
Musa, bishop for Youth, viii, 178–79
Youth Servants Training Center, 178
Yuhanna Abu Masri, 35, 36, 44
Yunis al-Nasrani, Sheikh, 12
Yusab II, pope, 86, 108, 111, 117, 123–26
banishment, 123, 125, 127
ecumenical developments, 124
election, 123
intra-communal strife and corruption, 124, 125–26
metropolitan of Girga, 112, 121, 122, 123
Sunday School Movement, 124–25
Yusab, bishop of Jirja and Akhmim, 50, 63
Yusuf Bek Mir al-Liwa, 44
Yusuf Makramallah, 34

Zaghlul, Sa'd, 100–101
al-Zawya al-Hamra', *see* Sectarian incidents

CPSIA information can be obtained
at www.ICGtesting.com
Printed in the USA
JSHW060800160922
30538JS00003B/5

9 781649 032454